I0394382

Miles Away From Home

What makes a true Pacific Islander?
Is it the beautiful brown skin?
The comb in your hair?
The long flower-plaited skirt?
The long silky black hair down to your feet?

Or is it the thick palms?
The thick soles, result of being barefoot half the time?
The bulging of betelnut at the side of your mouth?
The preference for zorries over tennis shoes?
The timid, violent eyes of being foreign?

Perhaps it's the nostalgia of being thousands of
miles away from home.

Michael Kigimnang
Xavier High School
Class of 2010

Education In Chuuk

stained walls
broken windows
not enough chairs,
we gotta stand for a while

does it matter
the teacher is not even here
how long does it take
might as well ring the bell

no homework again
maybe today will be different

12:30
school's out
that's early, but class cancelled

can't graduate, can't learn
off I go

drugs, I'll say
keeps me occupied.

Kayviann Hallers
Xavier High School
Class of 2010

School On The Hill

Micronesia's Remarkable Xavier High School

Floyd K. Takeuchi

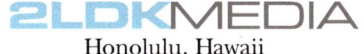
Honolulu, Hawaii

School On The Hill
Micronesia's Remarkable Xavier High School
By Floyd K. Takeuchi

Copyright © 2010 by Floyd K. Takeuchi
All rights reserved. No part of this publication may be reproduced or transmitted in any form or by any means without the permission of the publisher, except for the purpose of a review written for inclusion in a magazine, newspaper, broadcast or online service.

Published by 2LDK Media, Honolulu, Hawaii.

Second Edition
ISBN: 978-0-615-45835-9

Library of Congress Control Number: 2010913599

Designed by Malcolm Mekaru.

For more information on Xavier High School,
please visit: http://xaviermicronesia.org

www.floydtakeuchi.com

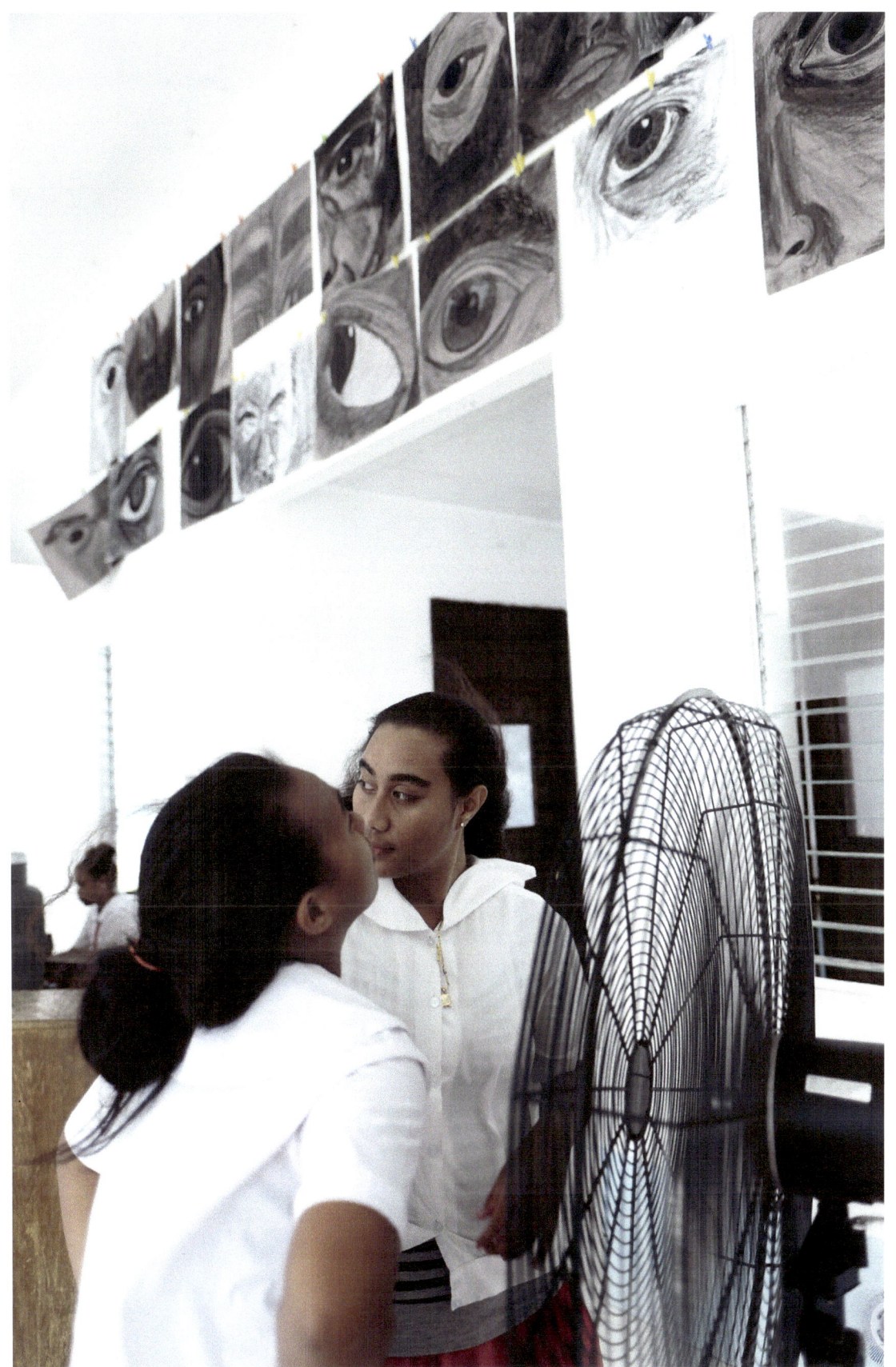
Cooling off in the Student Center.

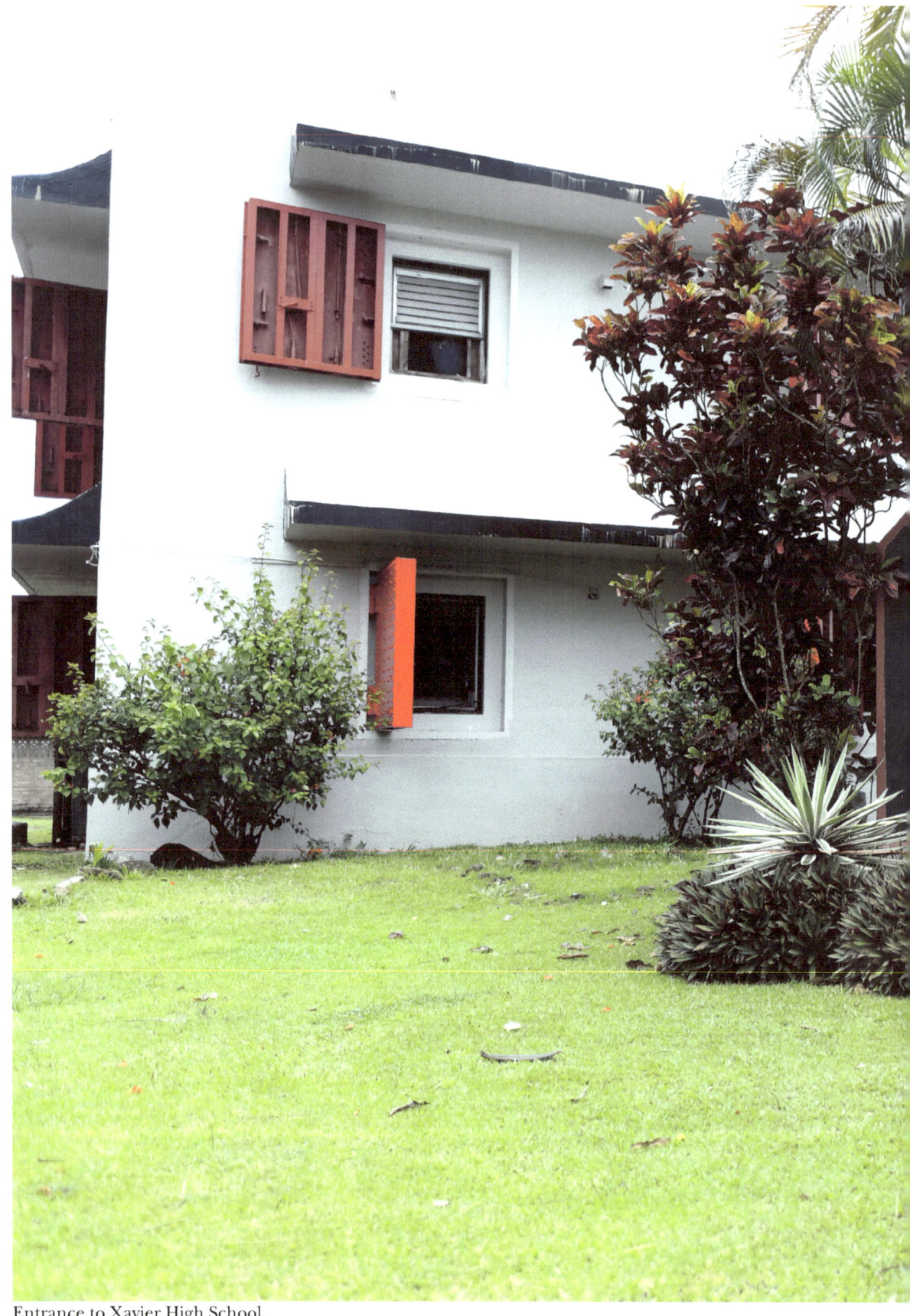

Entrance to Xavier High School.

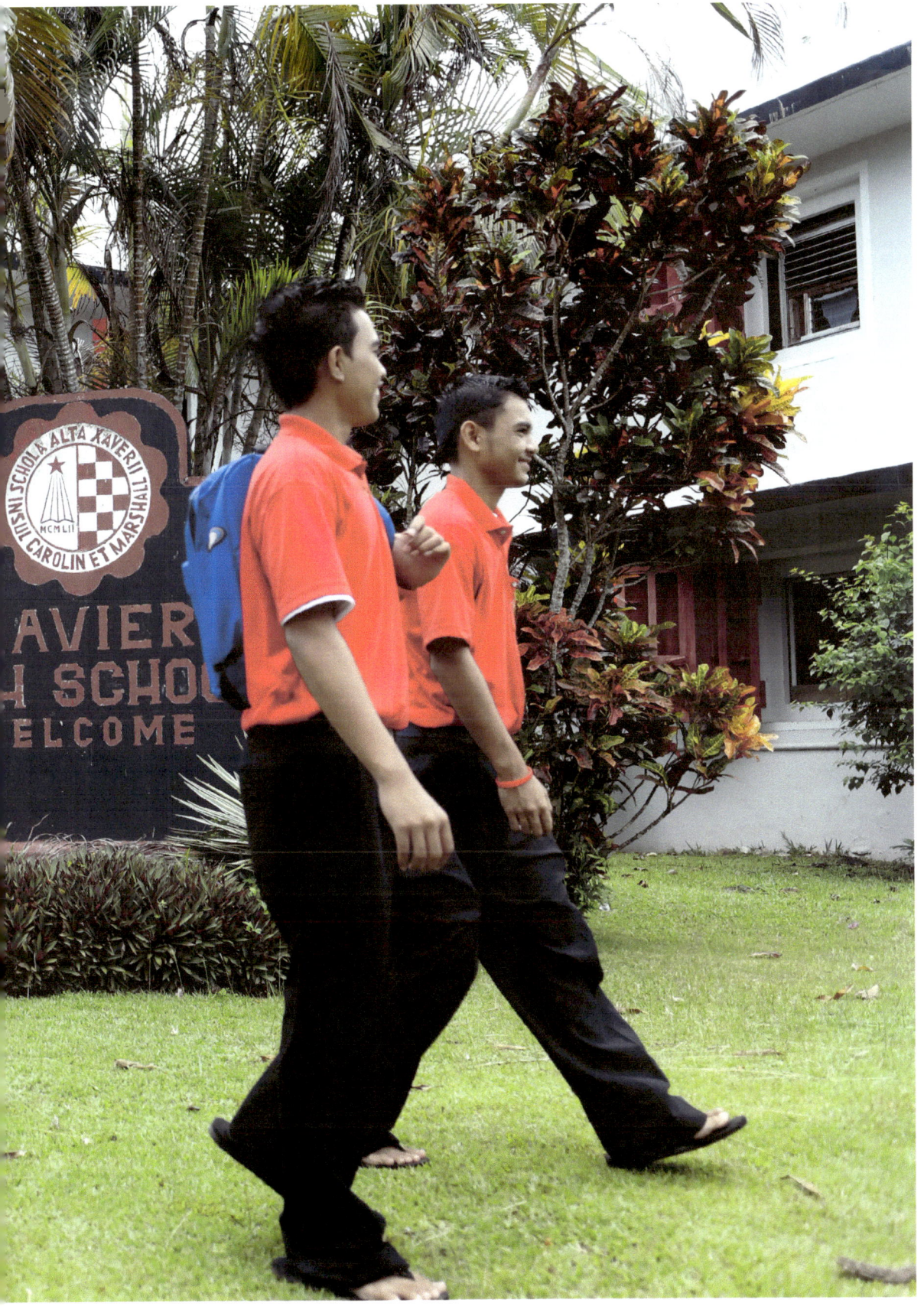

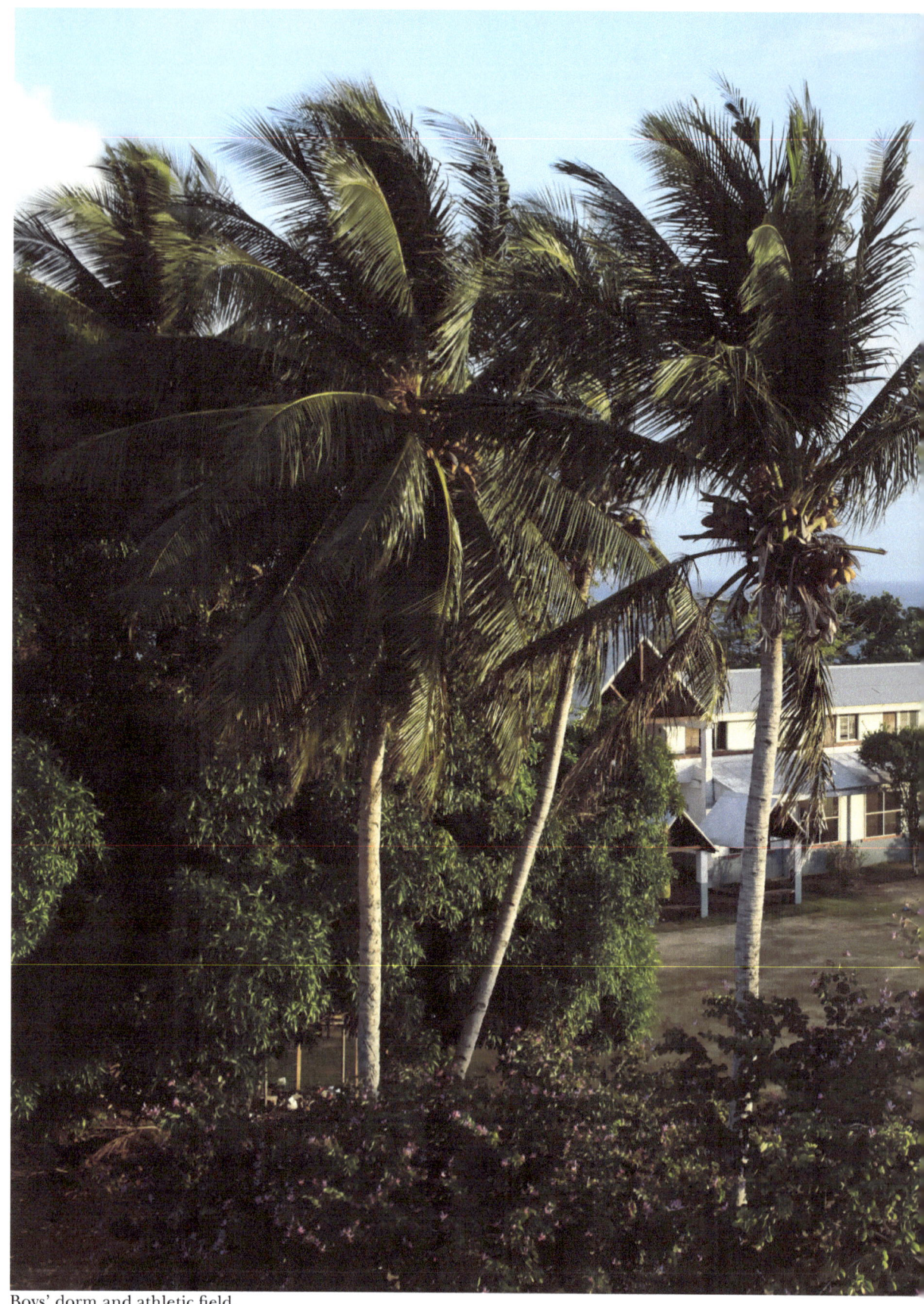

Boys' dorm and athletic field.

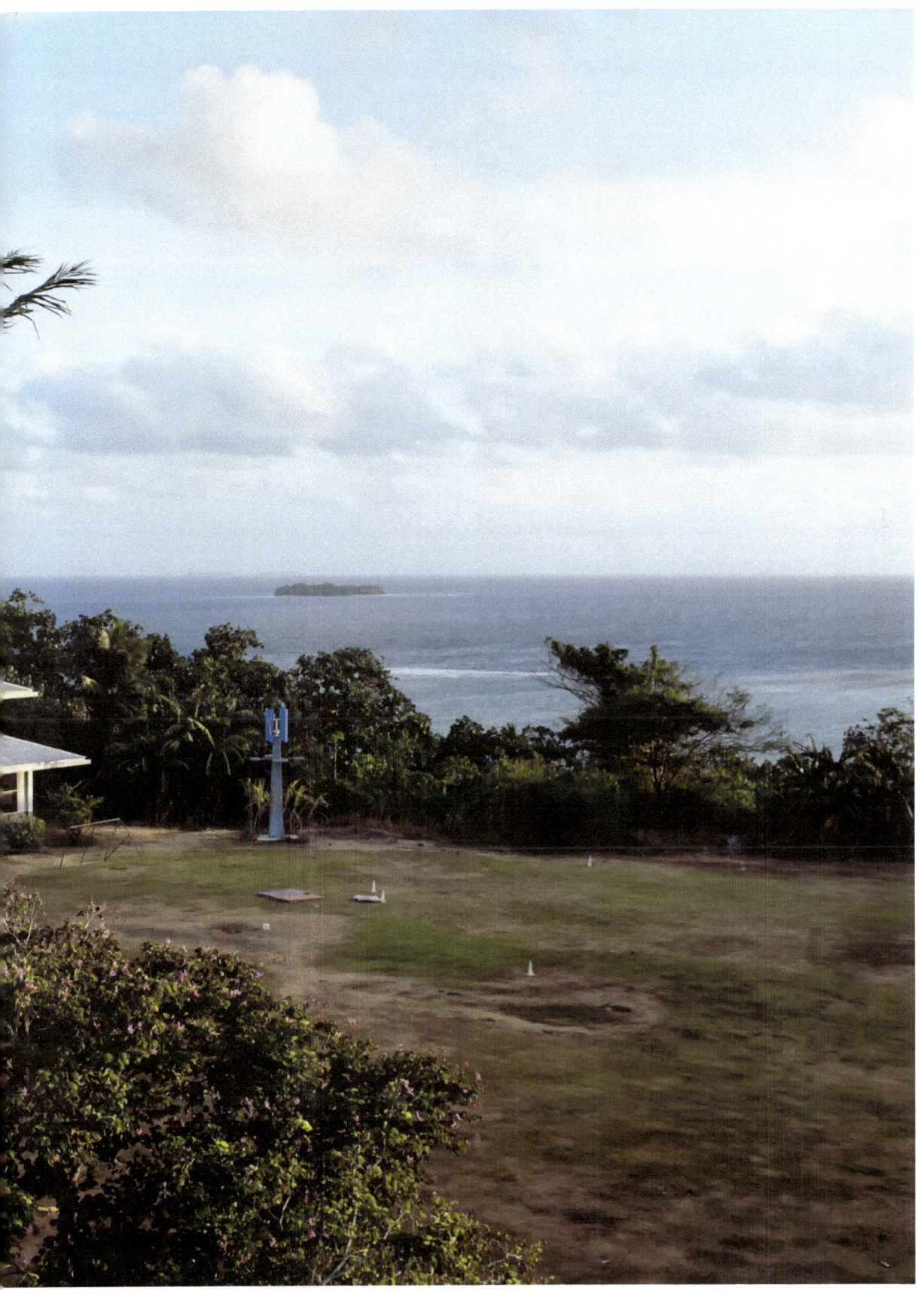

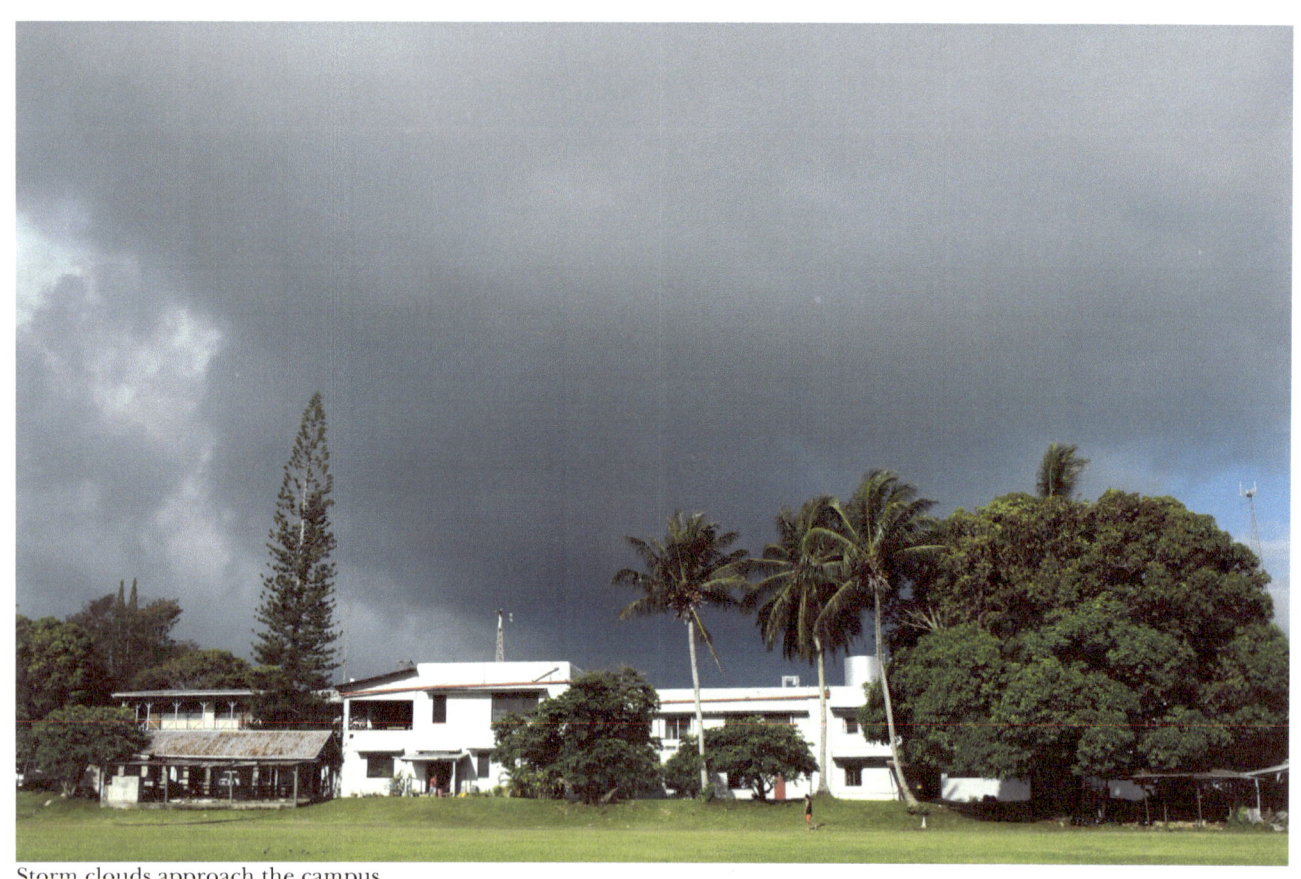

Storm clouds approach the campus.

Contents

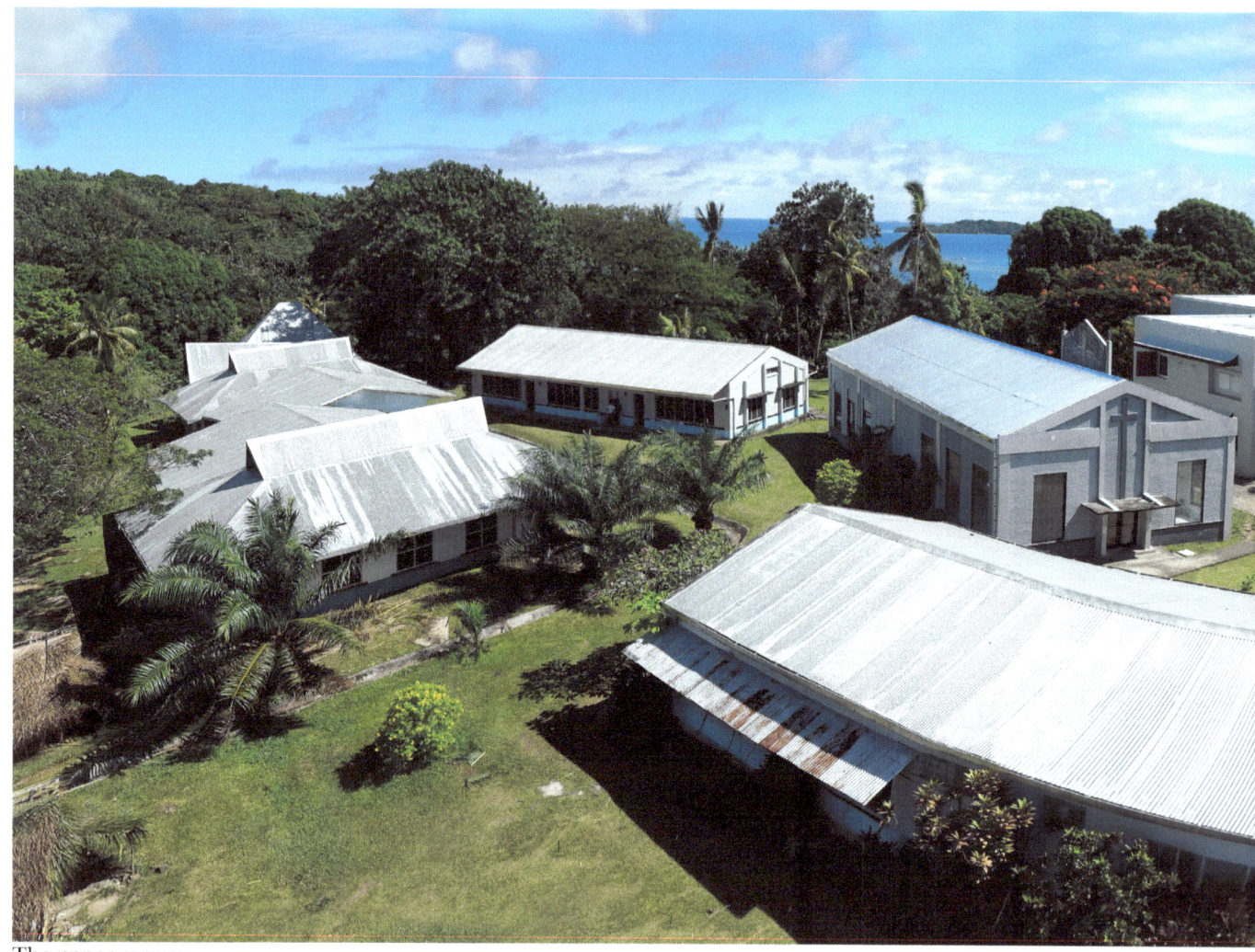

The upper campus.

Ut Omnes Unum Sint

Hands are raised, waving back and forth, as students shout out to be recognized. The teacher, Rey Dahilan, has the classroom under control, if barely. He looks across the small class and chooses two students. They rush to the front of the classroom, where they will compete to correctly answer the question Dahilan has carefully spelled out in dusty chalk.

On a blackboard. Not a whiteboard with brightly colored felt-tipped markers. And don't even think of looking for a SMART Board, not where municipal power is usually off for half the day. Or where the Internet connection is so slow that you could read half a chapter in a textbook by the time your Facebook home page loads.

Dahilan is teaching Math IV to the 29 members of the senior class of Xavier High School, which is located in the Federated States of Micronesia. The seniors at the blackboard are June Joy Lemaisei Laibeyal and Marson Elley. June Joy is from Woleai, a remote atoll in Yap State, population 1,000, at the western edge of the FSM. Marson is from Kosrae, a single island state at

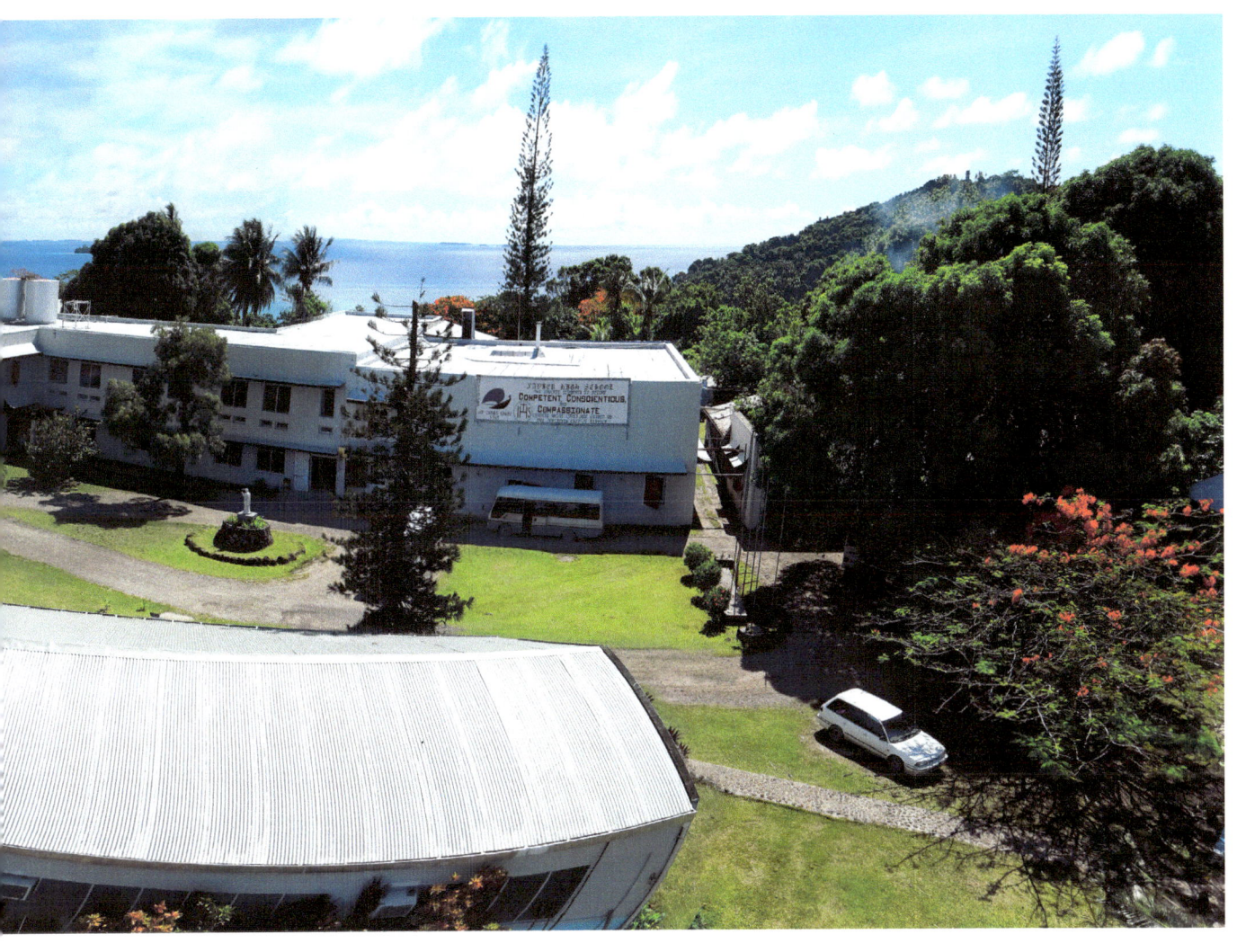

the far eastern edge of the FSM, home to some 7,000 residents.

June Joy and Marson grew up speaking different languages, learning different cultural traditions. But on this day, in their crisp red and white uniforms, they are speaking the same language, English, and are immersed in the rich cultural traditions of Xavier High School. The same holds true for their classmates, who come from Pohnpei and Chuuk, also part of the FSM, as well as the nations of Palau and the Marshall Islands. They are different, but after four years together at Xavier's hilltop campus in Chuuk, they are as close as

brothers and sisters.

There are a number of outstanding private schools in the Pacific Islands, institutions with traditions deeply immersed in local cultures. Queen Victoria School for boys and Adi Cakobau School for girls, which have trained generations of young leaders in Fiji, quickly come to mind. In the Western Pacific, Father Duenas Memorial School for boys and Academy of Our Lady of Guam for girls also are known for training leaders.

But none of those schools, or any other in Oceania, comes close to matching Xavier High School's combination of cultural diversity, rigorous scholarship, and tradition of preparing students for senior leadership roles in government, business and the community. The school is grounded in the Jesuit tradition of education framed by faith, discipline of intellect and values, and the call to service. But it is also shaped by the diversity of a cultural region that is as large as the continental United States, which has nine distinct languages and a host of dialects, just above the equator in the Western Pacific.

Xavier opened in 1952 as a Roman Catholic seminary. But in the wake of World War II, with the former Japanese-administered Mandated Islands now under U.S. control, it didn't take long for the Jesuits to figure out that the demand for general education outstripped their desire for training priests from the islands. The first graduates, all from Palau, received their high school diplomas in 1956.

In the years since, Xavier has earned a reputation as the premier high school in the Micronesian region. It remains the only U.S. accredited high school in what is now the Federated States of Micronesia, and one of the few accredited high schools in the Western Pacific. How Xavier maintains its high academic standards, despite meager financial resources and ever increasing needs, and produces disciplined, focused leaders is a story of hope and promise in a region of diminished expectations and standards, where "good enough" is usually as high as the bar is raised.

On another day, I was in the classroom of Stephanie Osborne, a young American from Maryland who was completing her second year at Xavier as a Jesuit Volunteer Corps teacher. Osborne is a gifted teacher, teaching science in laboratories and classrooms that often have no electricity or computers. In Osborne's sophomore science class that day, the lesson plan was understanding DNA.

Instead of computers with rotating 3-D images of a helix, the students had sheets of paper taped together to draw 2-D charts. They used pens, pencils, rulers and colored markers to develop the DNA analysis of a supposed victim of a crime, and of a host of suspects. The lesson: understand the components of DNA, chart them using markers and rulers, and then compare the DNA of the many suspects against that found on the murder victim.

Think CSI Chuuk. The students worked in teams, many huddled together on the floor, their DNA charts stretching three to four feet, all held together with clear tape. As Osborne laid out the DNA chart of the murder victim, she asked the students to compare their charts against that of the DNA found on the dead person. The students' eyes went wide, and many began to yell out answers, trying to be the first to identify the "murderer."

I looked around the classroom. Some of the glass louvers were broken or missing, others in desperate need of cleaning. The rusted ceiling fans were still, an anemic breeze providing the only relief from the tropical heat and humidity. The only light in the classroom came from soft reflections of the intense equatorial sun. It wasn't clear if the power was off – again – or if Osborne had decided there was no need to waste electricity, a necessary survival skill on this Pacific island. Regardless, the enthusiastic students were learning about DNA, and how to apply that knowledge. There was no sign of deprivation or despair.

The learning that takes place in Osborne's or Dahilan's classrooms isn't unique on the Xavier campus. I saw it in the art and physics classes taught by Jeff Pouzar, an American volunteer who came on his own from Texas. It was obvious in the required Latin classes that are taught by Brother Mario Tomi, SJ, an Indonesian who also taught freshmen how to dance with partners for a program in neighboring Sapuk Village. It was there in the Literature class taught by Mike Tedone, a Jesuit volunteer from California, where sophomores acted out scenes from Romeo and Juliet, reciting Shakespearean English with Micronesian accents.

Xavier High School has long had a reputation for rigorous scholarship. The school requires applicants to take a tough admissions test. Parents, some of whom are alumni, have been known to plead for special consideration for their children who did not do well on the test. Usually, the answer is "no."

The school is also known for setting high expectations for the behavior of its students, on campus and in the community. During my time at Xavier, there was still a buzz among some students about a group of junior boys who in the previous term had been expelled for drinking. What the students didn't see was the response from the parent of one of those juniors. She told Director Fr. Rich McAuliff, SJ, that her son finally understood why he was expelled, missed Xavier terribly, and was now enrolled and doing well at a private school on his home island.

It was harsh, but Xavier had taught the young man

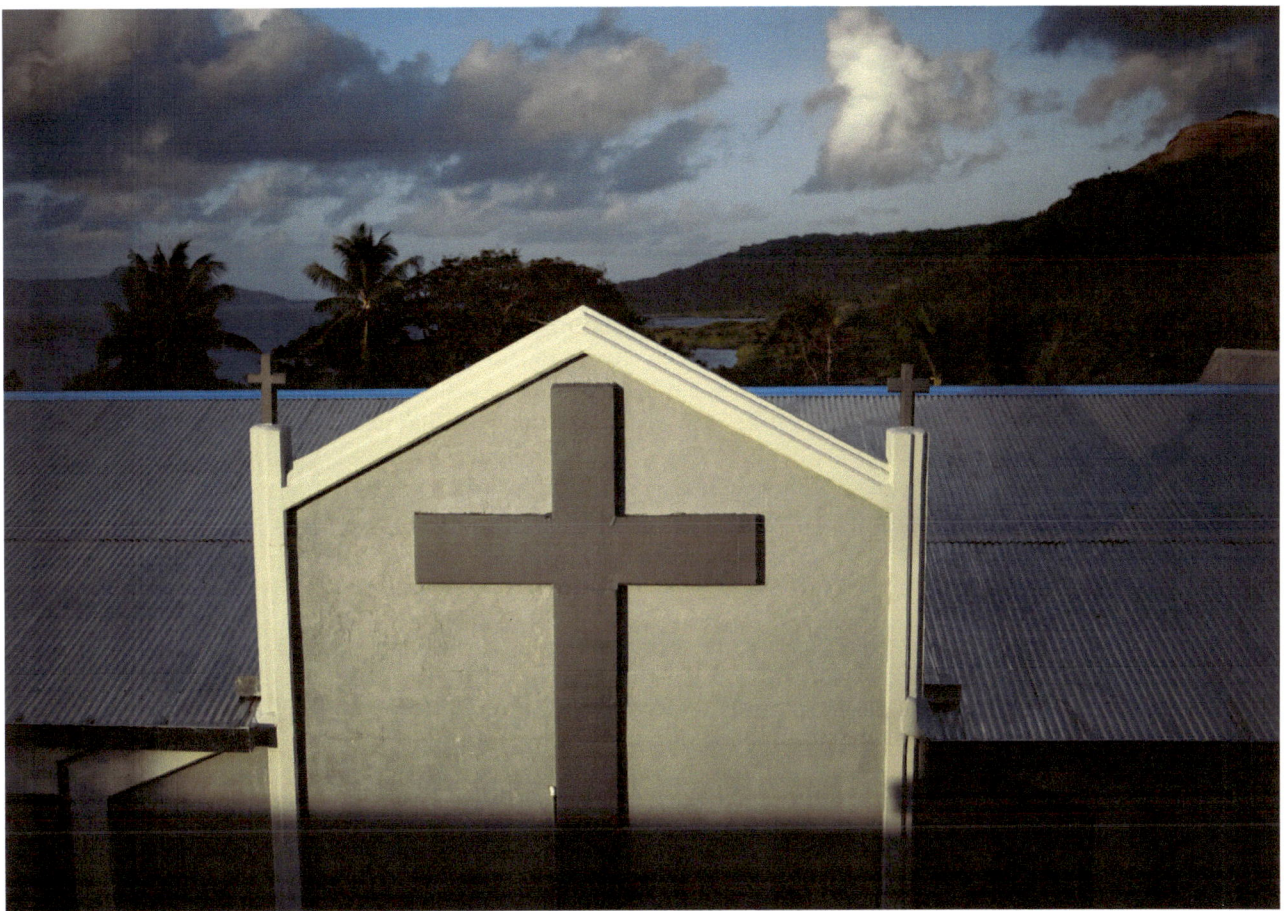
The Student Center in early morning light.

an important life lesson: there are consequences for your actions, and you are responsible for your behavior in the community of your peers, as well as in the larger community. It is a lesson, unfortunately, that isn't taught much these days in the broader community in the Micronesian region. Government teachers don't show up to work at public schools, but still get paychecks. Officials squander money on failed projects, or can't manage public services at an acceptable level of performance. They don't lose their jobs.

That's not the case at Xavier. The class that graduated in May 2010 is an example of the high expectations that Xavier places on its students. Some 900 youngsters competed for 50 positions in the class that enrolled in Fall 2006. Of the 50 who were accepted, 43 showed up to start their freshman year. When the class graduated in May 2010, there were 29 seniors.

The others had quit, been expelled for poor academic performance, or had been kicked out for infractions of the rules. That class wasn't unique; its story is usually repeated with each graduating class.

As one of the oldest private schools in the Micronesia region, Xavier High School has traditions that form the foundation of its experience. The boys, who make up slightly more than half of the school's 165 students, live in a dorm. The rituals of dorm life – from the bells that sound wake up in the morning, to the social skills one must learn living with so many strangers, to drying clothes on the weekends on the sun-baked tin roofs of school buildings – are central to their Xavier experience.

Some alumni say there needs to be a return to the strict discipline that governed dorm life in the 1960s, 1970s and 1980s. When I was on campus, Joe Saimon, a

17

graduate from the 1980s and a member of the school's board of governors, spent a long weekend at Xavier living in a Spartan faculty unit in the boys' dorm. With nothing to do that weekend, he asked Fr. Rich if he could oversee the cleaning of the dorm. Fr. Rich quickly said yes, and Joe went to work.

The dorm had been "cleaned" a few days before, overseen by an American teacher who was also the dormitory proctor. But the exercise was more Keystone Cops than Mr. Clean – the boys dragged bunk beds and foam mattresses outside to be aired, which then got soaked when the rains came. The bunk beds were left scattered on the athletic field, and it seemed as if half the boys were resting on the bunks rather than cleaning the dorm.

Joe, a Pohnpeian, took a different approach. He organized the boys by class – the freshman did the grunt work, the sophomores did major cleaning, and the juniors were to supervise and clean louvers and window screens. The seniors weren't included, as they were just days away from graduating.

Facing the boys, who had gathered in a large shed on campus, Joe told them they were going to clean the dorm again and, oh yes, clean the campus, too. When there were a few groans from the group, Joe looked at them and said, "This is a tradition at Xavier. We used to do this all the time when I was a student here. Boys, do you know why you do this? You do this so that you can learn to become men."

He had them; the boys worked from 9:30 a.m. to past 7 p.m. And the juniors, who thought they had it easy, were still working at 7 p.m. cleaning window screens that were thick with dust and grime. So much for being "supervisors." Another lesson learned.

There have been other changes over the years; the decision to enroll girls in the mid-1970s was a shocker to old-time alumni. Today, however, it is the girls who run the campus. They may let the boys hold elected office – Micronesian cultures, despite being matrilineal, still tend to give deference to males in such positions. But it is clear that the girls set the social and cultural agendas at Xavier.

But the essential experience at Xavier – learning to do much with relatively little – remains a staple of life on Mabuchi hill, as locals call the area. Everyone who lives on campus – the boys, faculty, staff, the priest – bathe using ladles to scoop cold water from plastic buckets. A talented teacher also makes tables, chairs and lockers from plywood. The door to the principal's office is decorated with brightly colored college banners, and peeling veneer that shows the damage caused by termites. Students have lots to eat, but the food is reminiscent of the simple staples of steamed rice and canned mackerel that generations of Xavierites remember with some fondness.

It is what you don't see that also impresses. Some of the Xavier girls made a pact to abstain from sex while they were in school. Not surprising at a Roman Catholic school? It was an initiative that took self-directed leadership and courage in a region where teen pregnancies are an epidemic, and the resulting broken dreams of not obtaining a high school diploma and going to college are commonplace.

What you do see, but may not realize it, is the reality that Palauans befriend Marshall Islanders, who become close to Pohnpeians, who live with host families in Chuuk. Or that Kosraeans and Yapese learn to speak Chuukese, which is taught as part of the Xavier curriculum. There is no other institution in Micronesia where this dynamic takes place to this extent on a daily basis.

There once was a time when the region's political leaders, many of whom were schooled at Xavier, espoused a vision of a "united Micronesia," one political entity of many languages and cultures. That dream of four decades ago fell victim to the realities of "nationalism." But to see these young Islanders, the grandchildren and great-grandchildren of that independence generation, living and studying together as brother and sister makes one realize the power of what might have been.

A high percentage of Xavier graduates go on to college, whether at the national College of Micronesia-FSM, Palau Community College or College of Marshall Islands, and beyond. I met one Xavier graduate who is studying for a Masters of Law at New York University. Two members of the class of 2010 received Gates Millennium Scholarships; full ride fellowships for four years of college. One is at the University of San Francisco, the other at Loyola Marymount University.

Xavier graduates have become diplomats, senators, government leaders, business executives, and lawyers. Four Xavierites have become presidents of Micronesian nations. All remain deeply attached to their second home on Mabuchi hill. My Facebook friends include a number of Xavierites, current and former. It

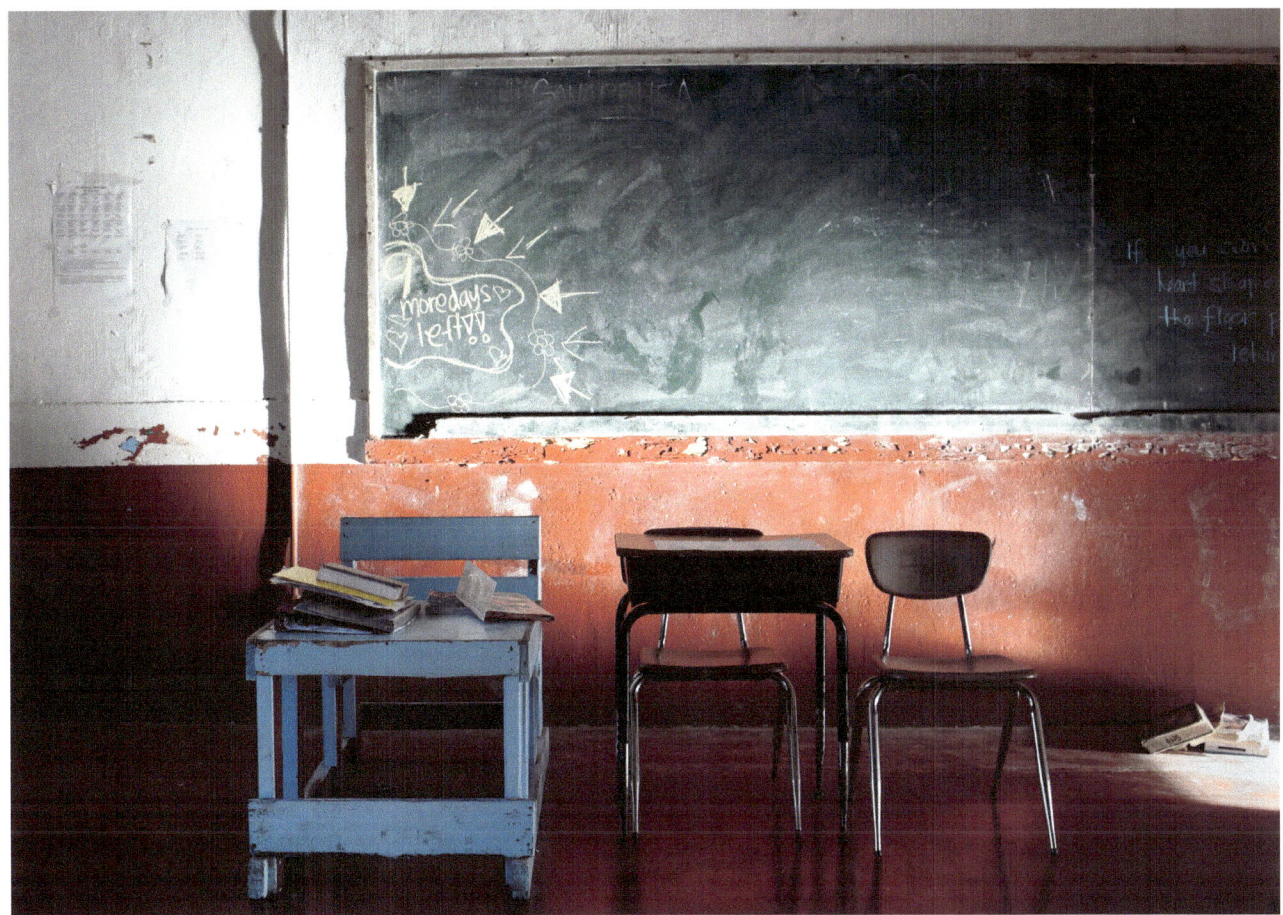
Desks and chairs in the freshman-sophomore study hall.

is fascinating to read their banter, well, some of it. I'm struck by how many times a graduate will write, "I miss that place," or "I want to go back." When I left high school, a private boarding school like Xavier, the last thing I wanted to do was go back. That's not the case for Xavier's graduates.

I finally understood why that was when I traveled with the senior class to Pisar Island, a spit of sand in the Chuuk Lagoon. They went there for their senior retreat, an annual ritual led by Fr. Jim Croghan, SJ, a former Director of Xavier. The two and a half day retreat was designed to give seniors a chance to reflect on their spiritual journey at Xavier, and to allow them one last time to be together as a class.

Amidst the usual teen-age joking and horsing around, I saw how students protected those who weren't socially adept or popular. I saw young people who found joy in friendships that were unencumbered by the usual teen-age issues of boys, girls and romance (though there were "couples" in the class). There was, above all, a level of transparent respect for their peers.

That is, I think, the key to the Xavier experience – respect gained from having together survived four years of demanding academics; respect earned from caring for each other as brother and sister; respect shared openly and without fear of embarrassment. That these young people could go on to any college or university and thrive is almost immaterial. At this small school in the middle of Micronesia, atop a hill called Mabuchi overlooking the Western Pacific, young people from diverse Island backgrounds learn how to respect others, and perhaps most important, they learn how to respect themselves.

The experience makes real Xavier High School's central value, "Ut Omnes Unum Sint." That all may be one.

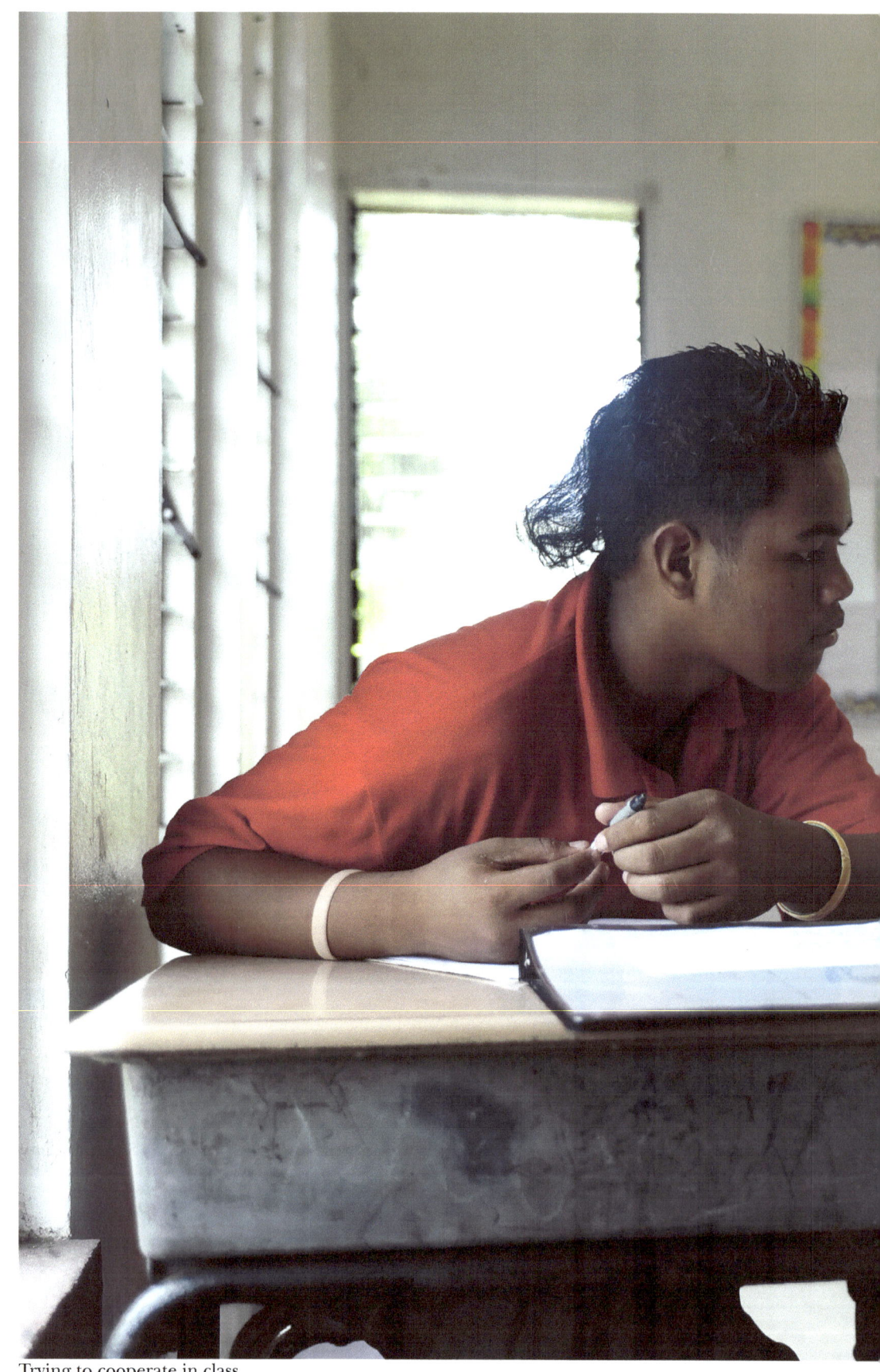

Trying to cooperate in class.

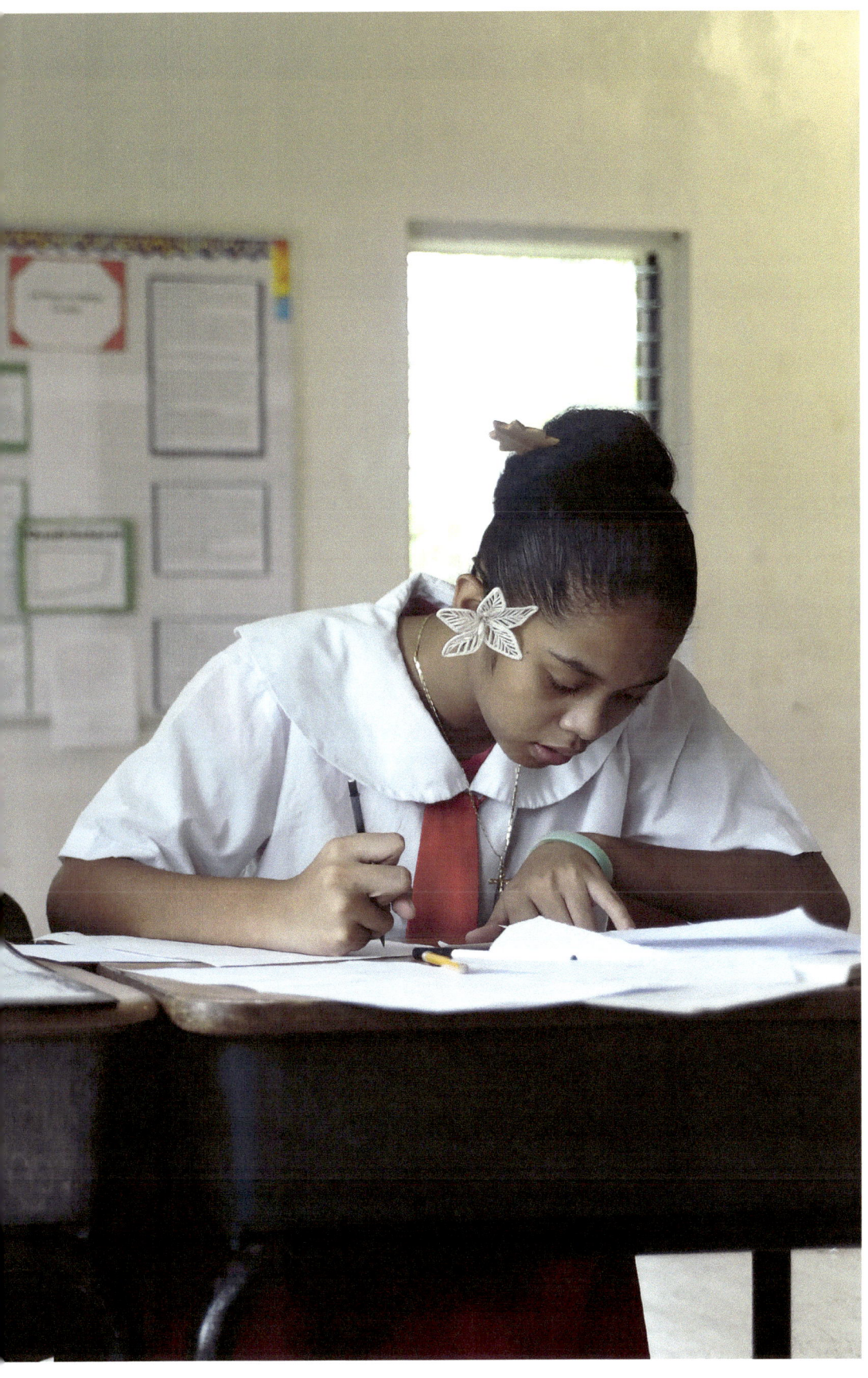

Mind

How do you challenge high school seniors to understand what calculus is, and then apply the language of mathematics to everyday life? At Xavier High School, teacher Rey Dahilan has the answer.

His final exam for Math IV, a required class for all 29 seniors, consisted of two parts. First, use calculus to determine whether the population of a certain island would increase or decrease over a set period of time. Second, what will the impact of that answer be on the consumption of a specific food, and beyond that, prepare a report on the nutritional value and cultural importance of that food to the island community.

The students divided into teams. They were assigned foods such as breadfruit, taro, fish, pork and coconuts. They chose their best mathematician to answer the calculus question – it would be done at the black board – and the rest of the group researched their assigned food.

On the morning of the final exam in Math IV, the students were busy slicing tuna filets, frying pork steaks, completing charts and PowerPoint presentations. One group uprooted a seven-foot taro plant and brought it to the classroom. Three faculty members – Dahilan, English teacher Megan Bell and Japanese language instructor Manabu Nakano – judged the presentations.

I can't recall a final exam in my 18 years of formal education – K-12, university and graduate school – where I was required to show in a tangible way the real-world value of what I learned in class. Ever. Nor was I ever then allowed with my classmates to eat our final exam for lunch.

At Xavier High School, the extraordinary is often commonplace in the classroom.

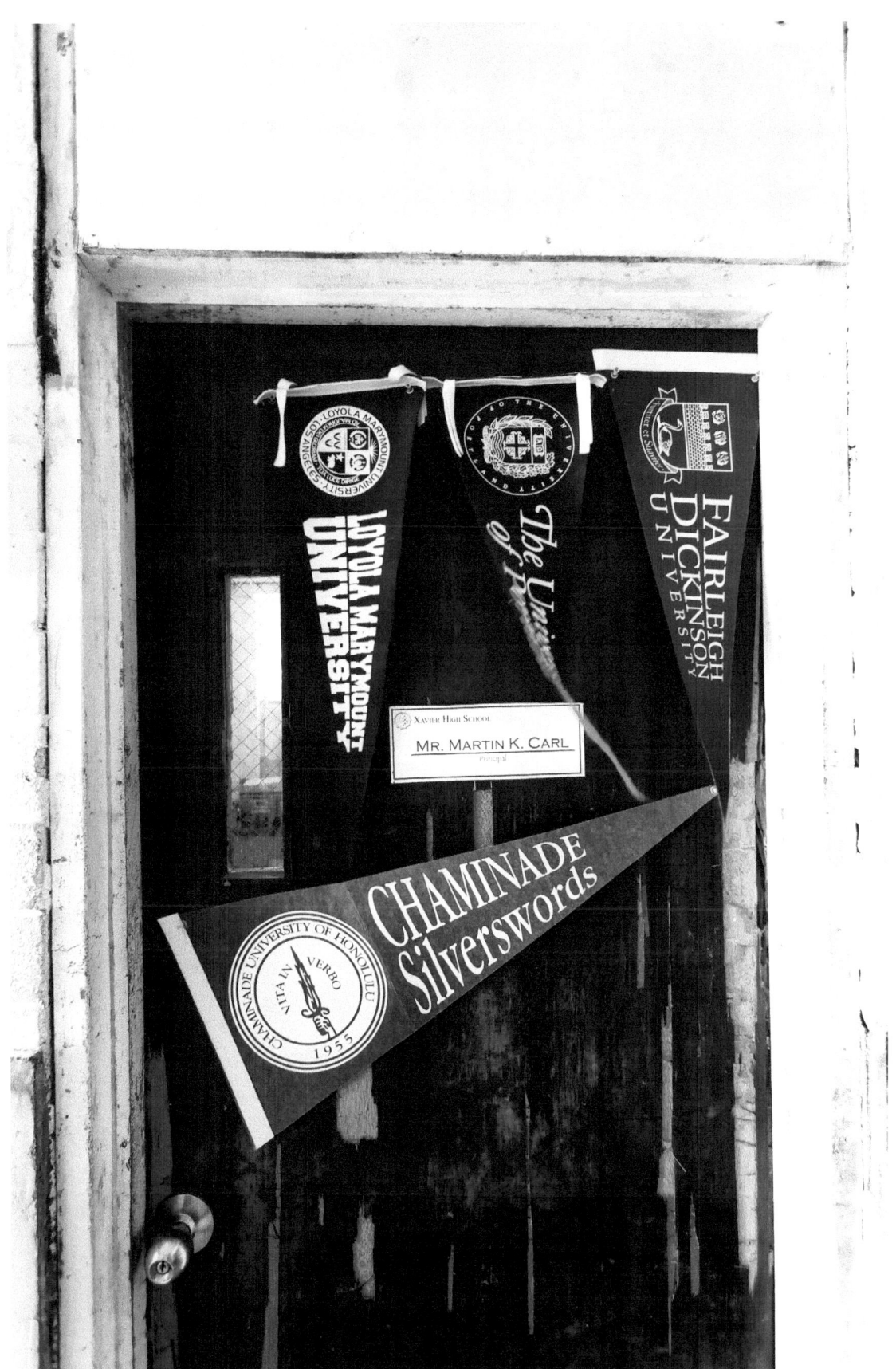

Door to the office of Principal Martin Carl.

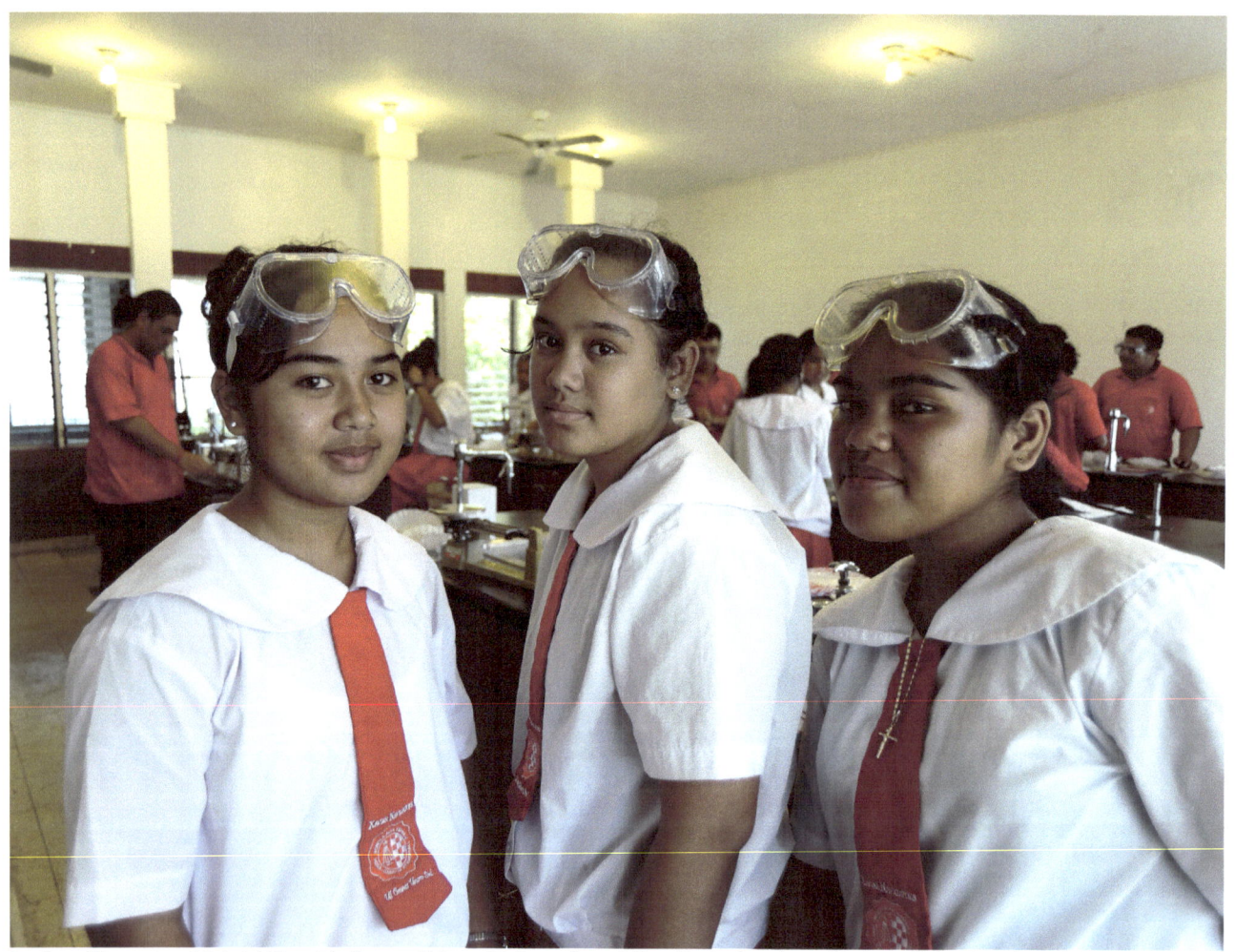

Juniors Cherotine Maipi (Chuuk), Renee Edgar (Pohnpei) and Rosalinda Lambert (Pohnpei) in chemistry lab.

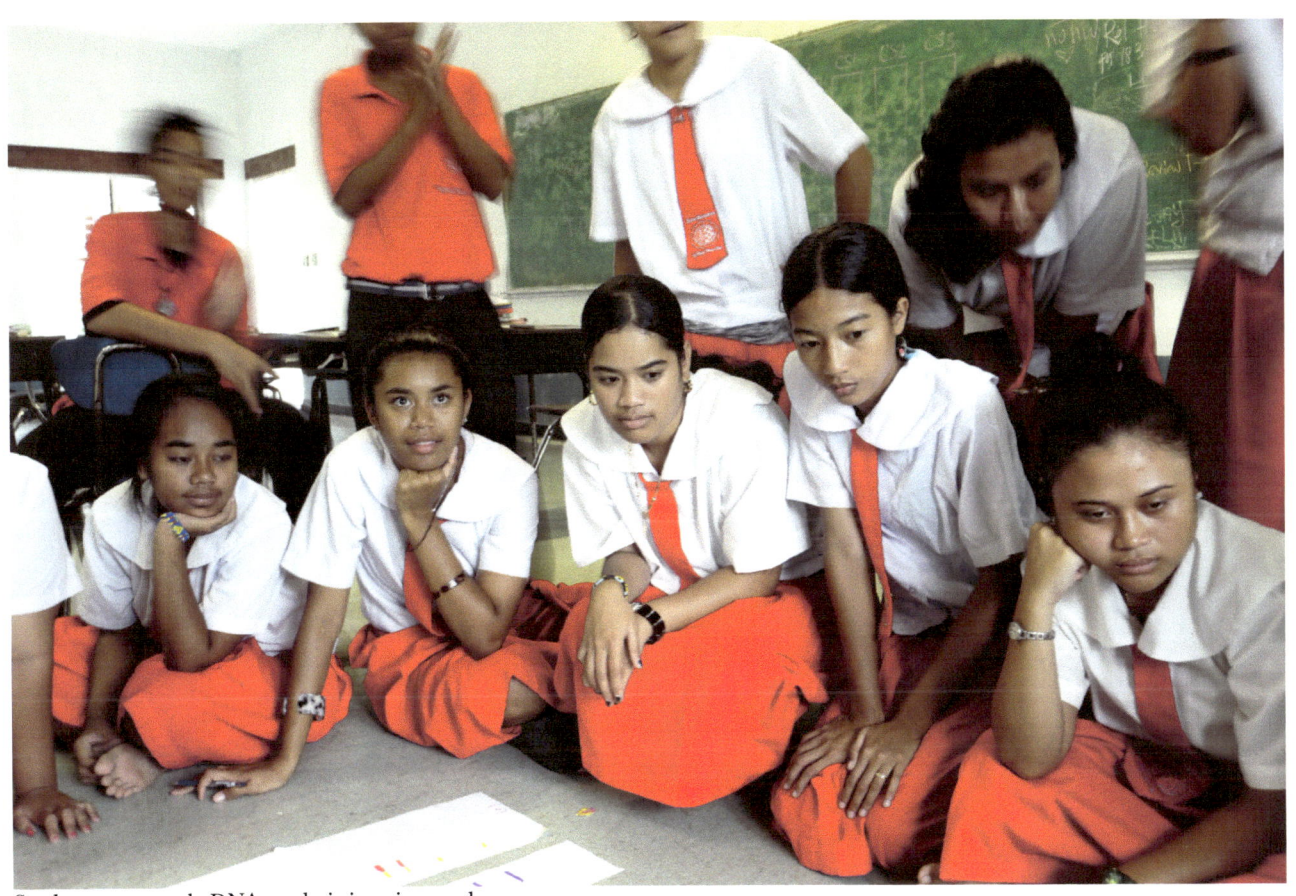
Sophomores study DNA analysis in science class.

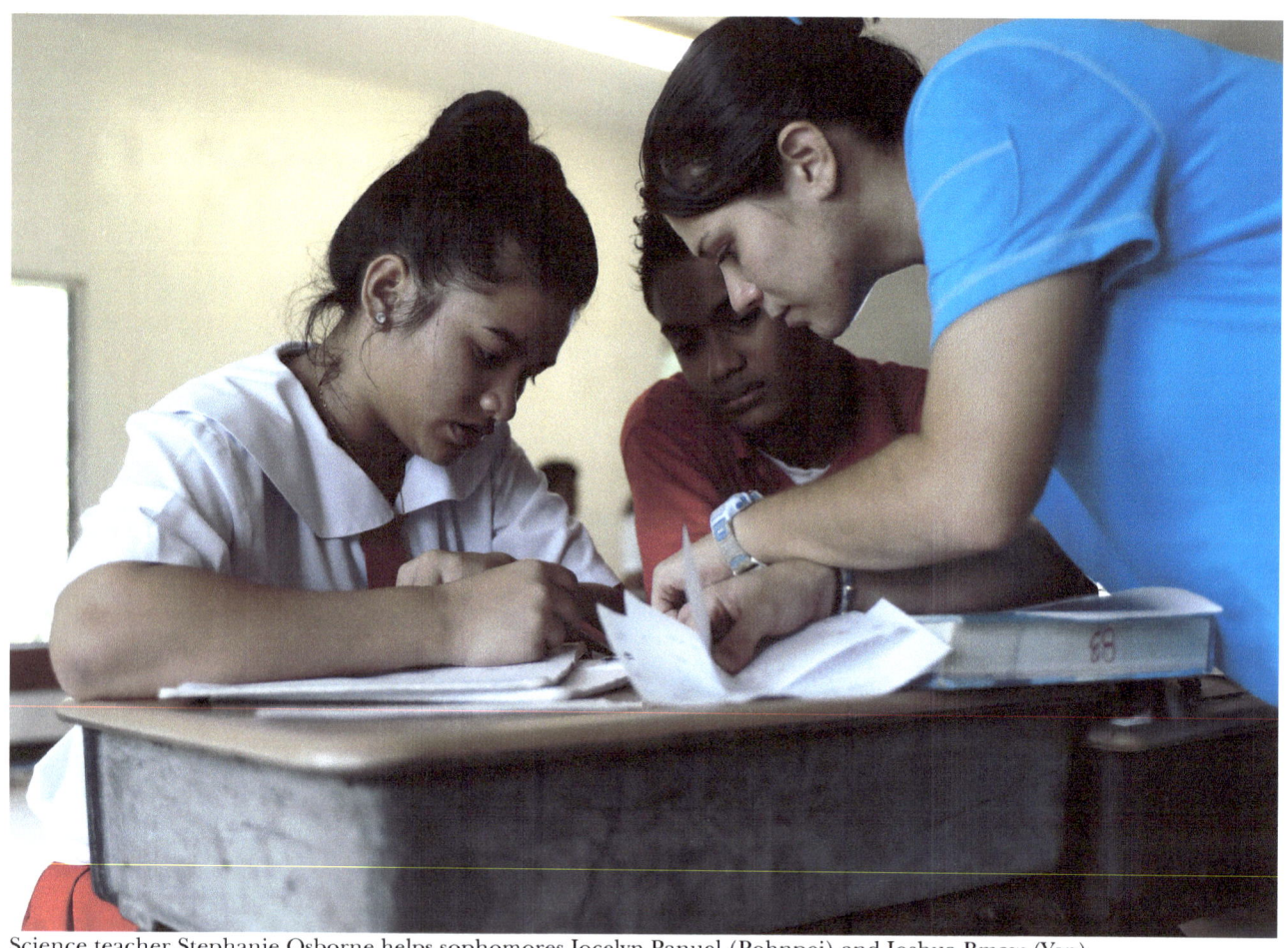

Science teacher Stephanie Osborne helps sophomores Jocelyn Panuel (Pohnpei) and Joshua Bmaw (Yap).

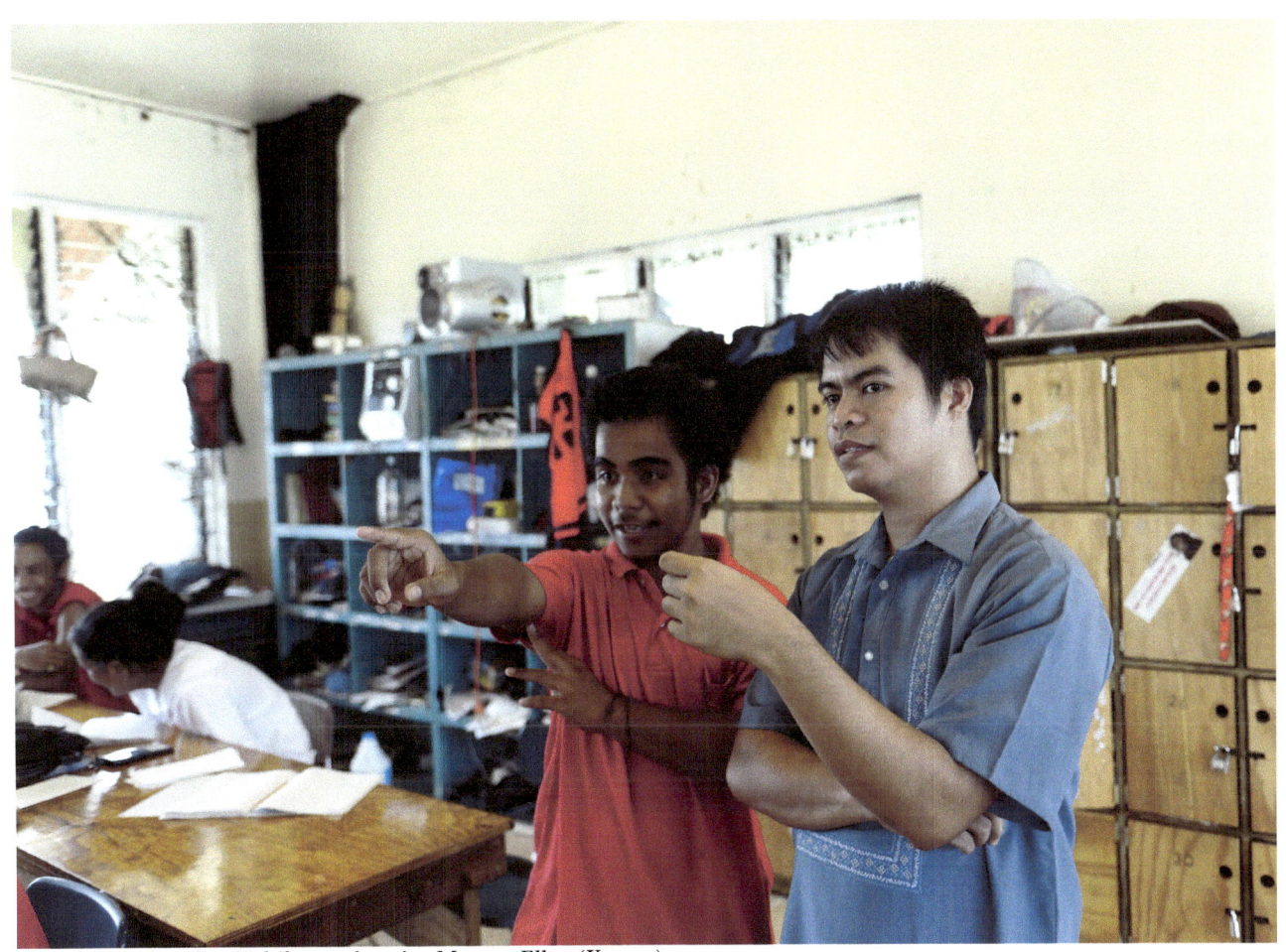

Calculus teacher Rey Dahilan and senior Marson Elley (Kosrae).

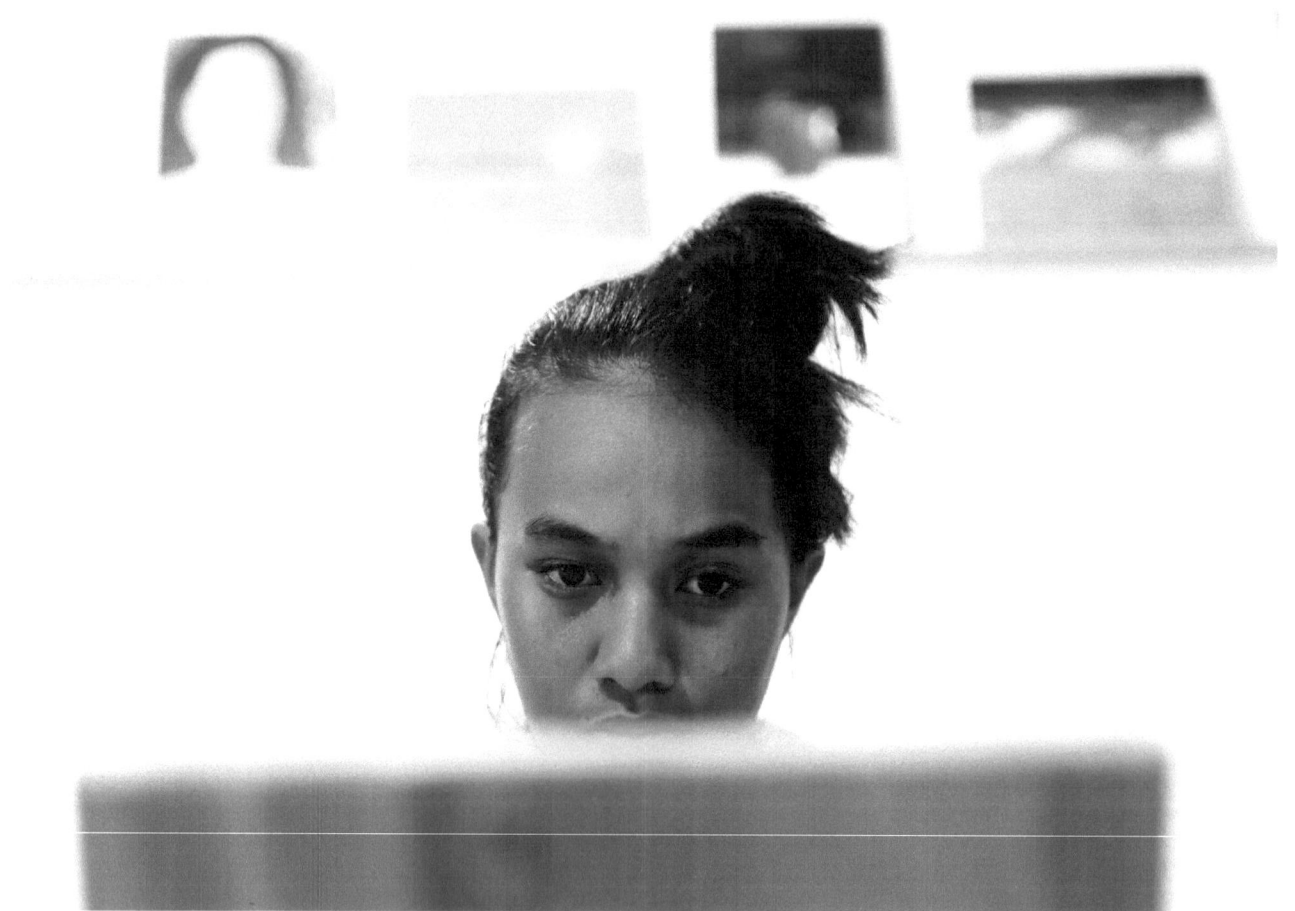

Junior Gayle Hallers (Pohnpei) uses a mirror to draw a self-portrait in art class.

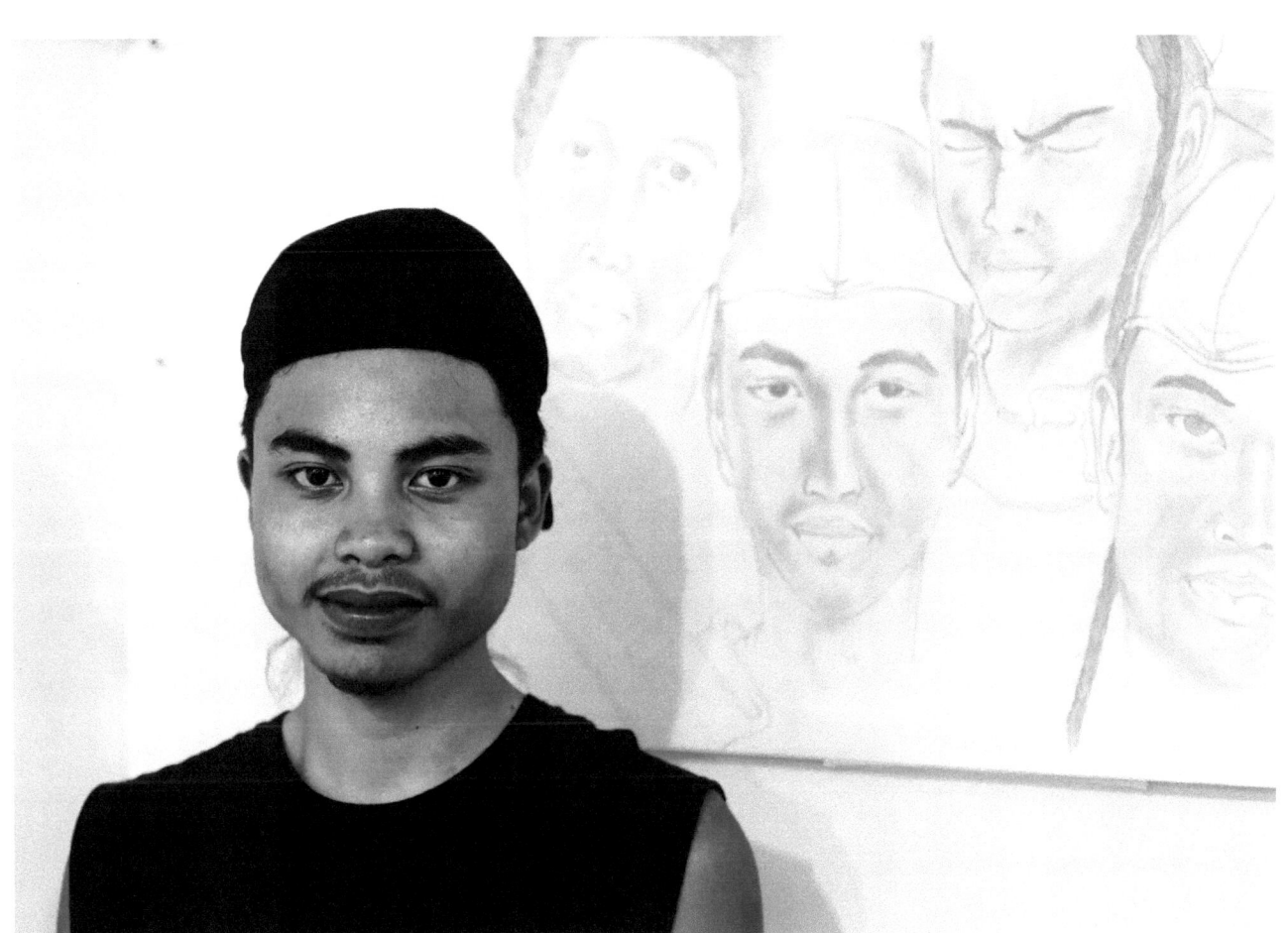

Senior Takamasa T-Bo Mori, Jr. (Chuuk) and a drawing he did in art class.

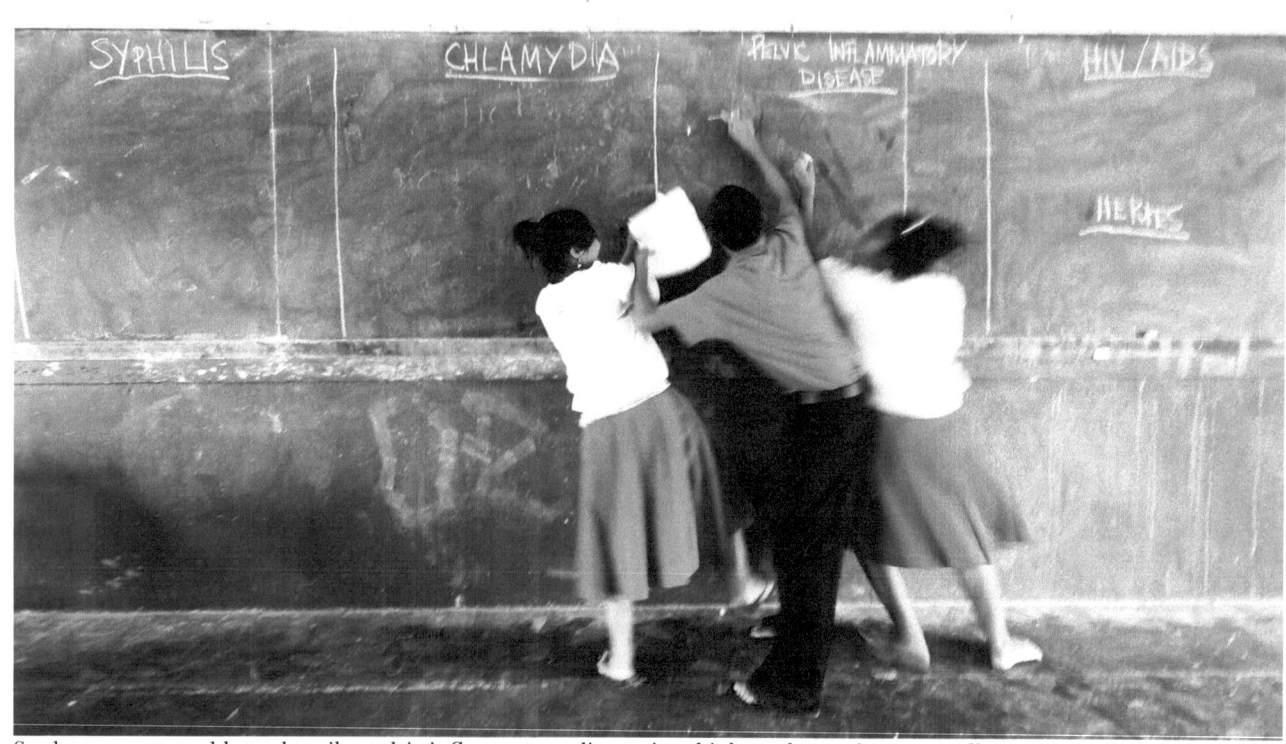

Sophomores scramble to describe pelvic inflammatory disease in a biology class unit on sexually transmitted diseases.

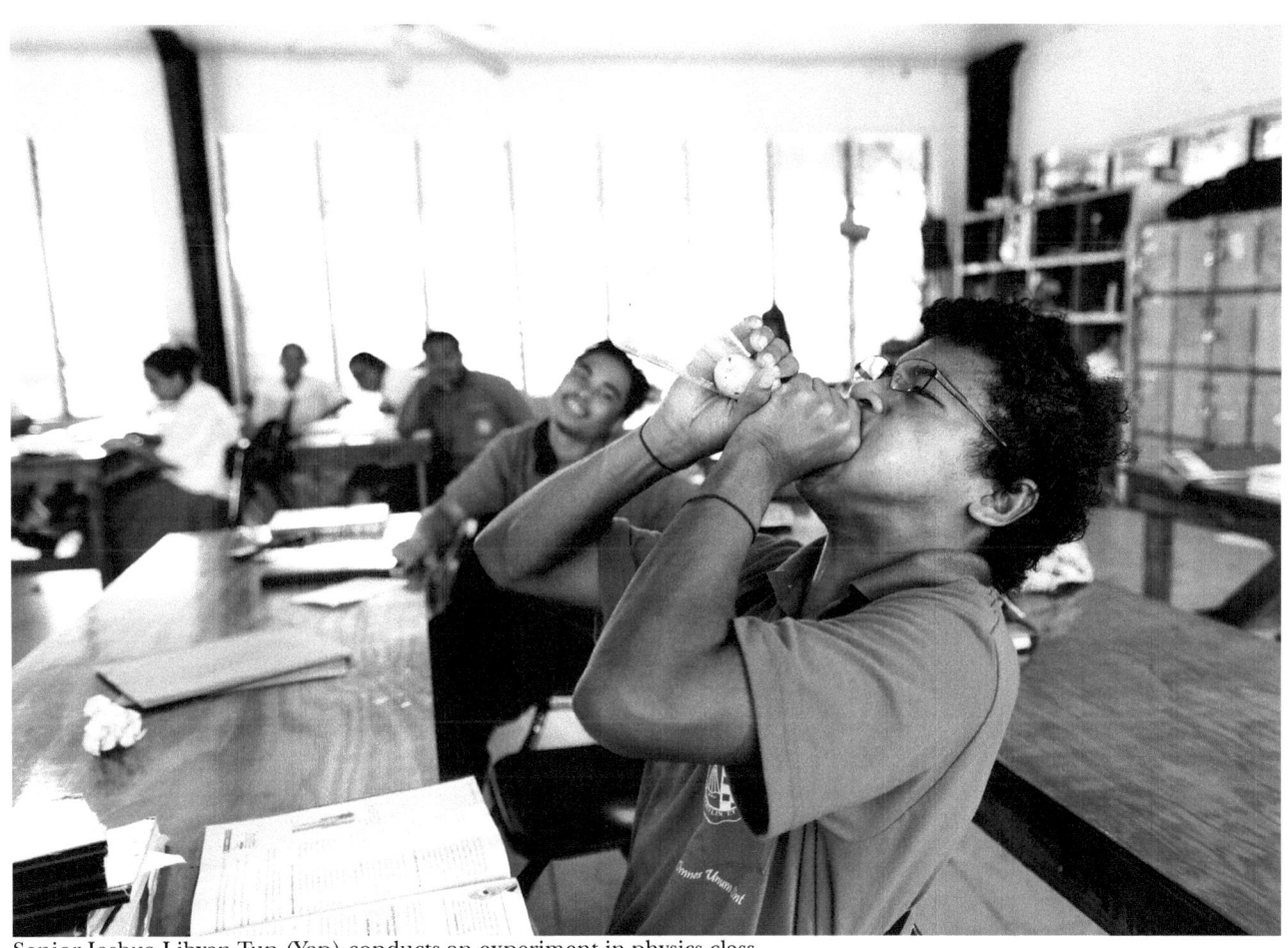

Senior Joshua Libyan Tun (Yap) conducts an experiment in physics class.

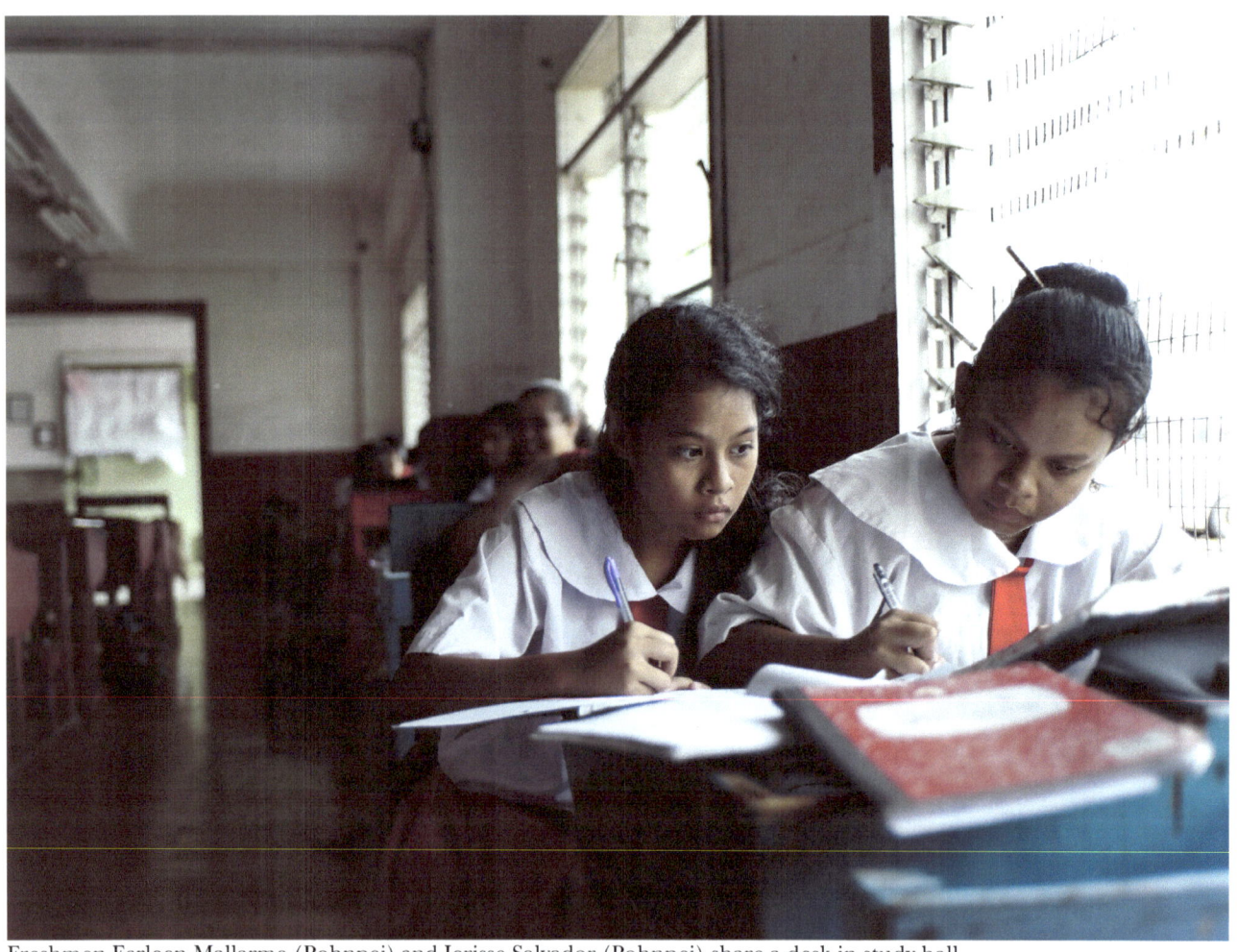

Freshmen Ferleen Mallarme (Pohnpei) and Jerisse Salvador (Pohnpei) share a desk in study hall.

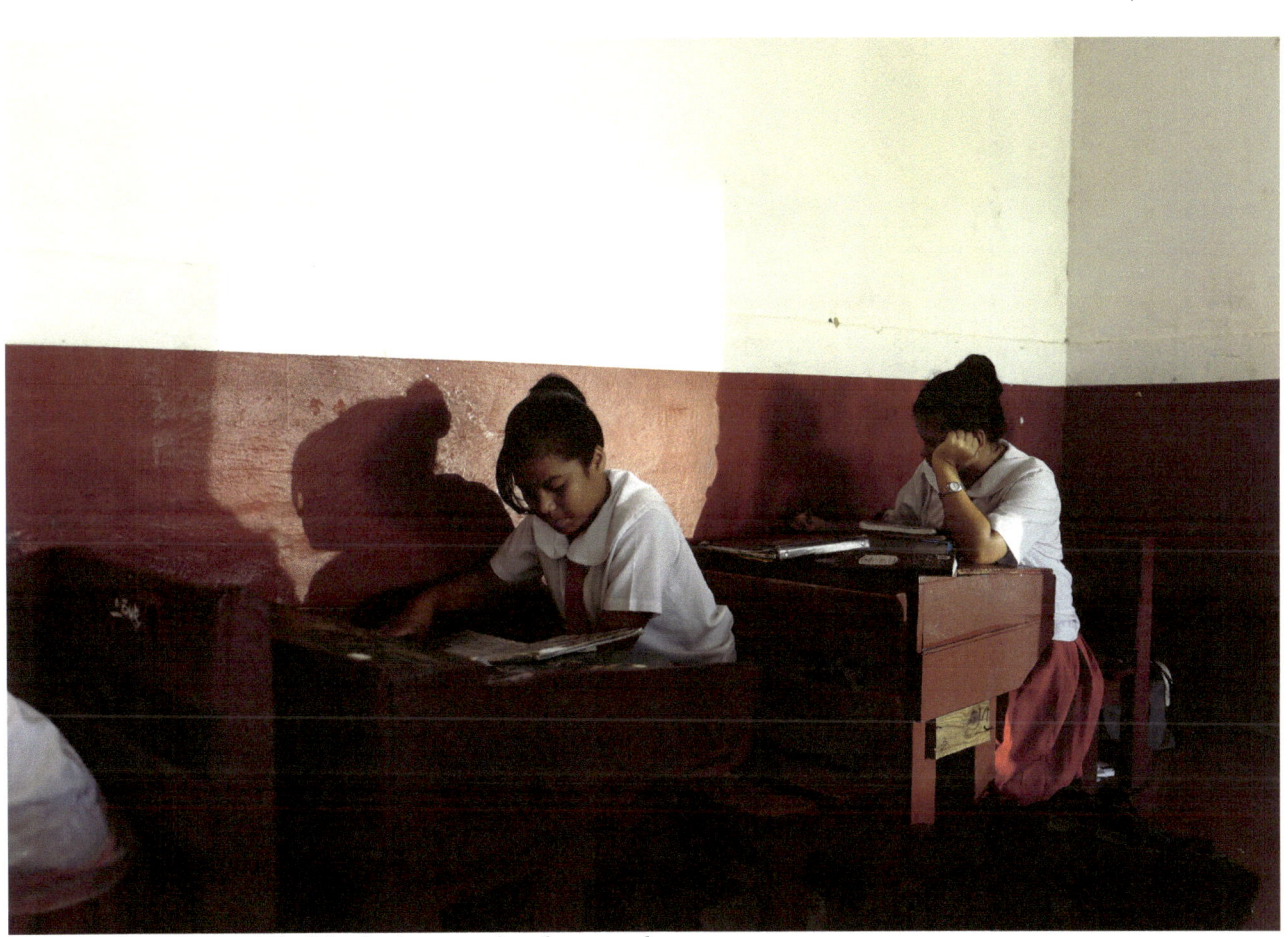

Combined morning study hall for freshman and sophomore classes.

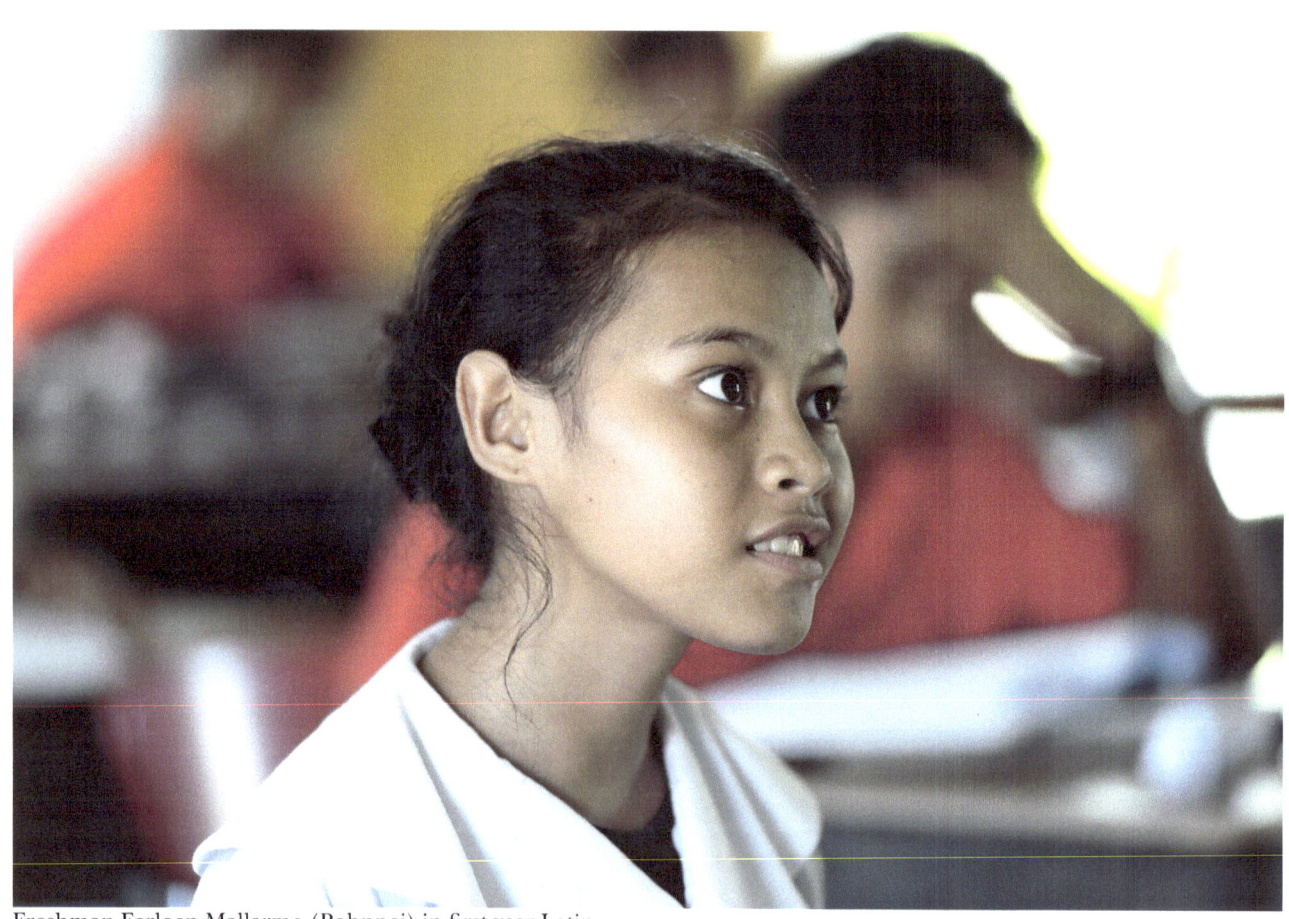

Freshman Ferleen Mallarme (Pohnpei) in first-year Latin.

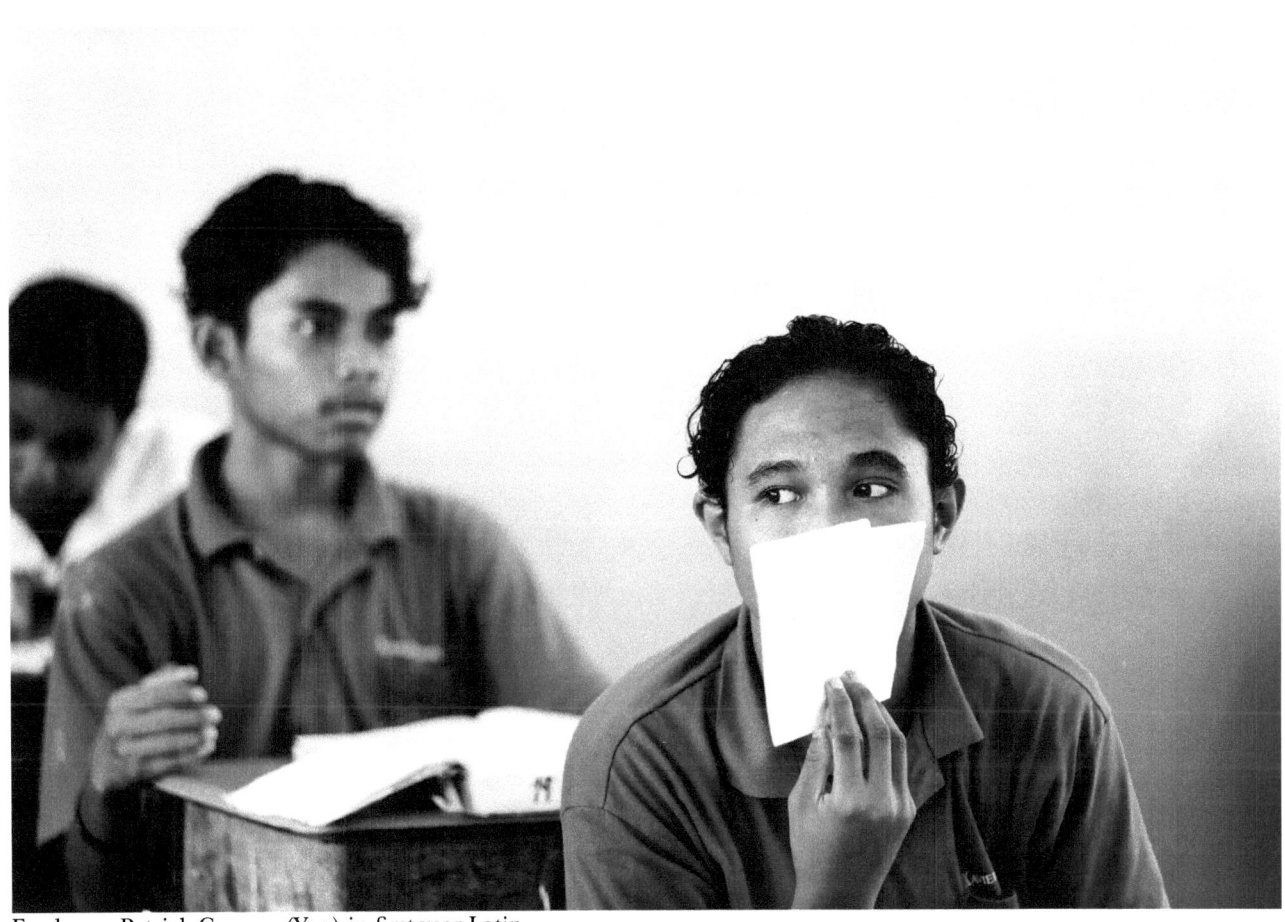

Freshman Patrick Gorong (Yap) in first-year Latin.

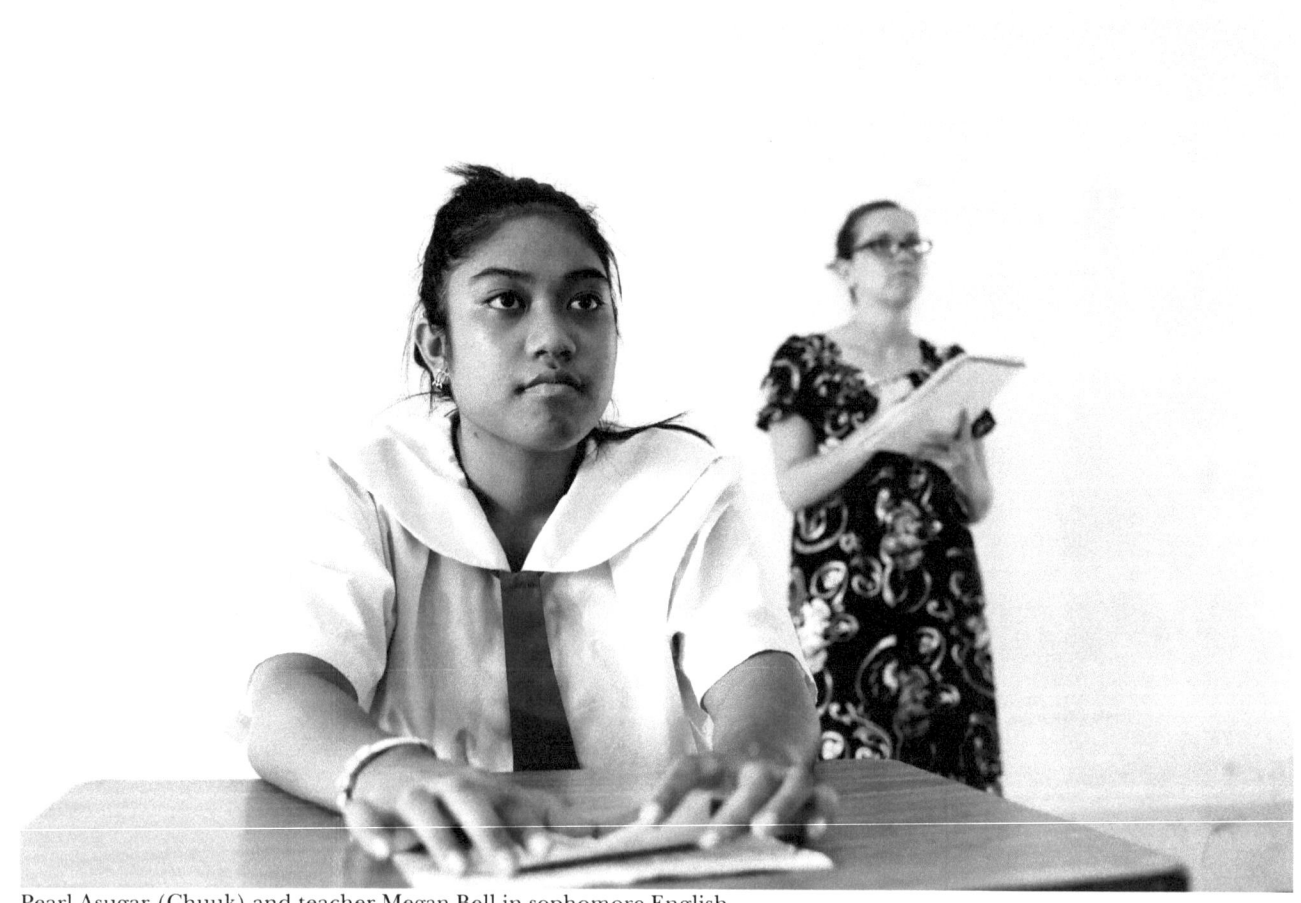

Pearl Asugar (Chuuk) and teacher Megan Bell in sophomore English.

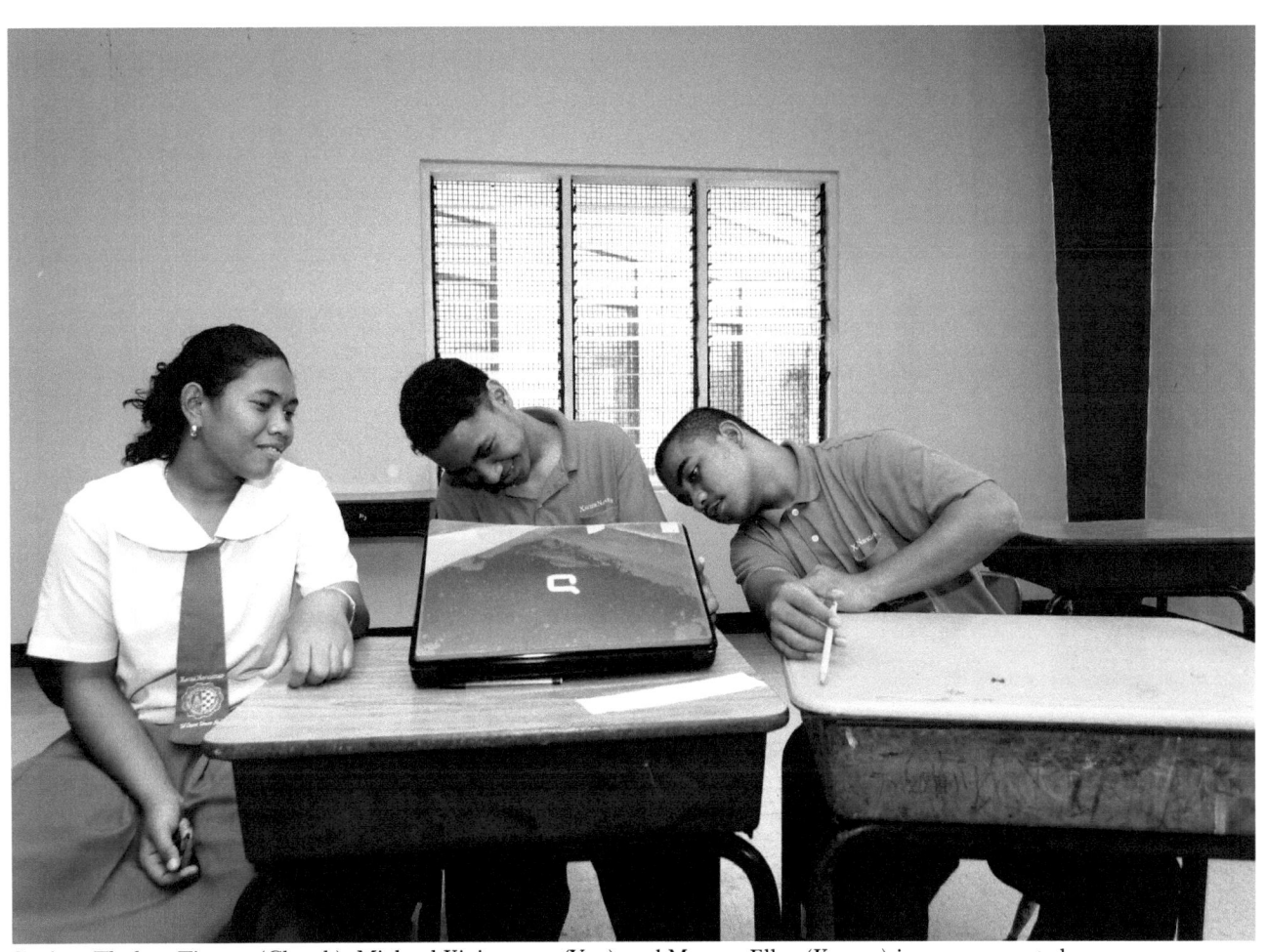

Seniors Thelma Tipeno (Chuuk), Michael Kigimnang (Yap) and Marson Elley (Kosrae) in government class.

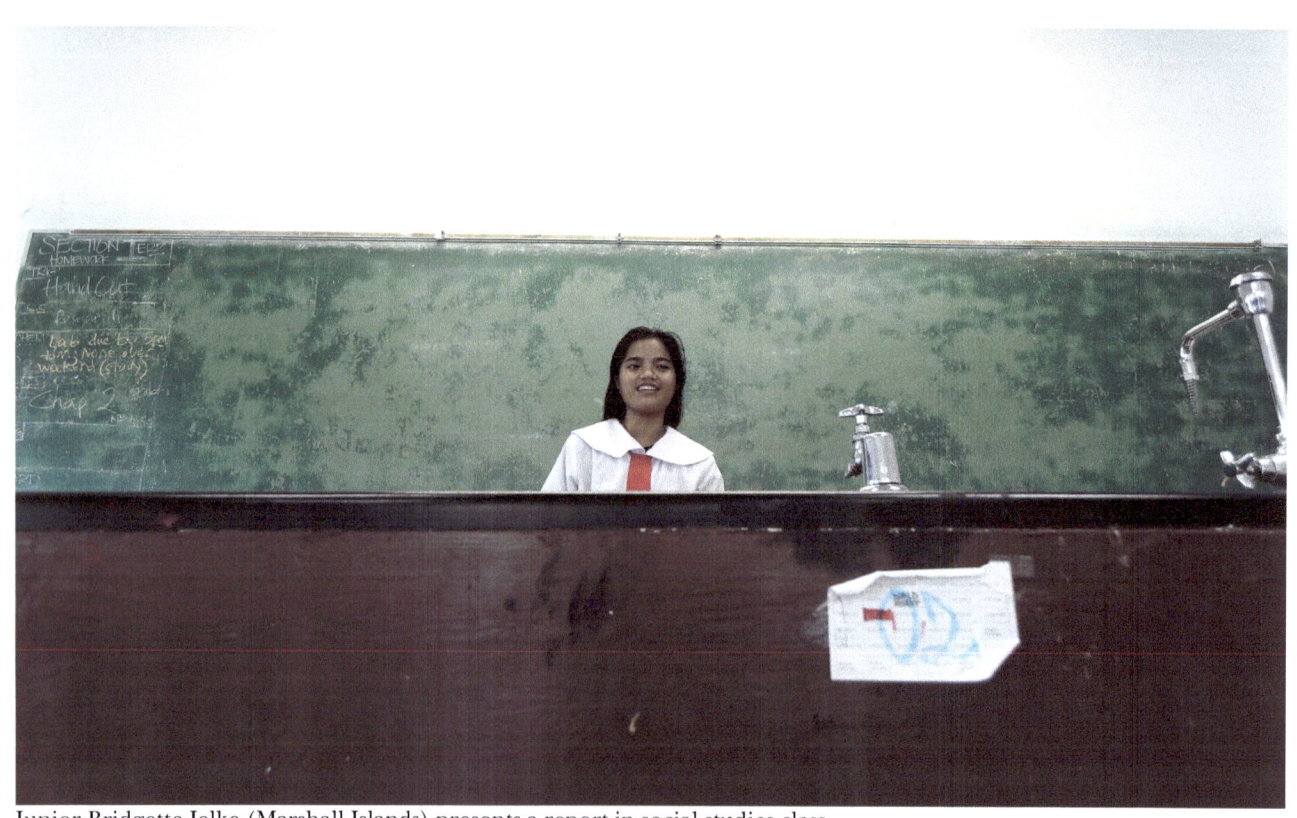

Junior Bridgette Jelke (Marshall Islands) presents a report in social studies class.

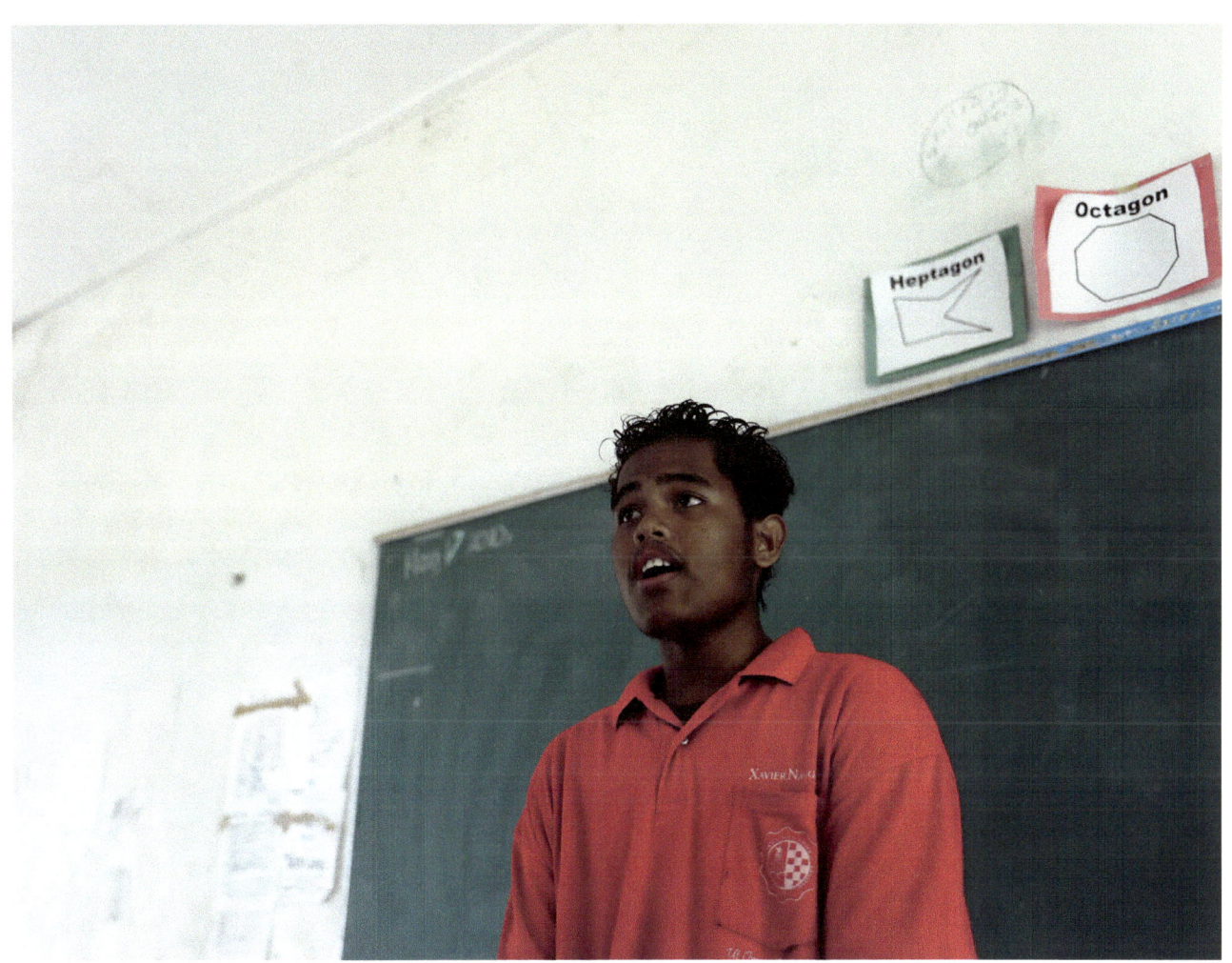

Sophomore Anfernee Mallarme (Pohnpei) gives a speech during the public speaking unit in English.

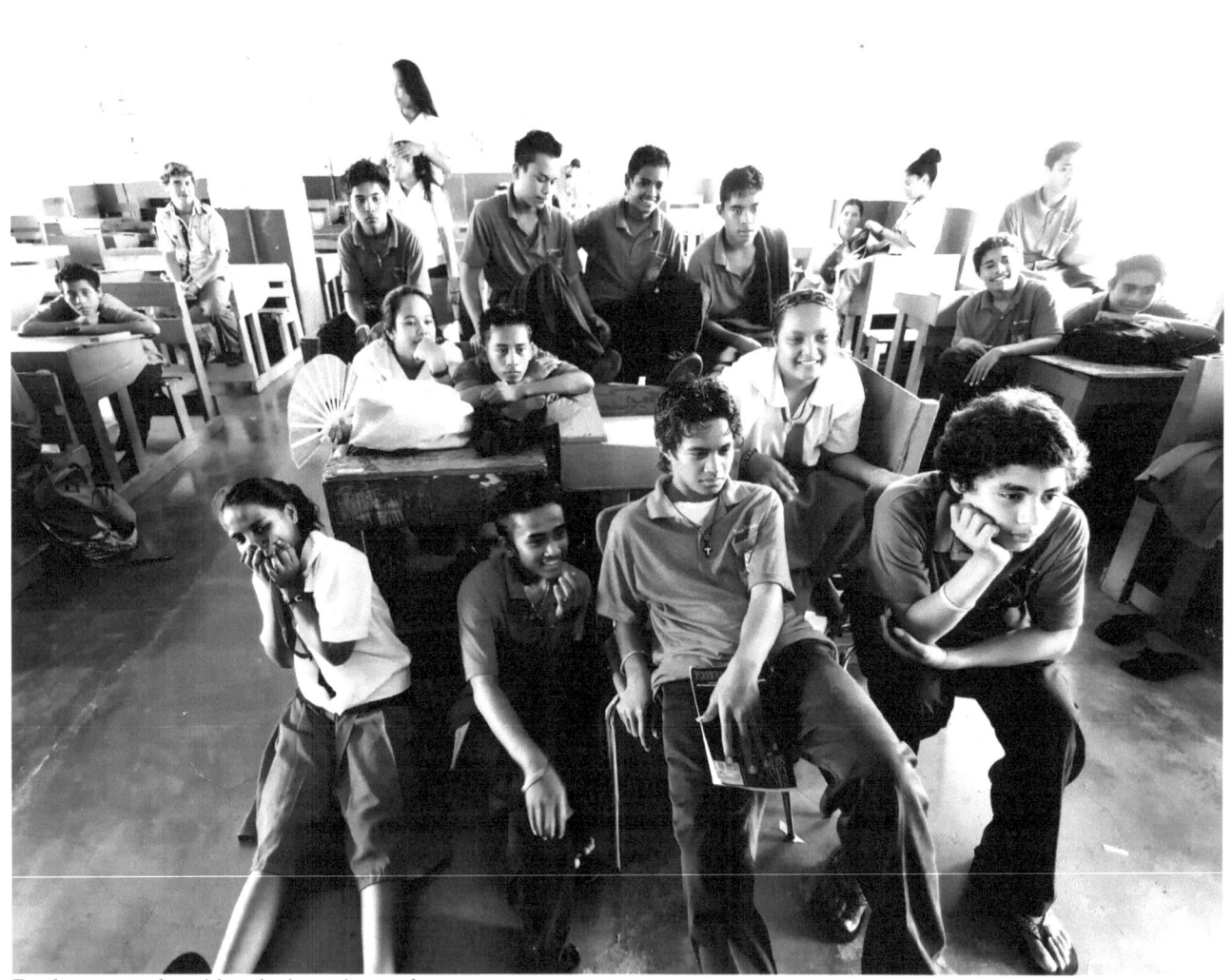

Freshmen watch a video during science class.

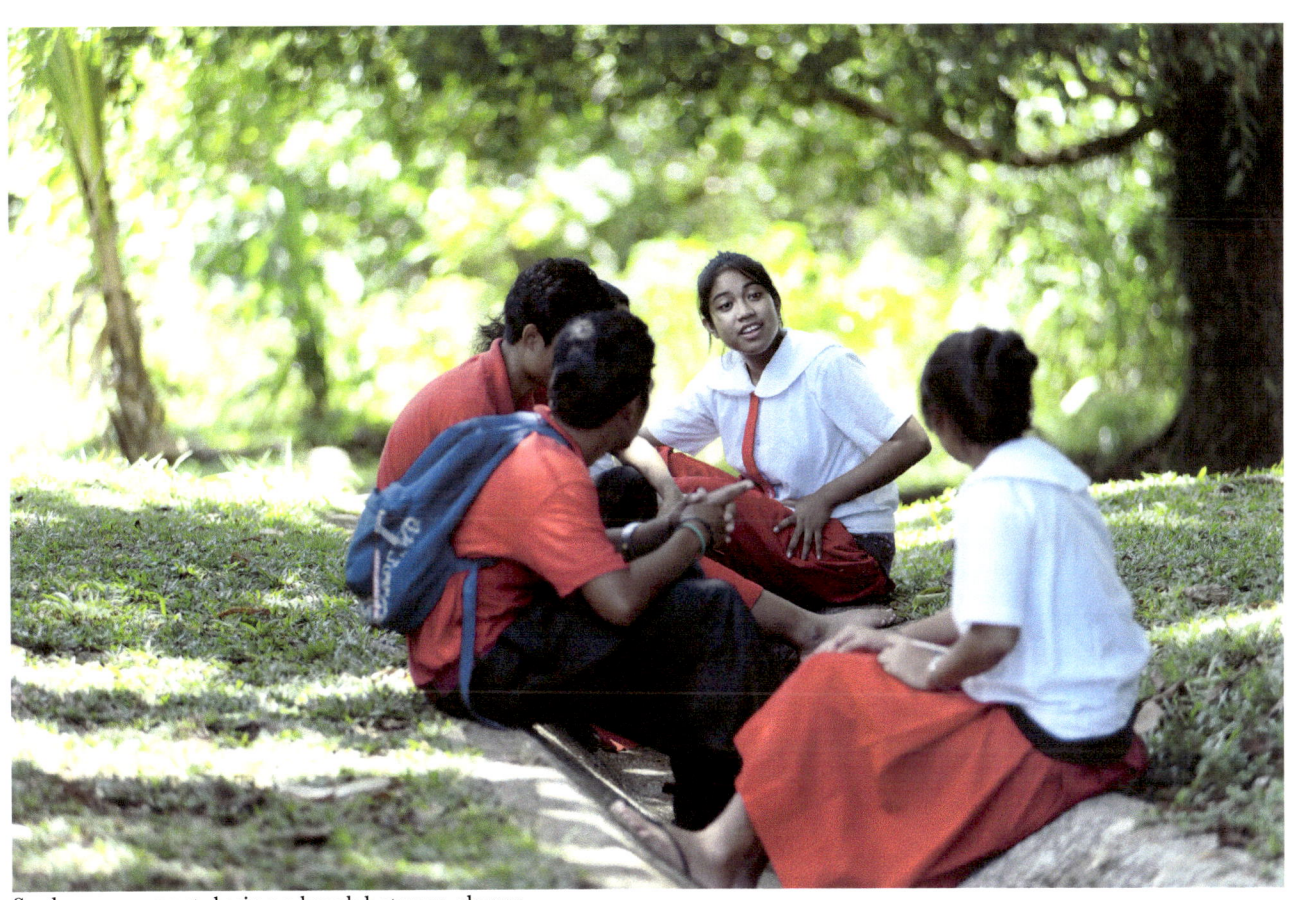
Sophomores meet during a break between classes.

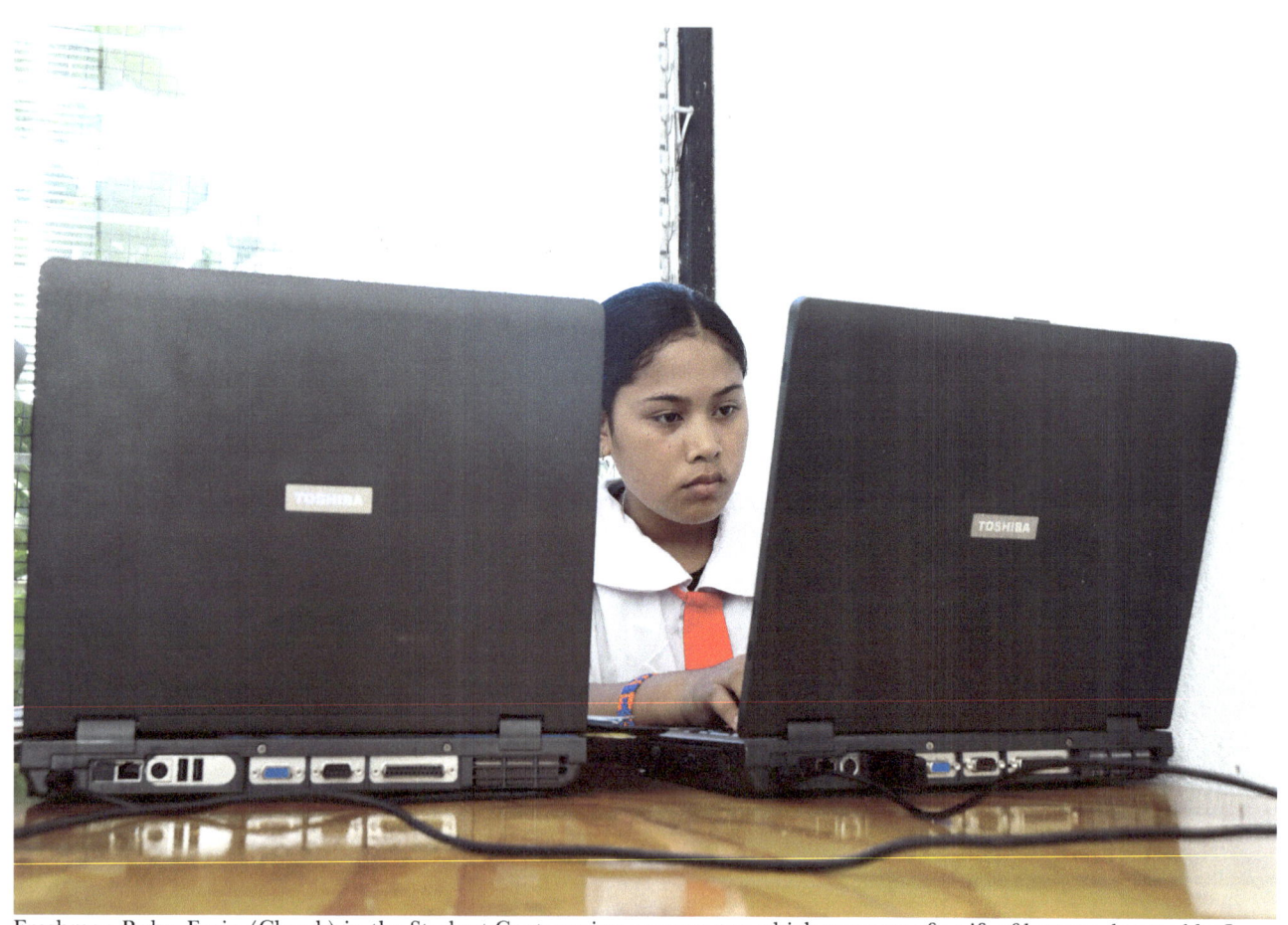

Freshman Rolyn Esein (Chuuk) in the Student Center using a computer, which was part of a gift of laptops donated by Japan.

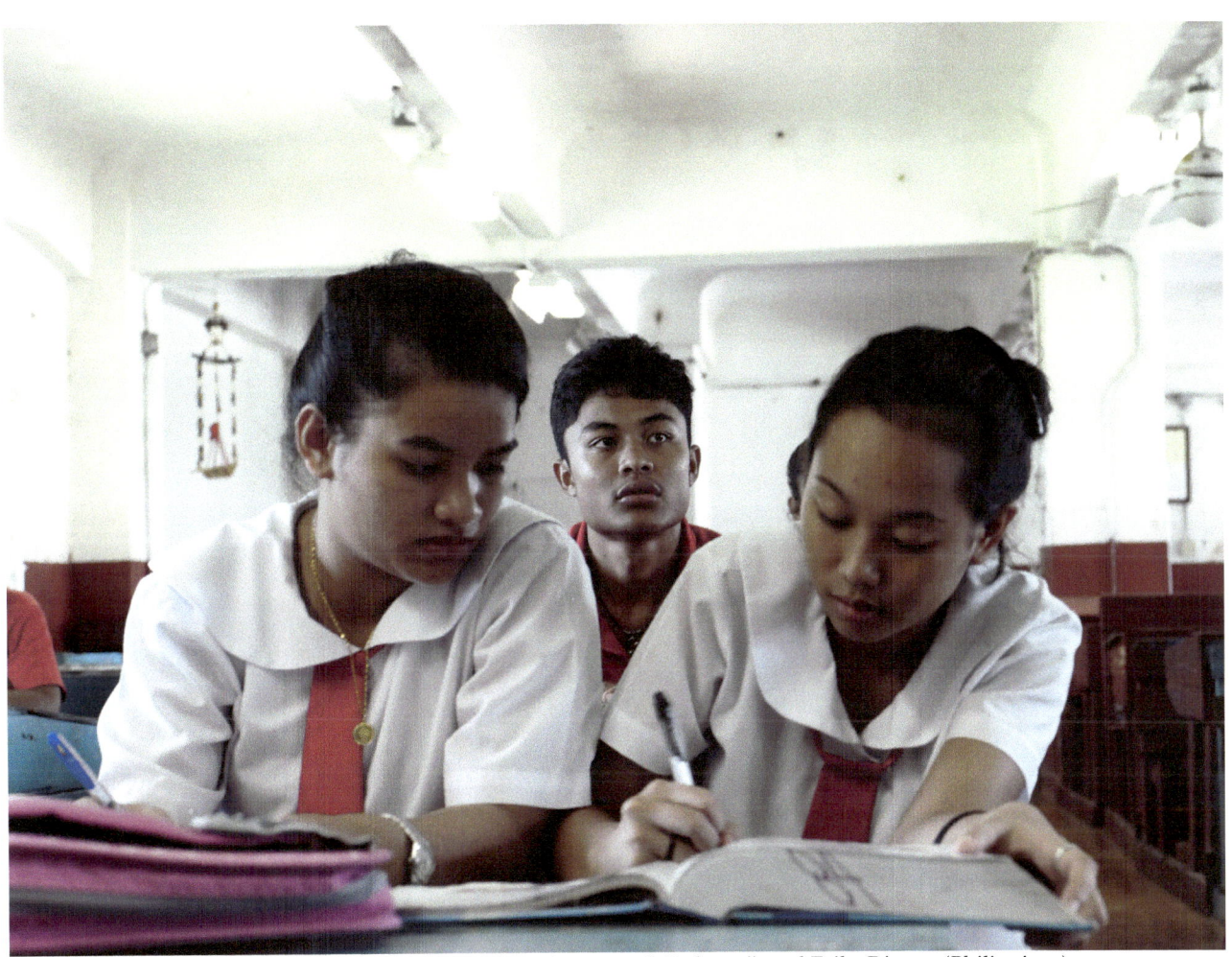

Sophomore Joyful Noket (Chuuk) with classmates Jocelyn Panuel (Pohnpei) and Erika Diones (Philippines).

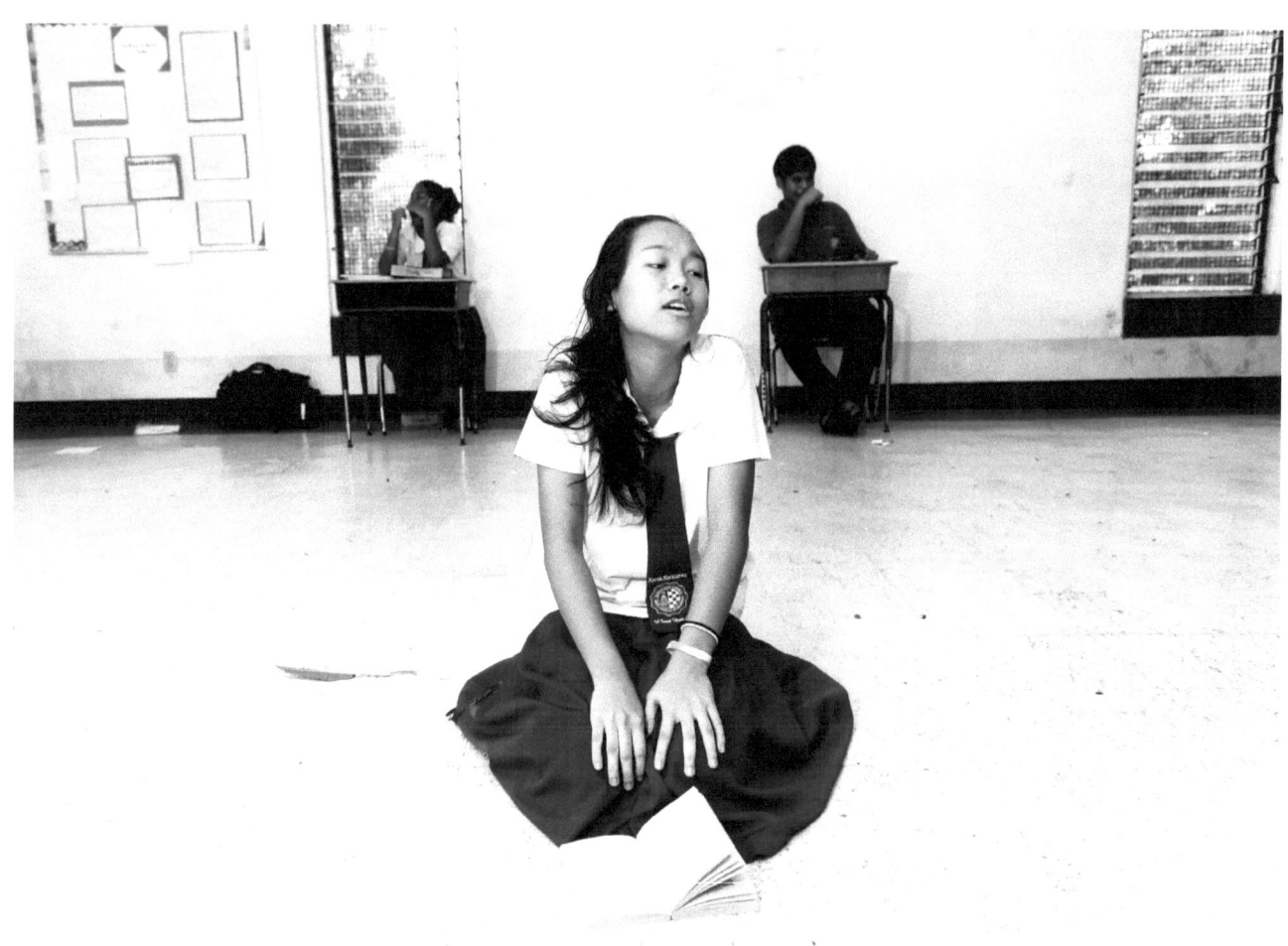

Sophomore Erika Diones (Philippines) plays Juliet during a literature class unit studying Shakespeare's "Romeo and Juliet."

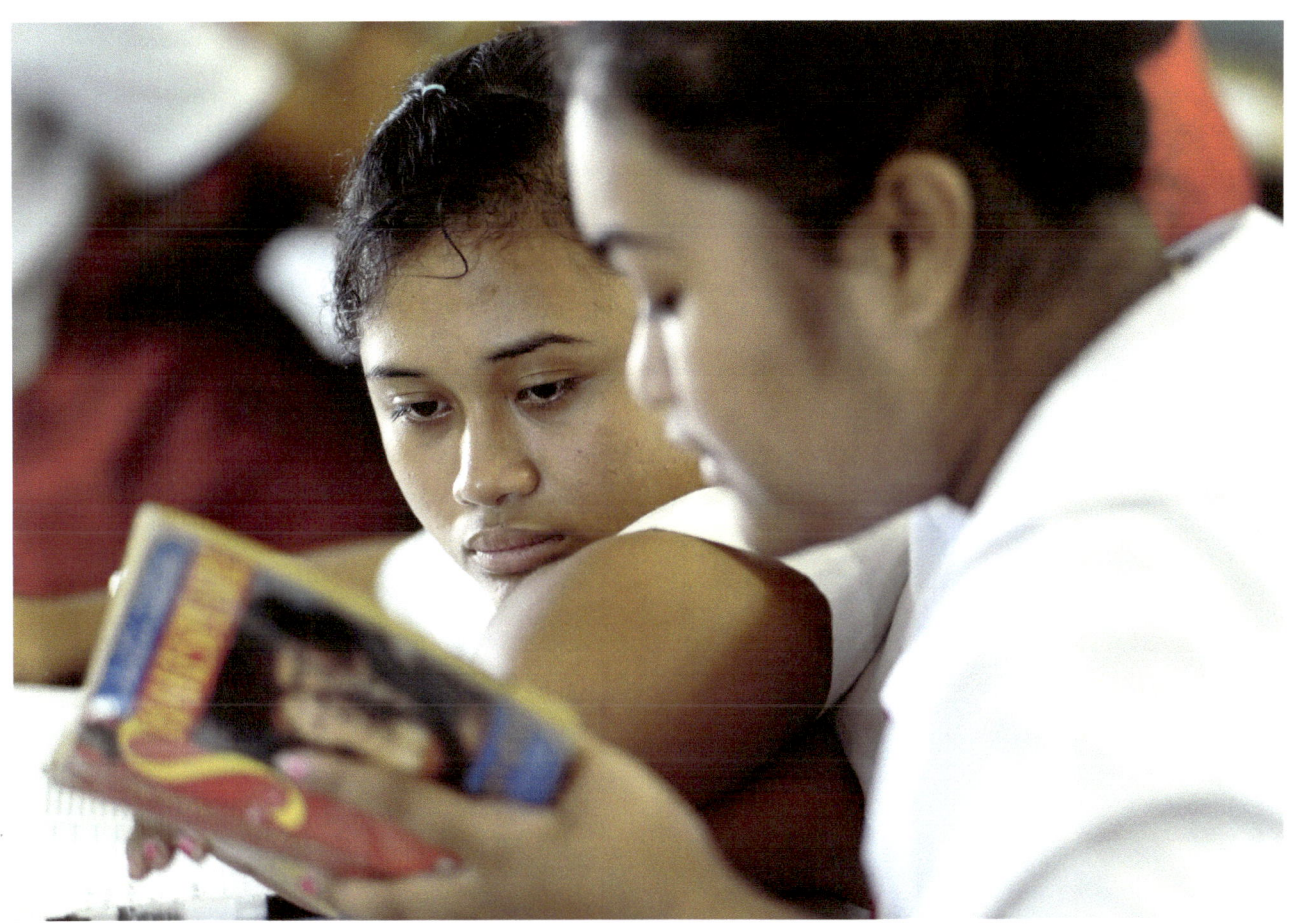

Sophomores V-ann Nakamura (Chuuk) and Kerina Eria (Chuuk) study Shakespeare in literature class.

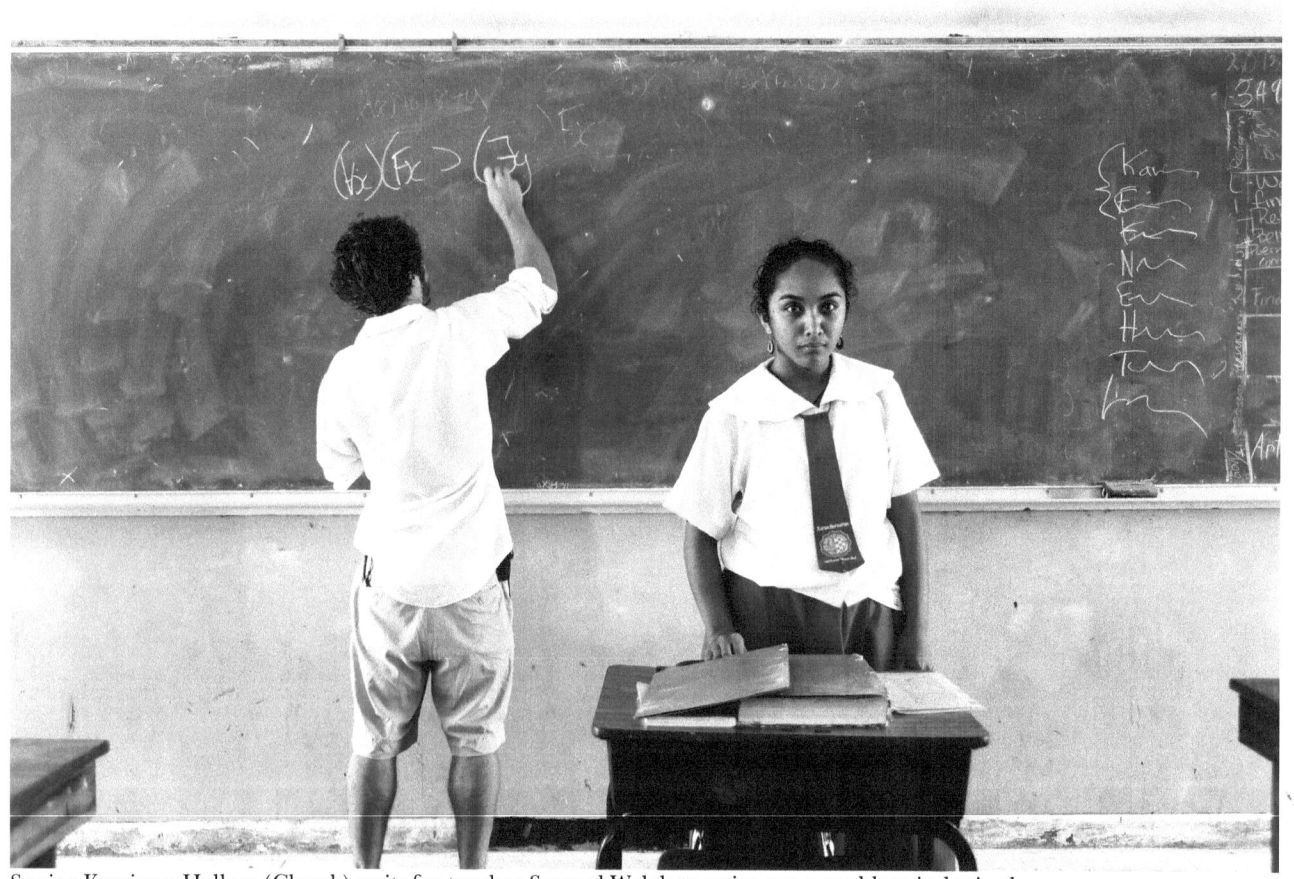

Senior Kayviann Hallers (Chuuk) waits for teacher Samuel Welch to write out a problem in logic class.

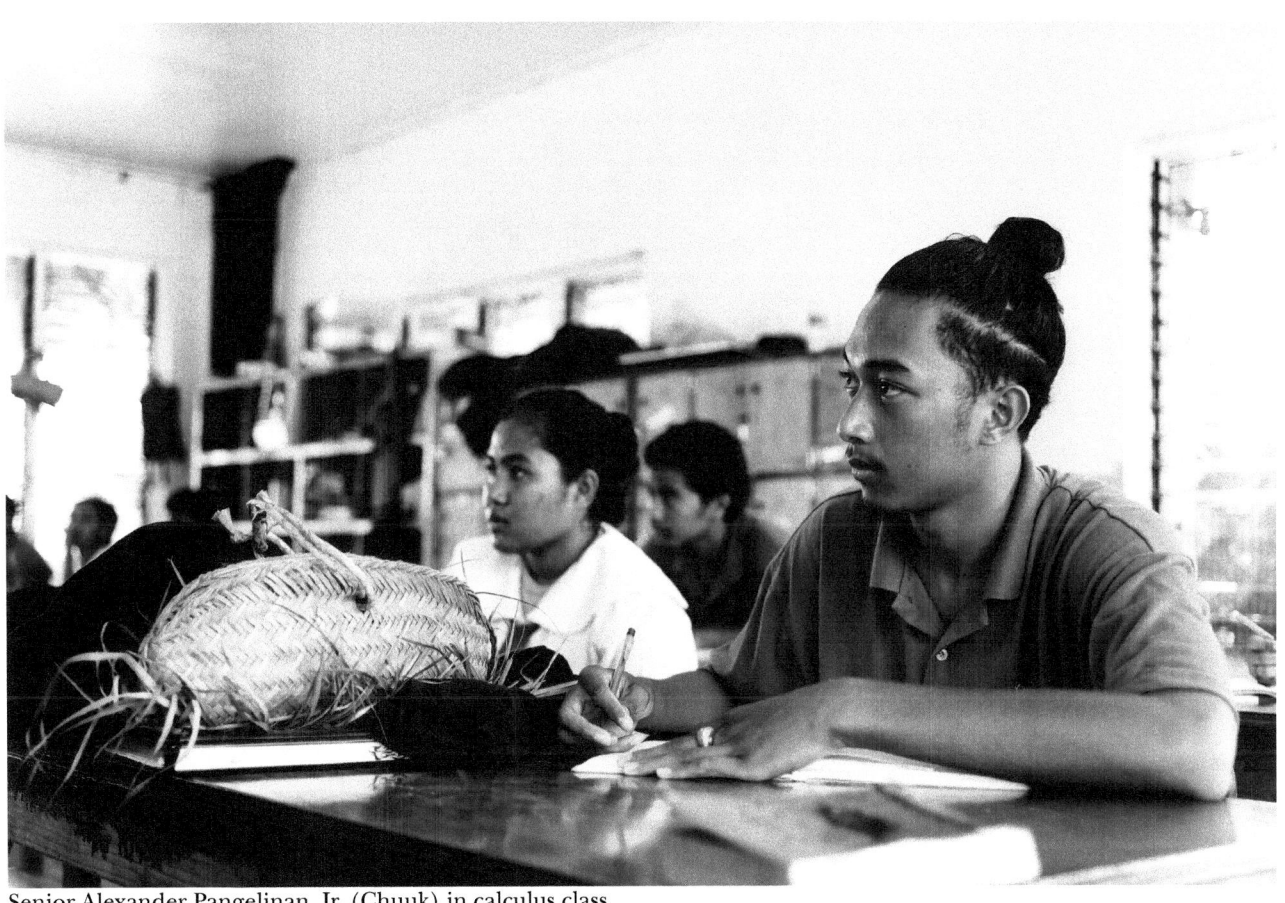

Senior Alexander Pangelinan, Jr. (Chuuk) in calculus class.

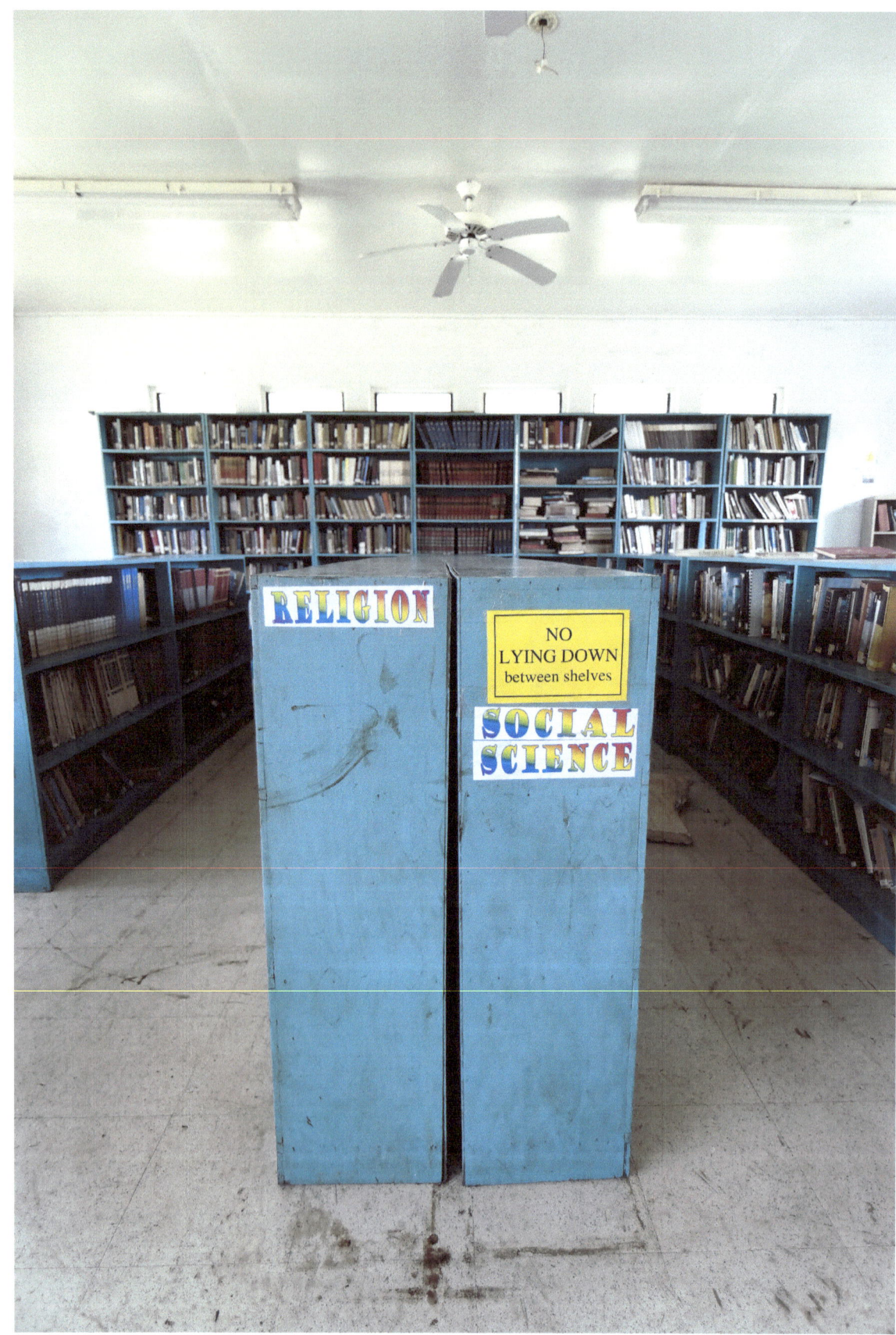

Despite the warning sign, a cushion for relaxing is visible in the library.

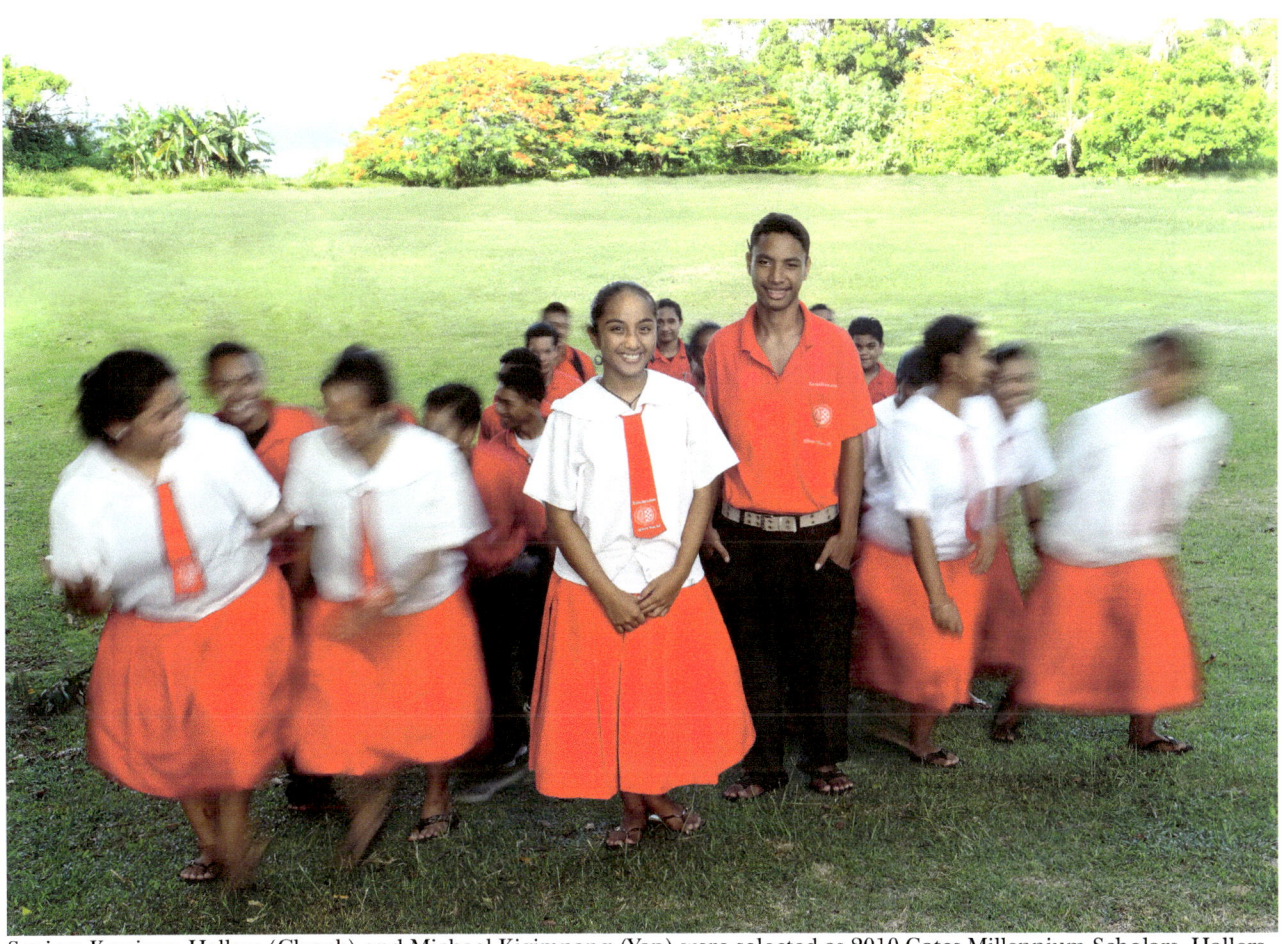

Seniors Kayviann Hallers (Chuuk) and Michael Kigimnang (Yap) were selected as 2010 Gates Millennium Scholars. Hallers now attends Loyola Marymount University and Kigimnang studies at the University of San Francisco. The full-ride fellowships are from the Bill and Melinda Gates Foundation.

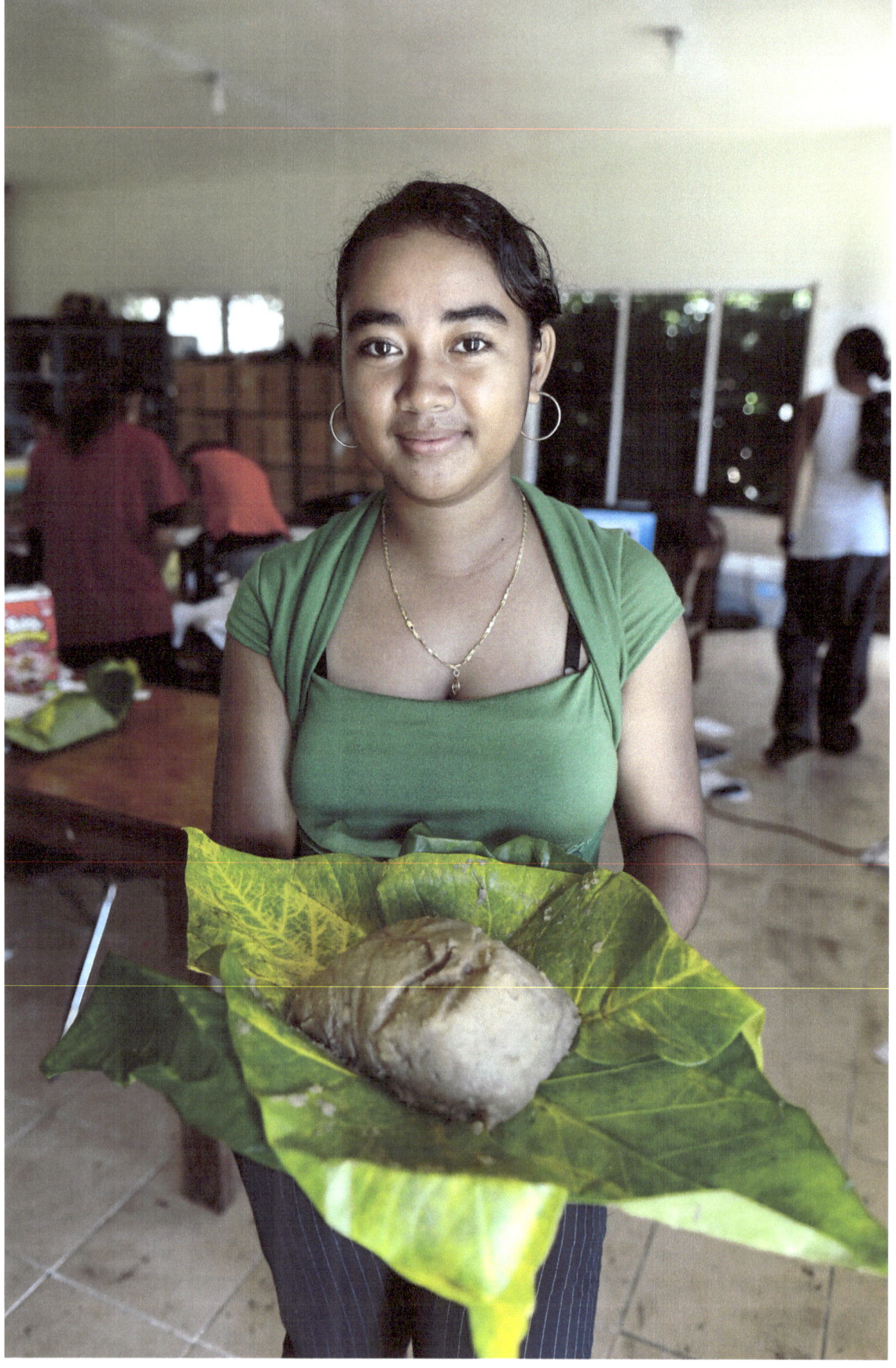

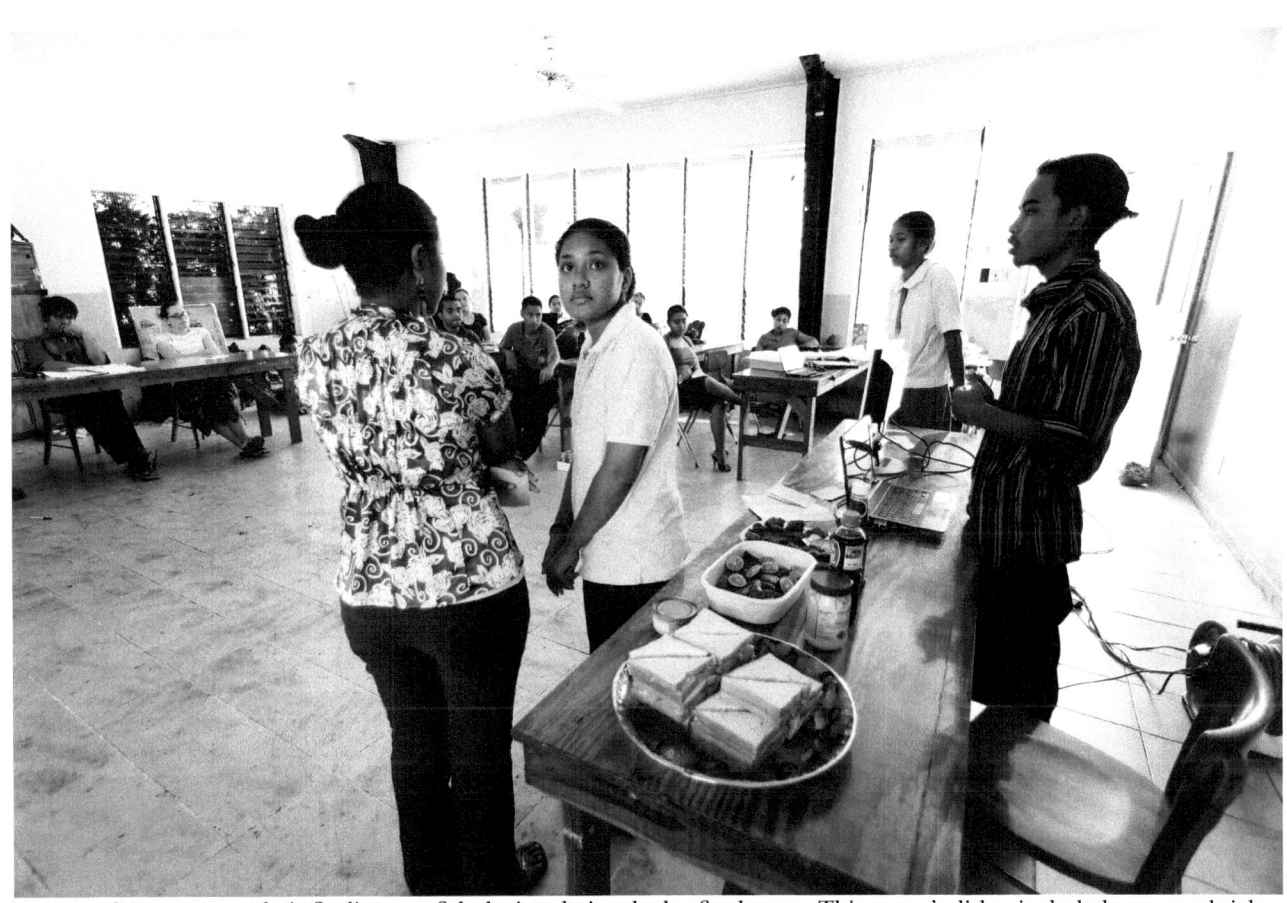

Seniors, above, present their findings on fish during their calculus final exam. This group's dishes included tuna sandwiches, sashimi and fried fish.

Senior Stephanie Ham (Chuuk), left, prepares a traditional taro dish as part of the calculus final examination. The class used calculus to determine whether an island population would increase or decrease, and the impact of that result on the supply of certain foods. Each group had to research the foods they were assigned and also prepare dishes. At the end of the exam, the students ate the dishes they prepared.

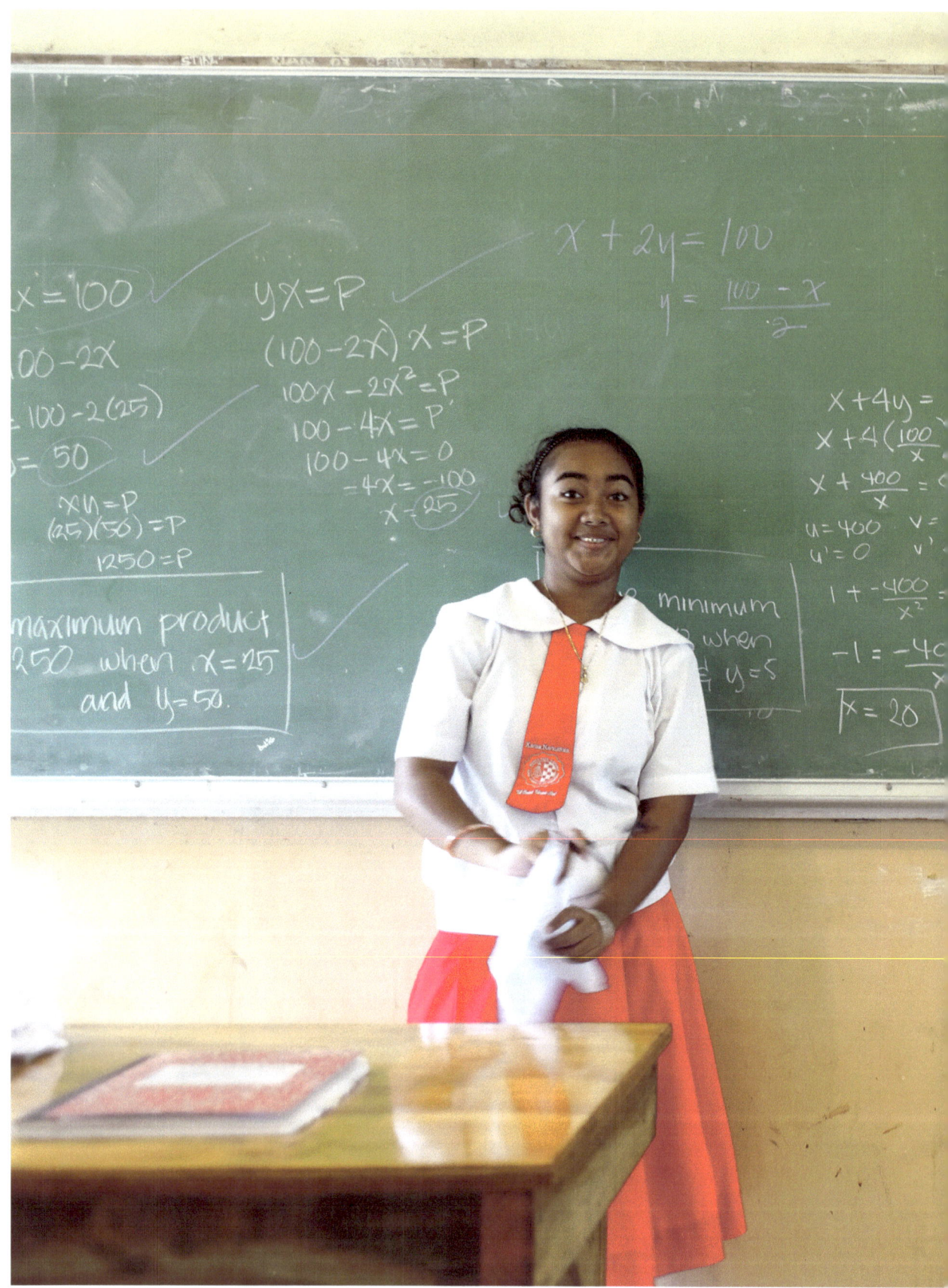

Senior Stephanie Ham (Chuuk) after completing an exercise in calculus class.

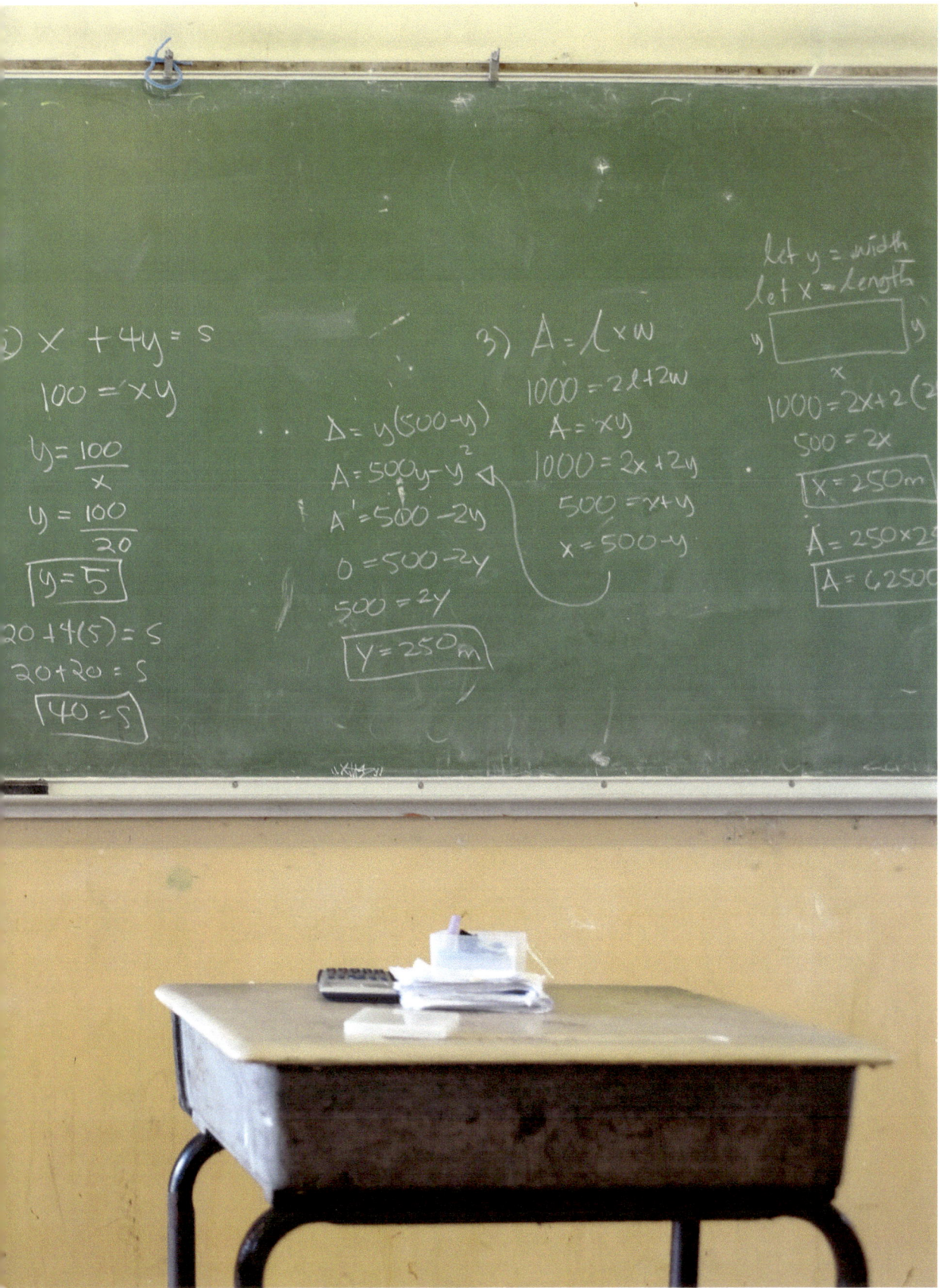

2) $x + 4y = s$

$100 = xy$

$y = \dfrac{100}{x}$

$y = \dfrac{100}{20}$

$\boxed{y = 5}$

$20 + 4(5) = s$

$20 + 20 = s$

$\boxed{40 = s}$

3) $A = l \times w$

$A = y(500 - y)$

$A = 500y - y^2$

$A' = 500 - 2y$

$0 = 500 - 2y$

$500 = 2y$

$\boxed{y = 250\,m}$

$1000 = 2l + 2w$

$A = xy$

$1000 = 2x + 2y$

$500 = x + y$

$x = 500 - y$

let y = width
let x = length

x

$1000 = 2x + 2(2$

$500 = 2x$

$\boxed{x = 250\,m}$

$A = 250 \times 2$

$\boxed{A = 62500}$

53

Spirit

Xavier High School is a Roman Catholic school, and most of the students who attend are of that faith. But anywhere from a quarter to a third of the student population are members of other churches, predominantly Protestant. That's been the case since the early days of the school.

But a religious divide isn't evident at Xavier, even during the daily (and non-mandatory) Mass held at 8 a.m. On some days the Chapel is packed; on other days, there is a scattering of students and faculty members.

When students are expected to attend Mass, Catholics and Protestants mix easily in the Chapel, where everyone sits on the tile floor. Protestants often actively contribute – preparing songs, doing readings – alongside their Catholic peers.

At a time when most of the Western world has become enthusiastically secular, most of the Micronesian students at Xavier are comfortable expressing their faith in small but tangible ways. I discovered that as I roamed the campus with my camera. A photographer looks for both the vistas as well as the details.

At first, it was the crucifixes that many students wore, not as a gaudy fashion statement like a hip-hop singer, but as a small symbol of faith. And then I noticed the students who wore a small crucifix and rosary beads around their wrists. One student even wrapped her rosary beads and crucifix on her pen. It was a quiet but important detail, easily missed, not done to impress others but to be reminded of one's God.

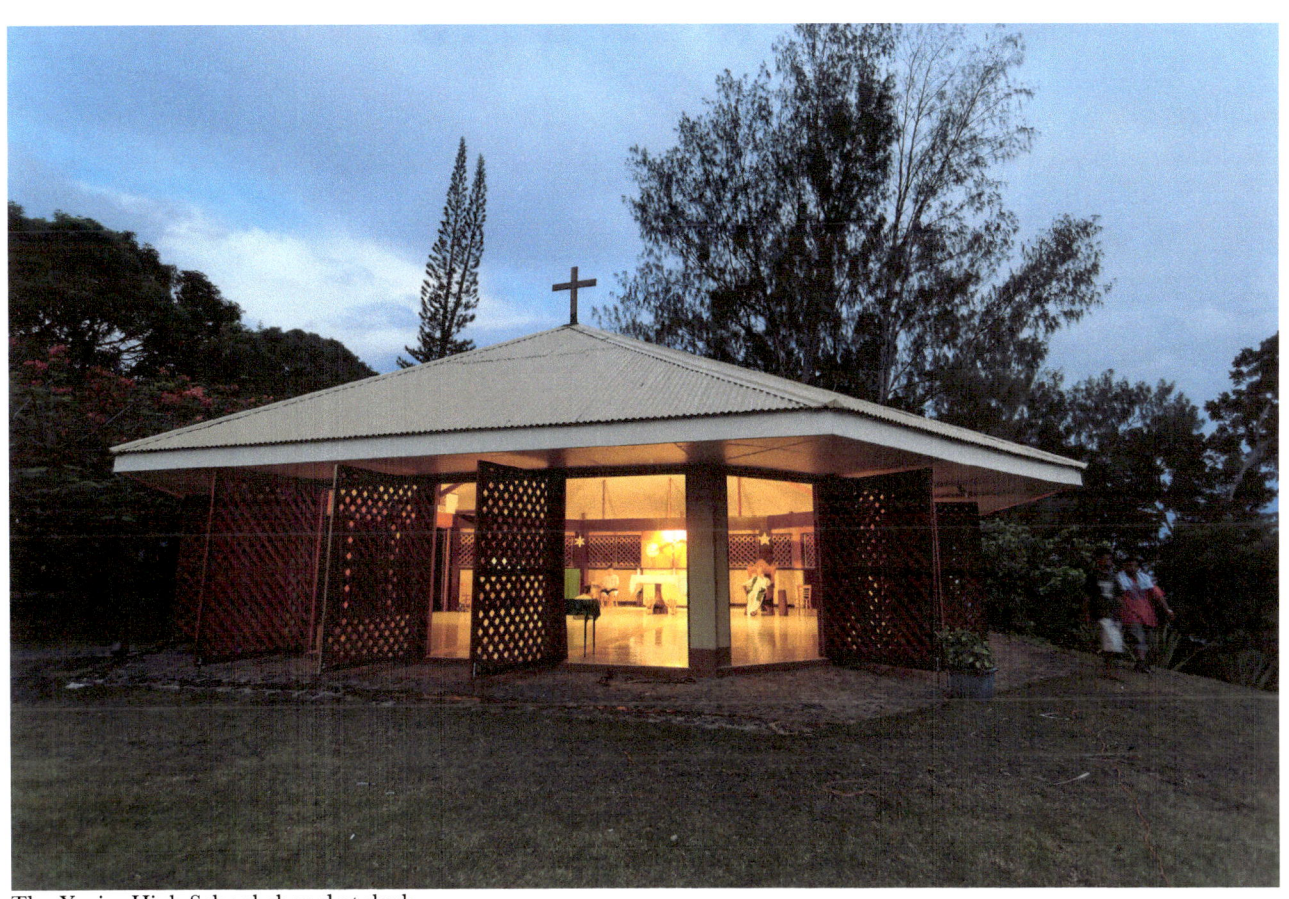

The Xavier High School chapel at dusk.

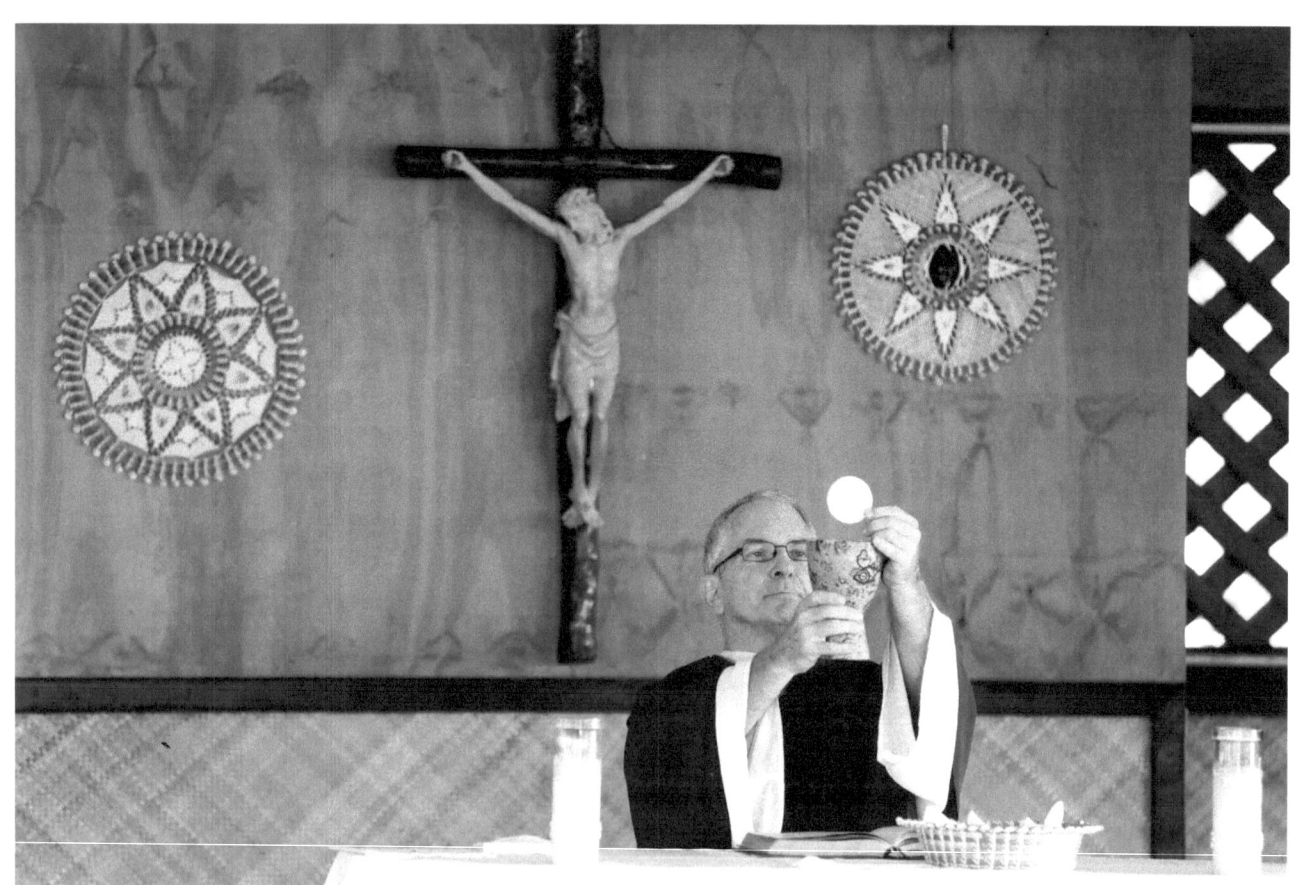

Xavier Director Fr. Rich McAuliff, SJ, celebrates Mass in the chapel.

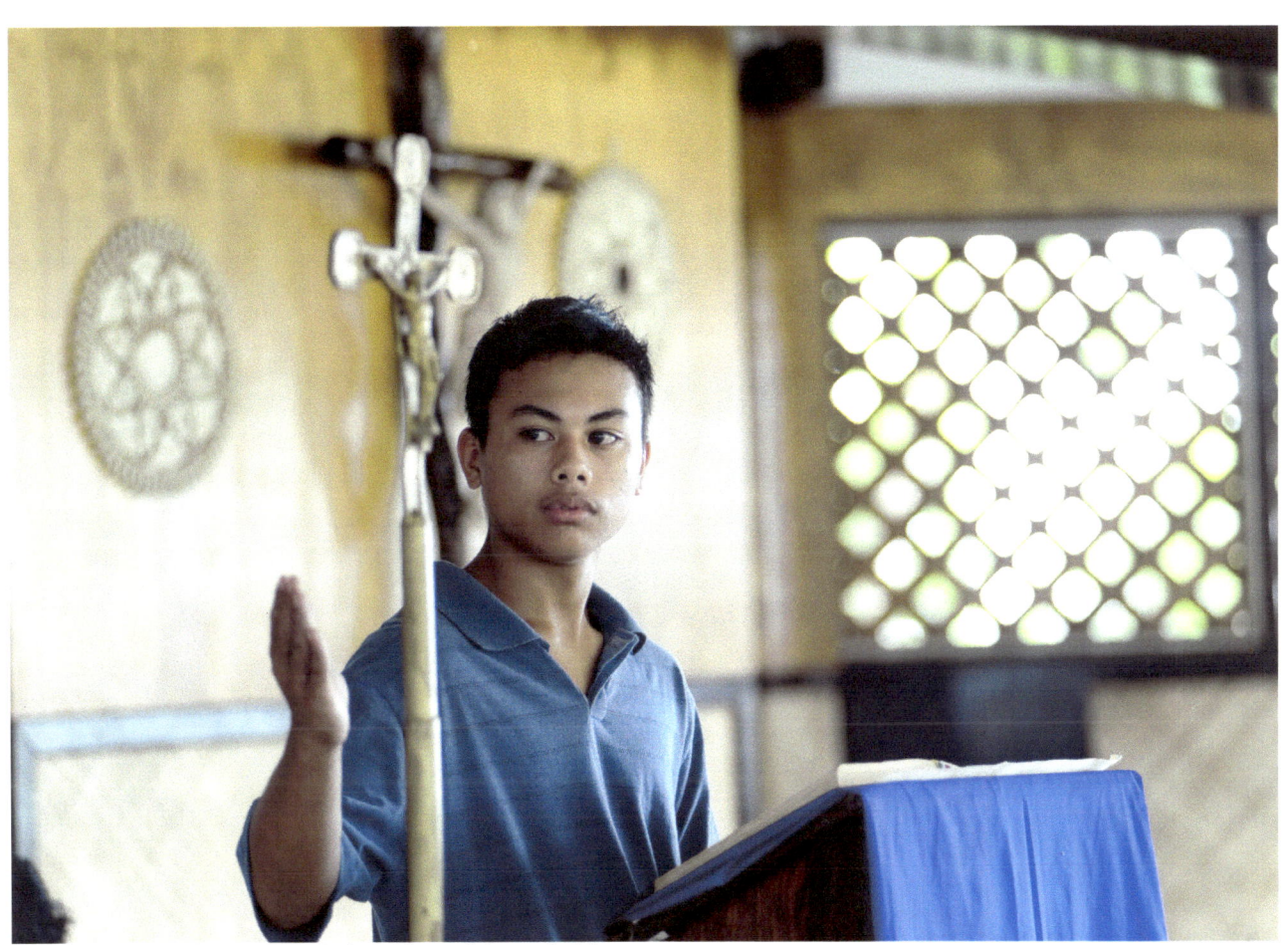
Freshman Kenneth Edmund (Pohnpei) participates in Mass.

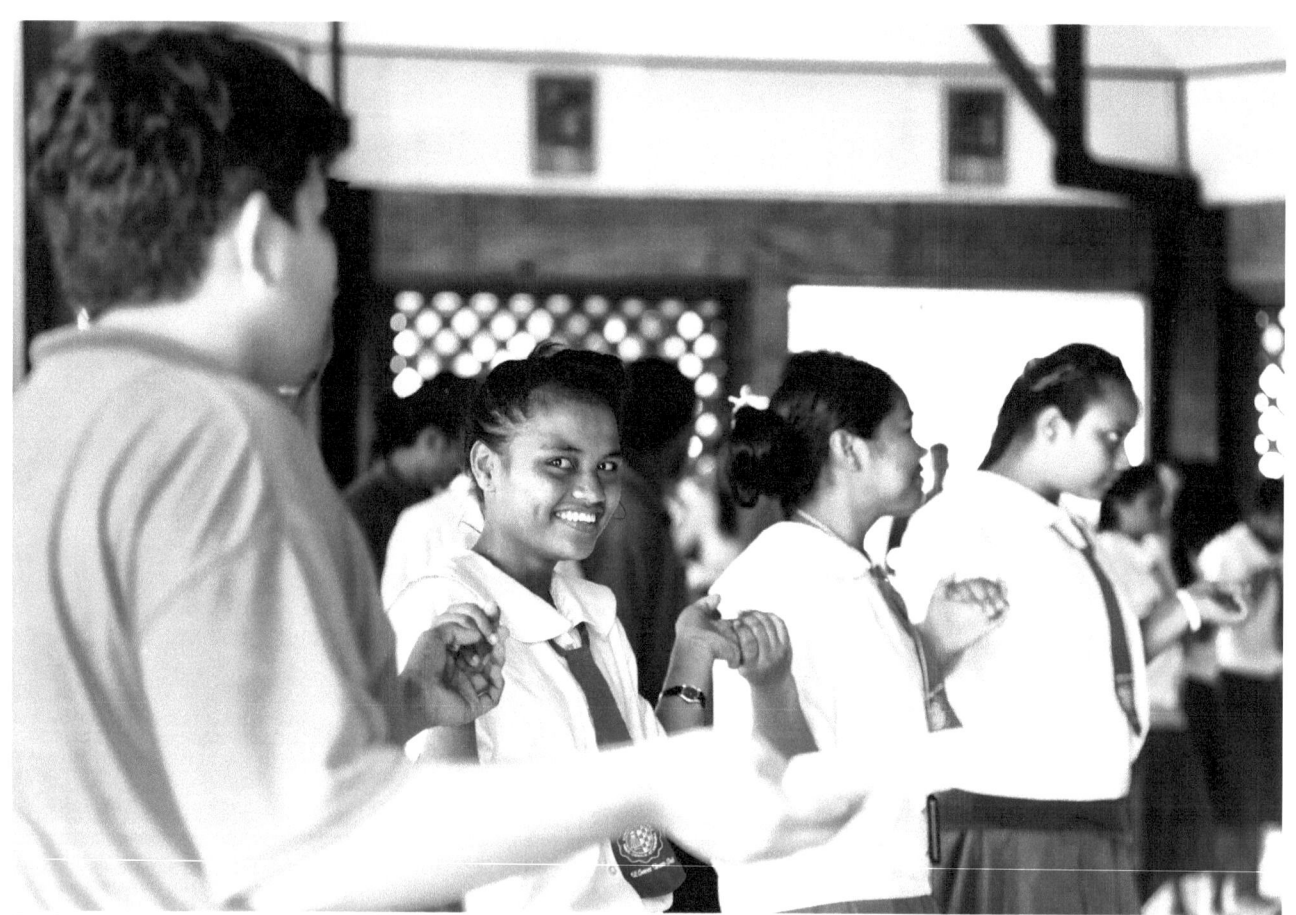

Freshmen during Mass in the chapel.

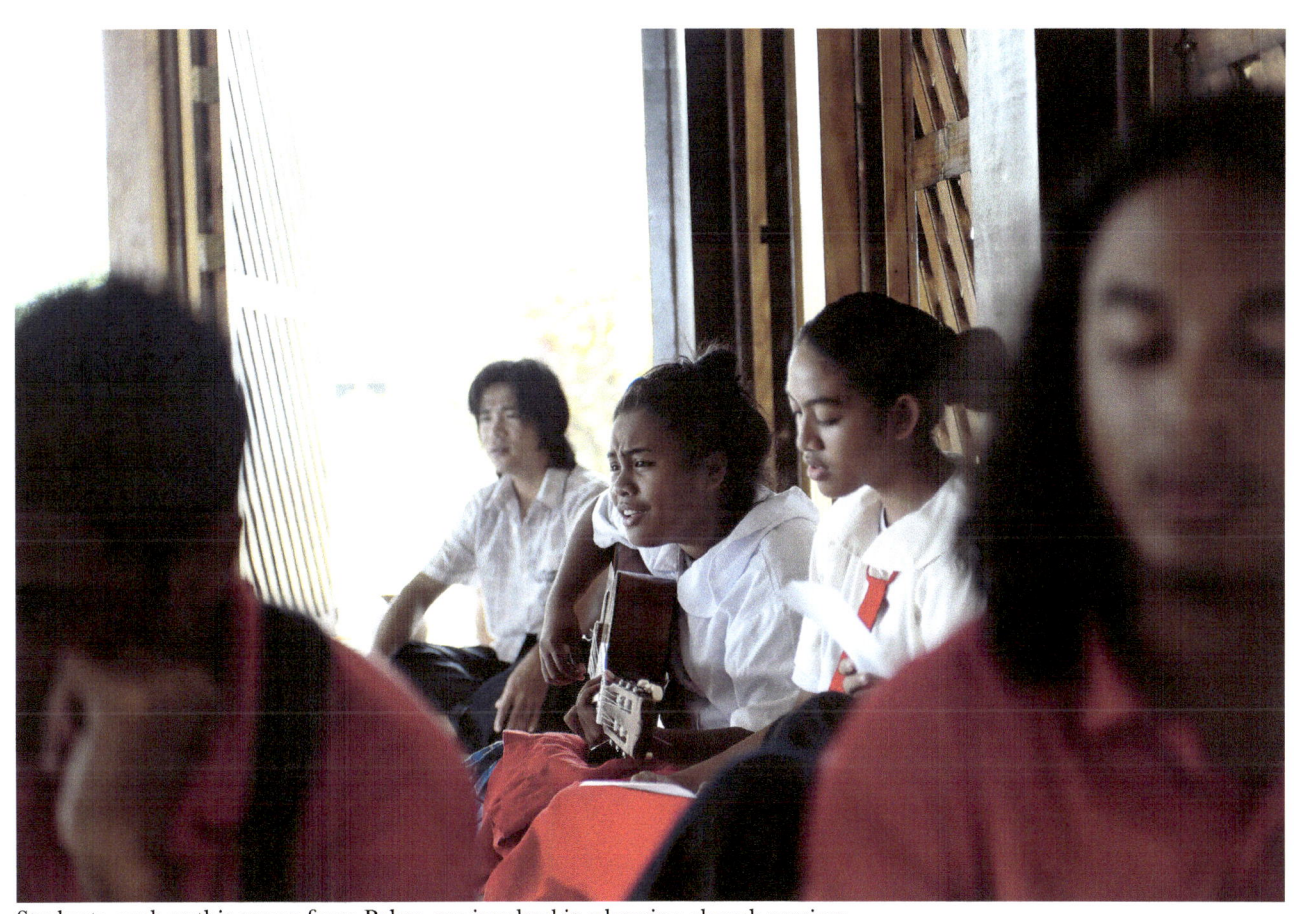
Students, such as this group from Palau, are involved in planning church services.

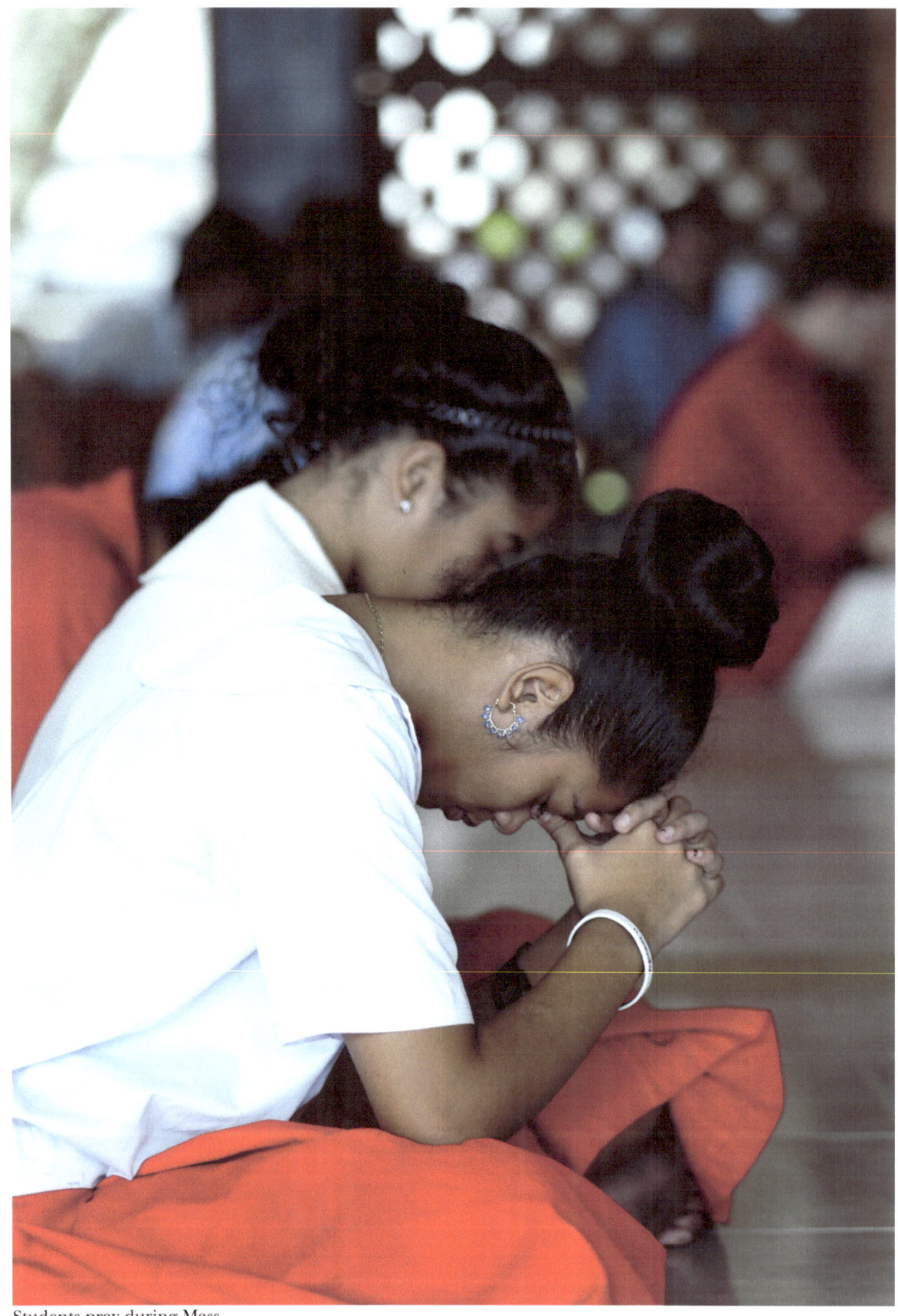

Students pray during Mass.

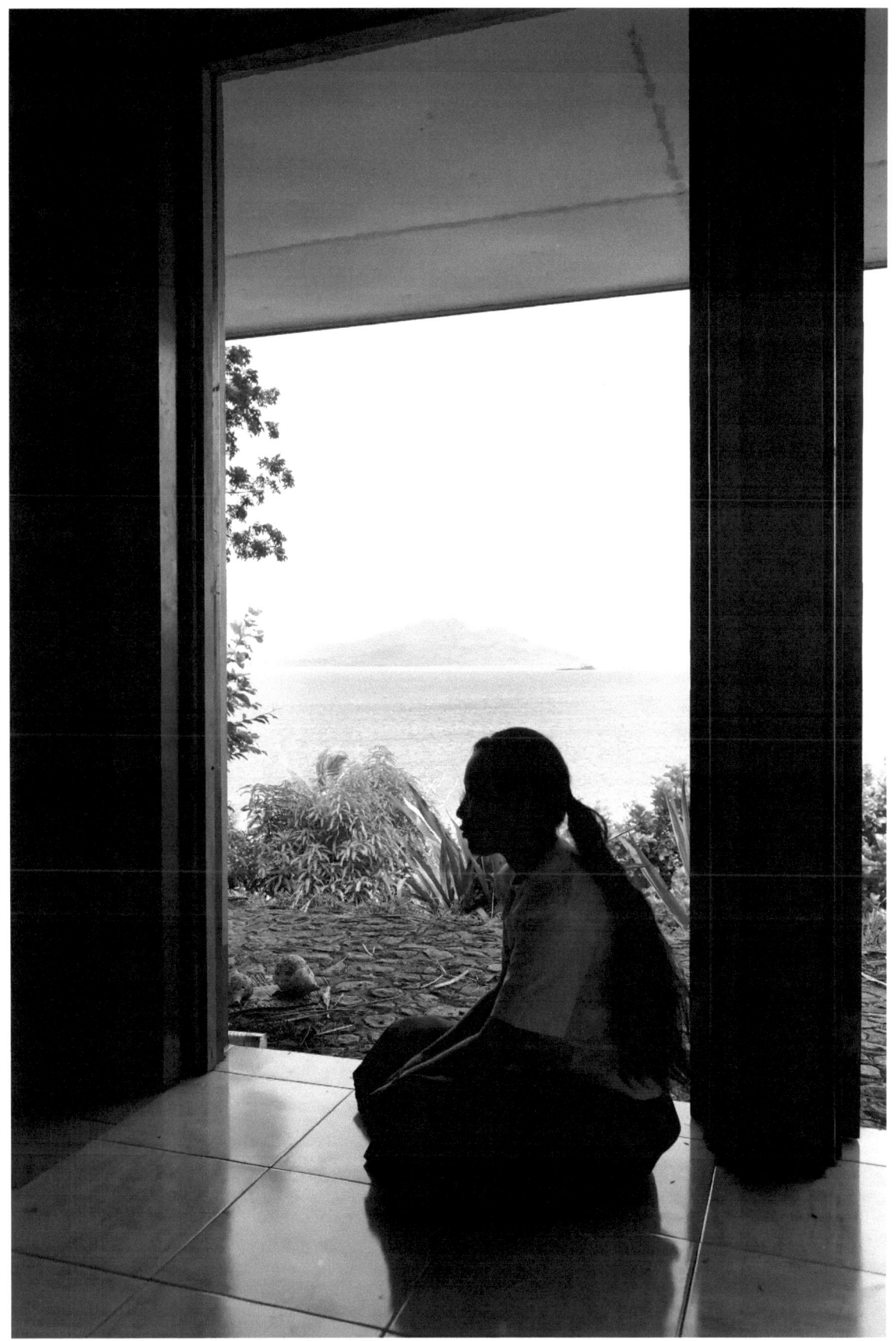

The view from the chapel overlooks Chuuk Lagoon.

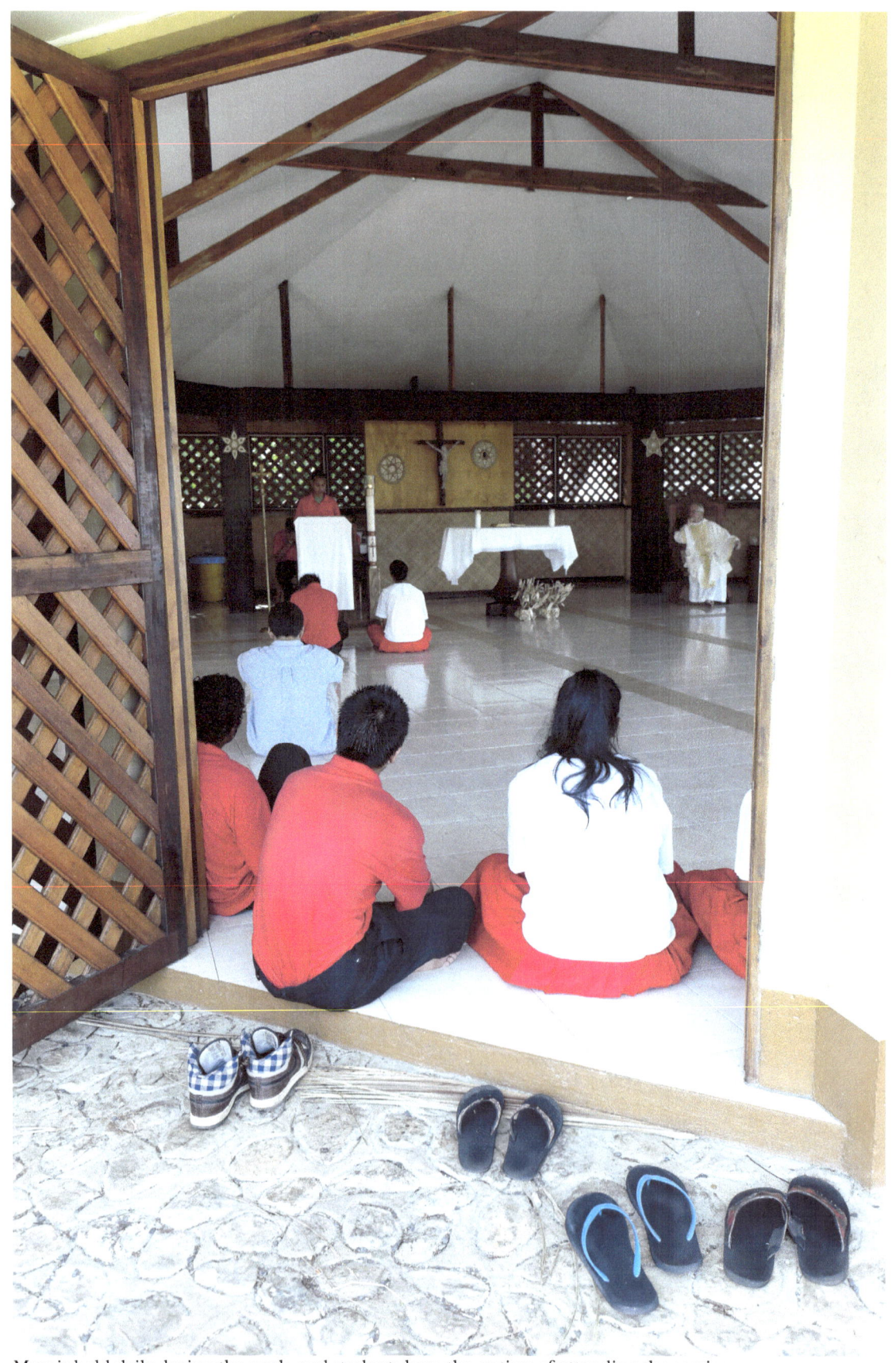

Mass is held daily during the week, and students have the option of attending the service.

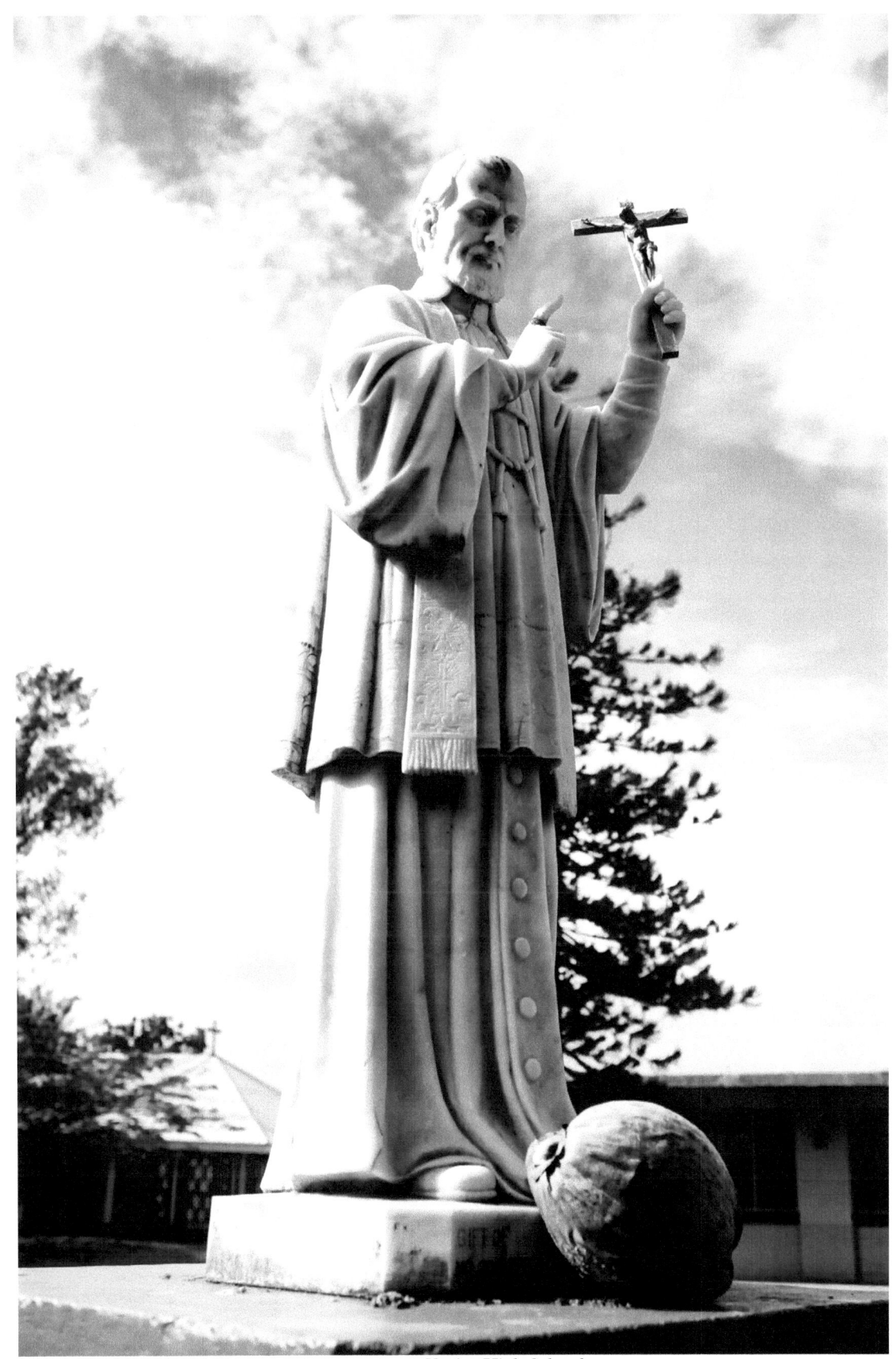

A statue of Saint Francis Xavier at the entrance to Xavier High School.

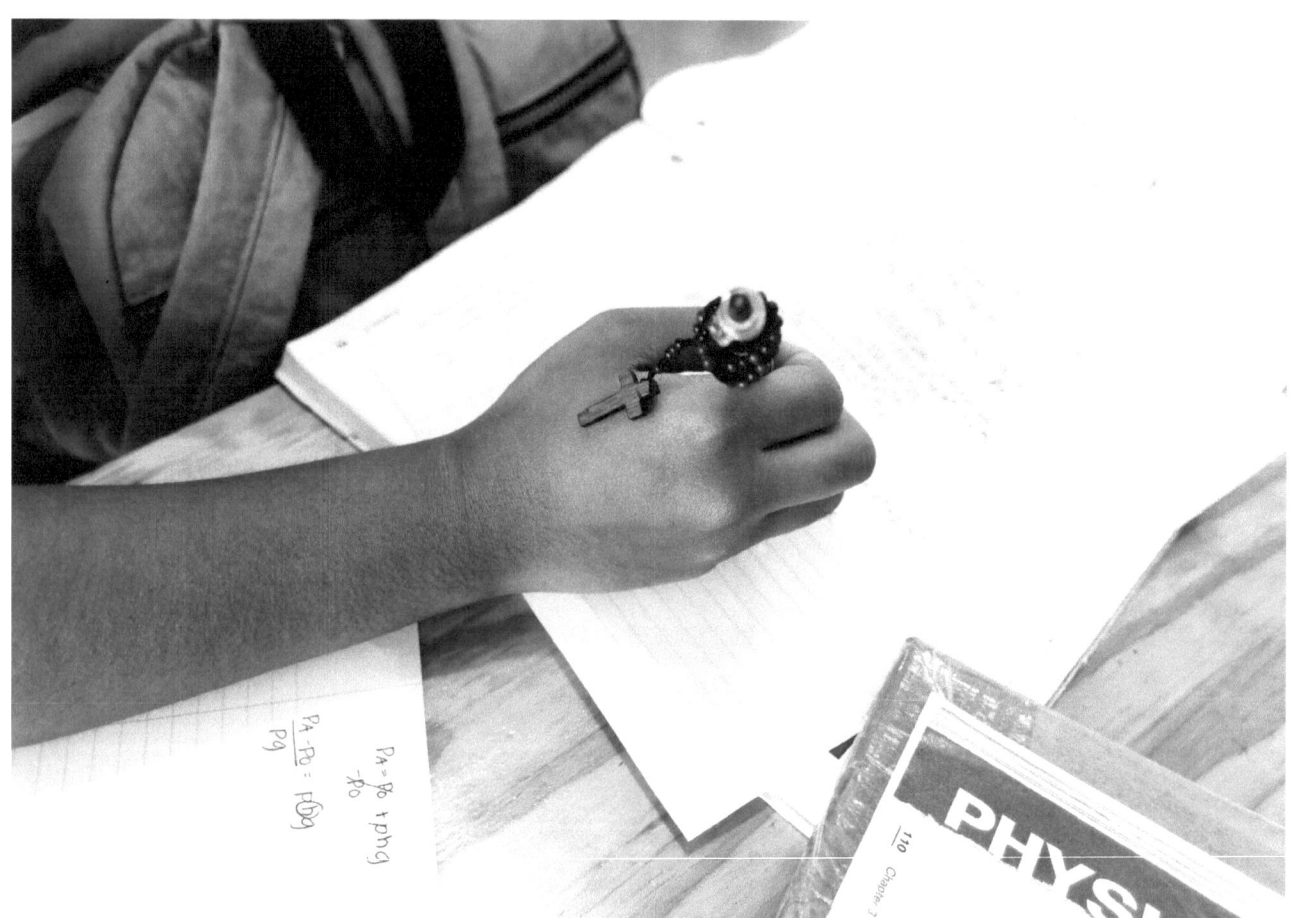

Senior Jeanelle Omi Adelbai (Palau) expresses her faith with a rosary and crucifix attached to her pen.

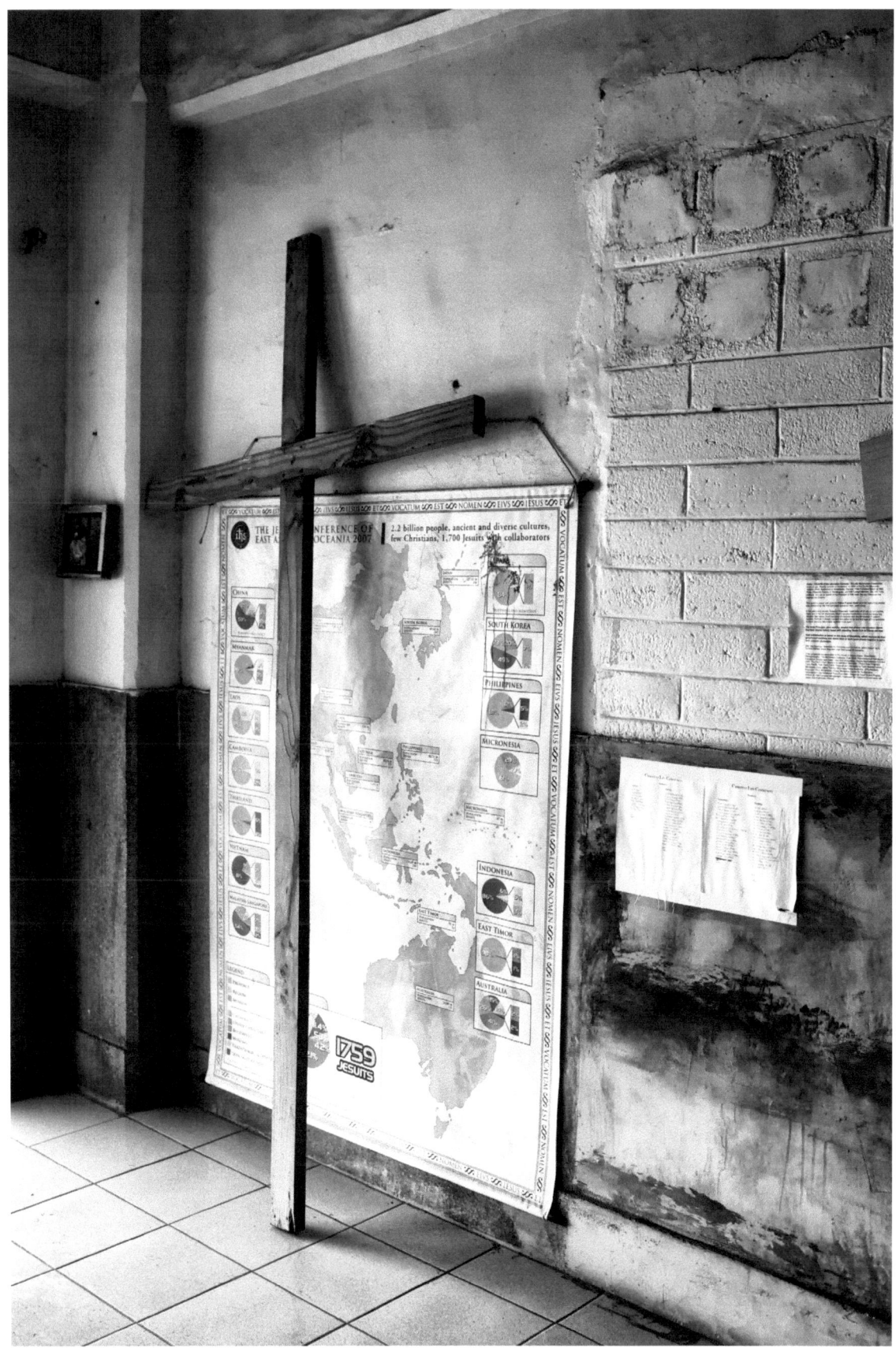

A cross used by students in Easter processions is placed near the Director's office.

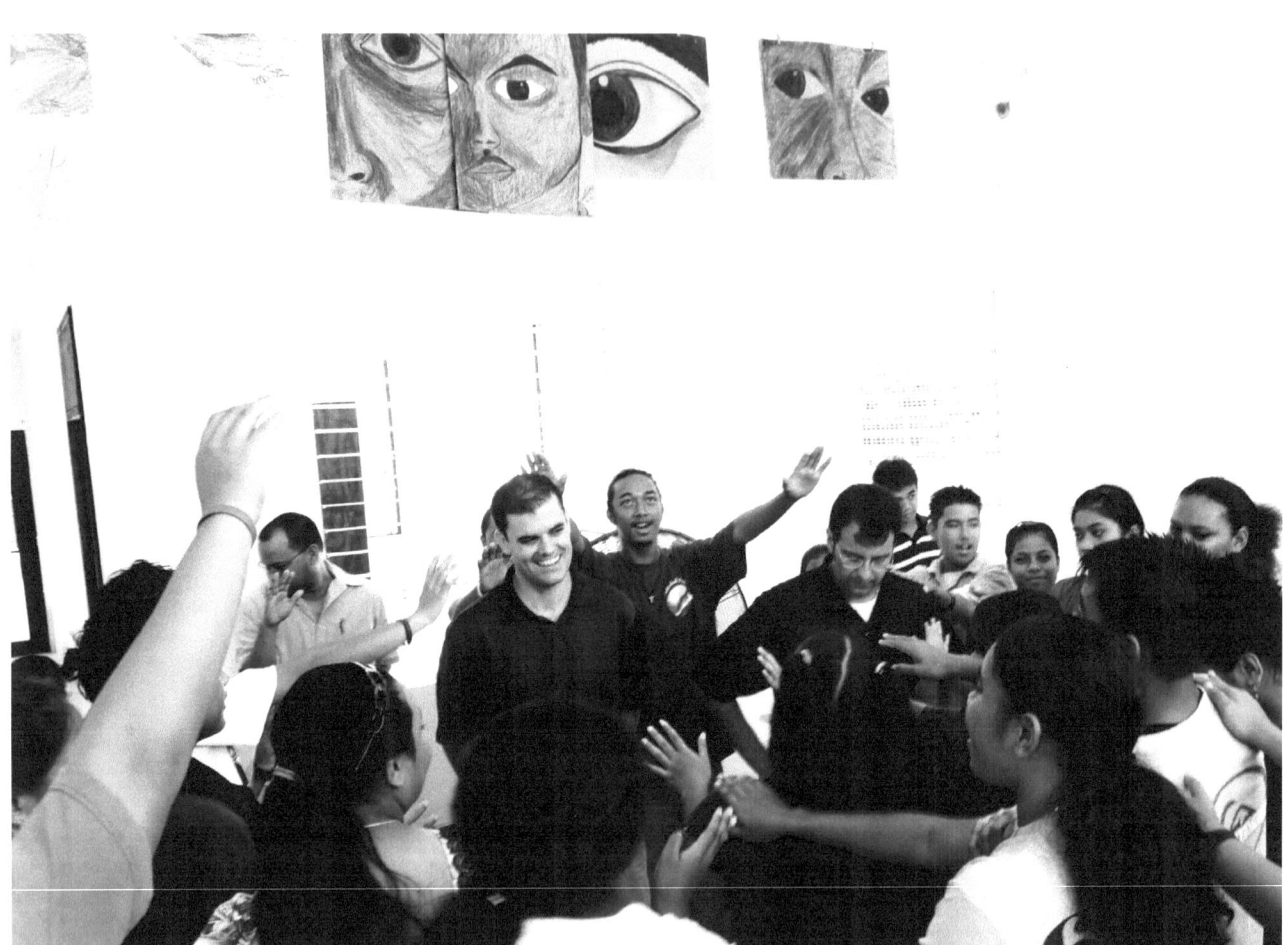

Students sing and pray for departing teachers, Brother Patrick Nolan, SJ, and Brother Ricardo Avila, SJ.

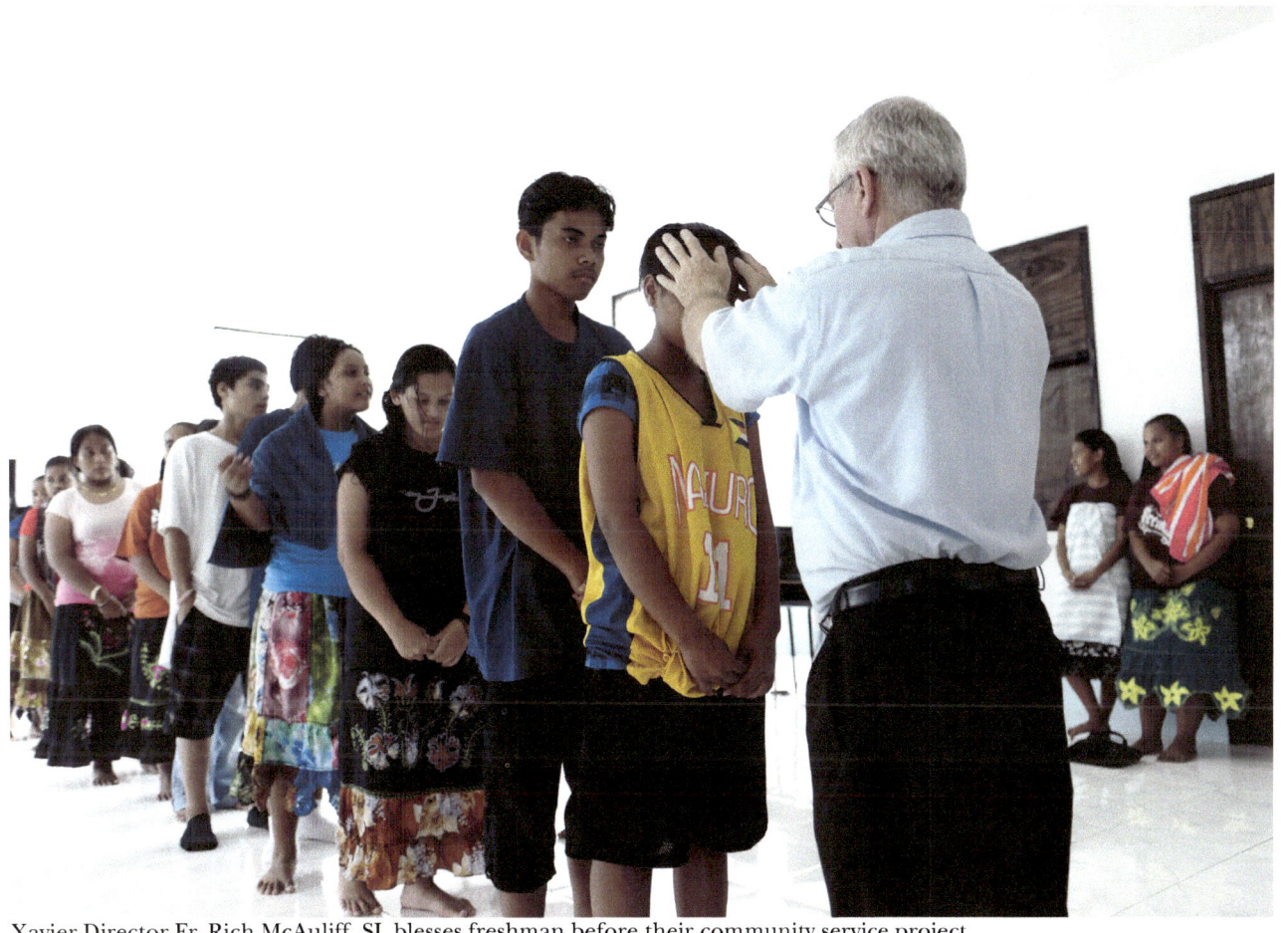

Xavier Director Fr. Rich McAuliff, SJ, blesses freshman before their community service project.

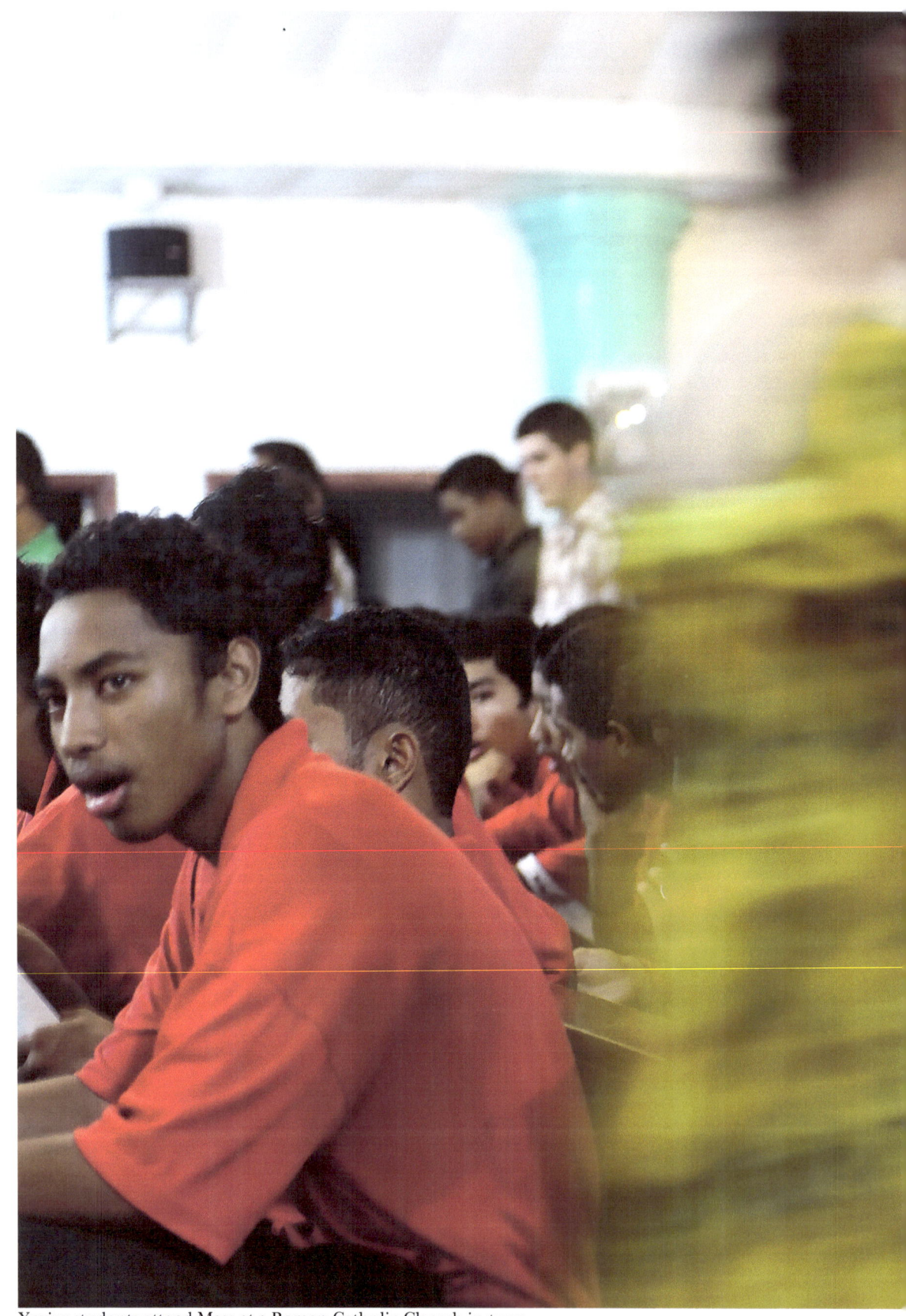

Xavier students attend Mass at a Roman Catholic Church in town.

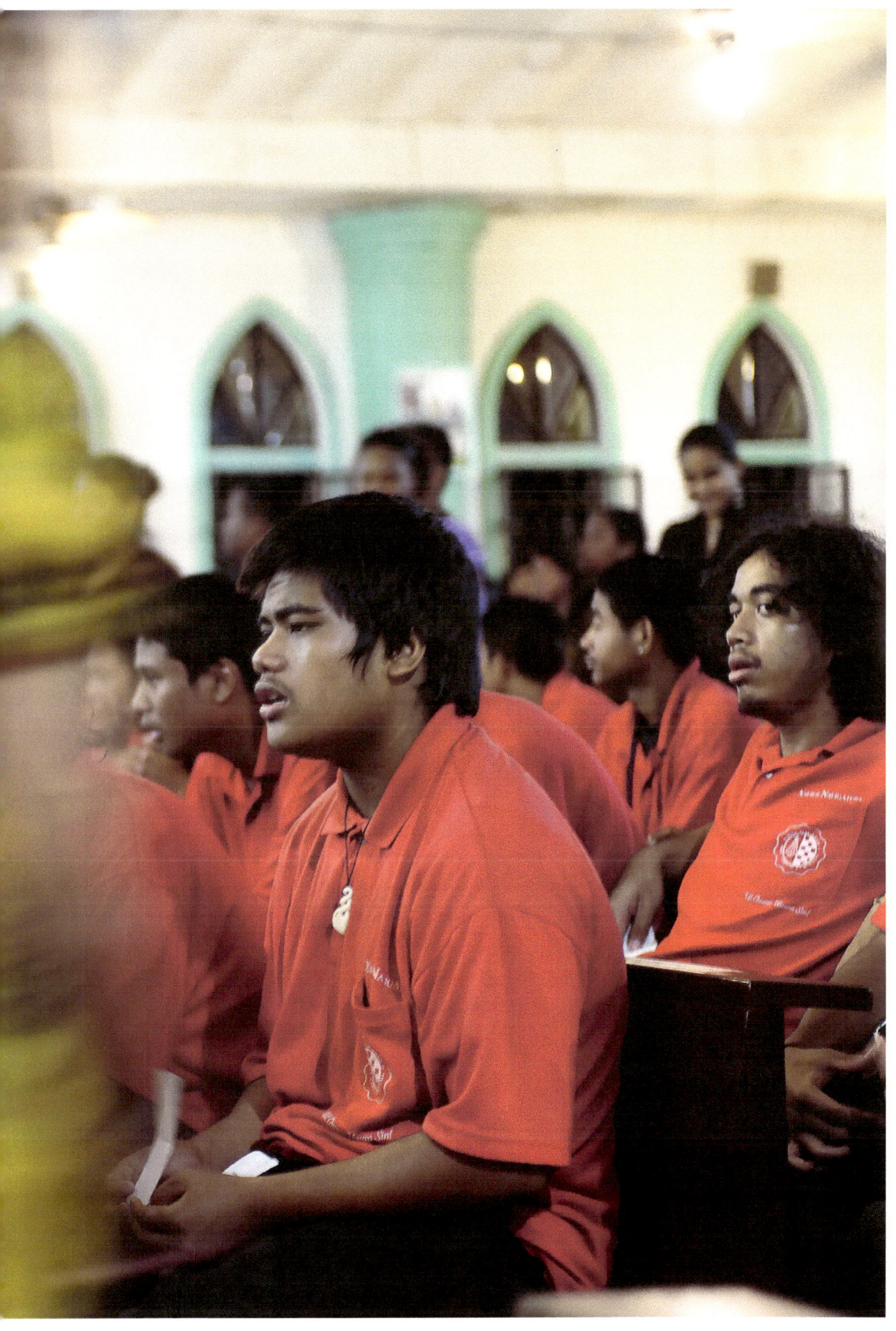

Community

The sun rises early in the equatorial tropics, and by 6 a.m. the sky is bright. I was up early on my first full day on the Xavier High School campus. I shared Jesuit House with the school's Director, Fr. Rich McAuliff, SJ. At a few minutes past 6 a.m. as I was shaving, I heard the sound of raking outside my window

It was one of the Xavier boys, a freshman I later learned, wearing shorts but no shirt, barefoot, raking the leaves under a tree. As I looked out over the campus, I could see other boys with rakes and trash bags.

This was my introduction to "Morning Glory," part of Xavier's tradition of self-reliance and hard work. Students are assigned to work around the campus, and are expected to keep the grounds clean. Over the month that I spent at Xavier, the sound of raking leaves was my early morning accompaniment as I shaved by the window in my room.

Students run "Morning Glory," and that says much about the culture of the school. Adults play an obviously important role in the life of the Xavier, but I saw how much initiative students take to manage their lives. It reminded me of what you see in villages across Oceania: older children, still in grade and middle school, caring for the infants and younger kids, usually one carried on a hip. And not a parent in sight.

A more serious example played out later during my stay on campus. As the school year ended, it was discovered that two of the school's laptop computers were missing. This was a major problem – most Xavier students do not have their own computers. Fr. Rich conferred with the incoming student body president, Benigno Sablan of Palau. The Director made it clear that unless both laptops were returned, no student would be allowed to take final exams.

Within a day, Sablan and other student leaders resolved the crisis. They did a massive campus search and found one of the missing laptops. They also recommended that every Xavier student be fined a portion of the cost of replacing the last missing computer. The crisis was resolved. Final exams were held.

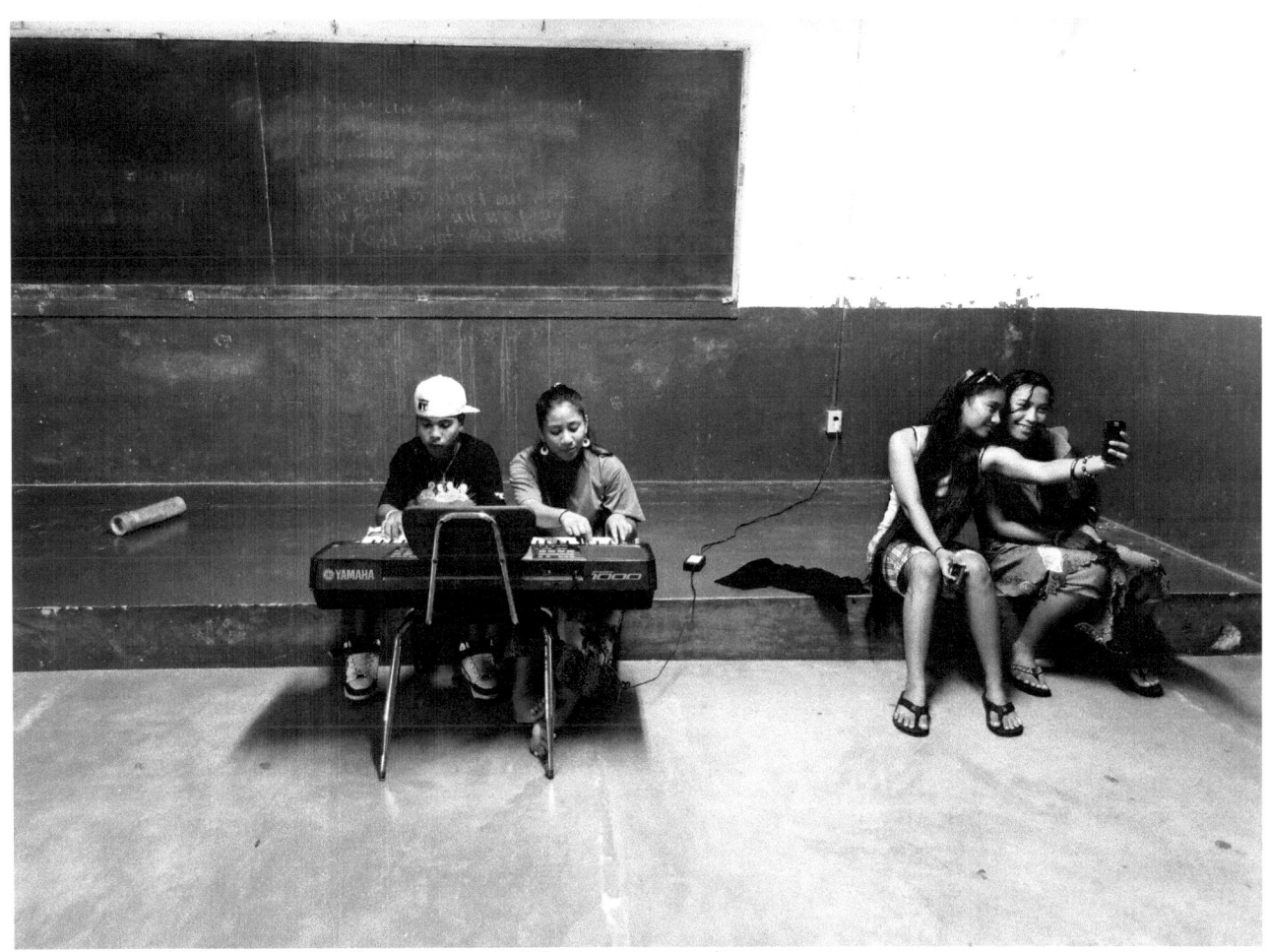

Students relax in the study hall following an end-of-the-year campus cleanup.

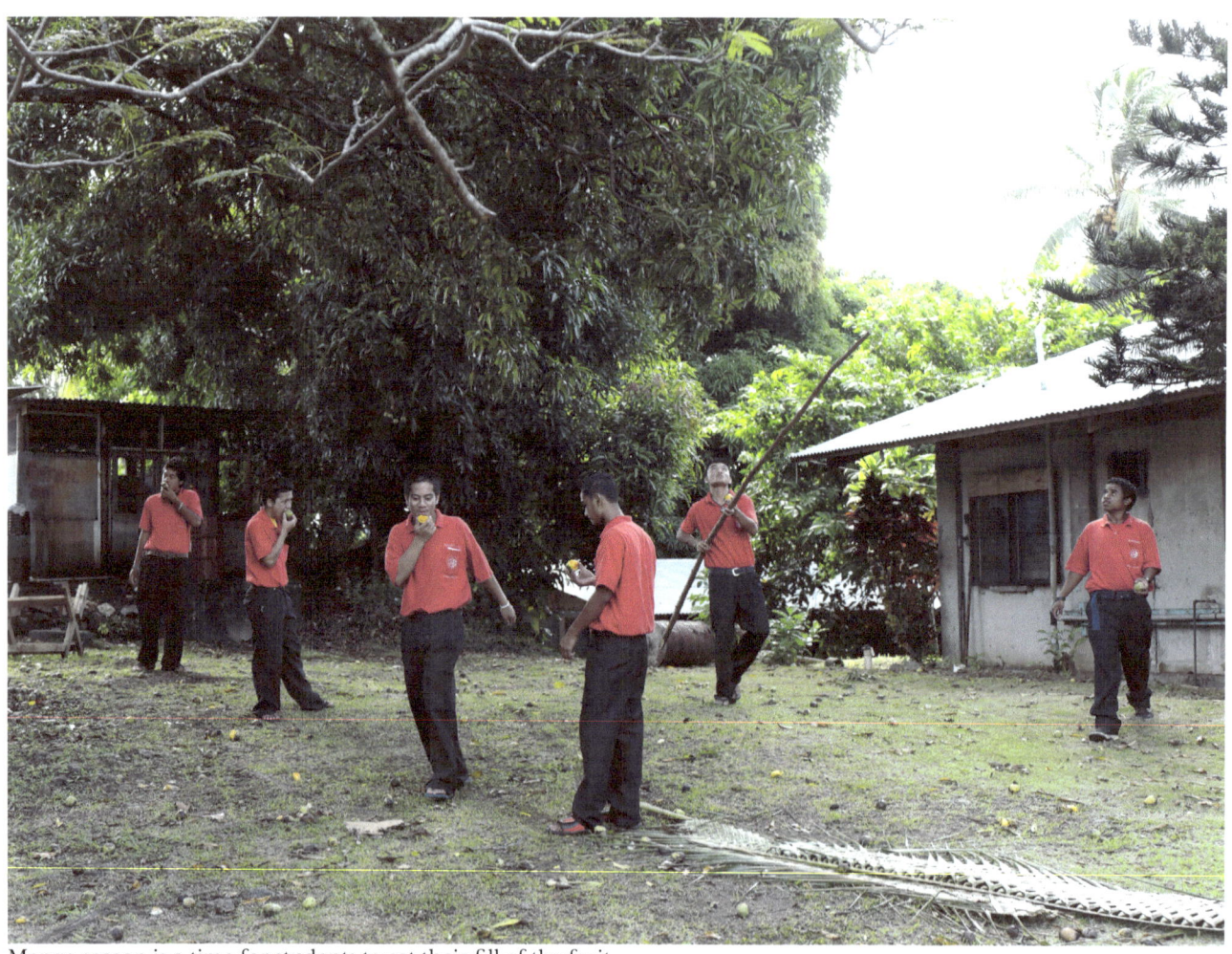

Mango season is a time for students to eat their fill of the fruit.

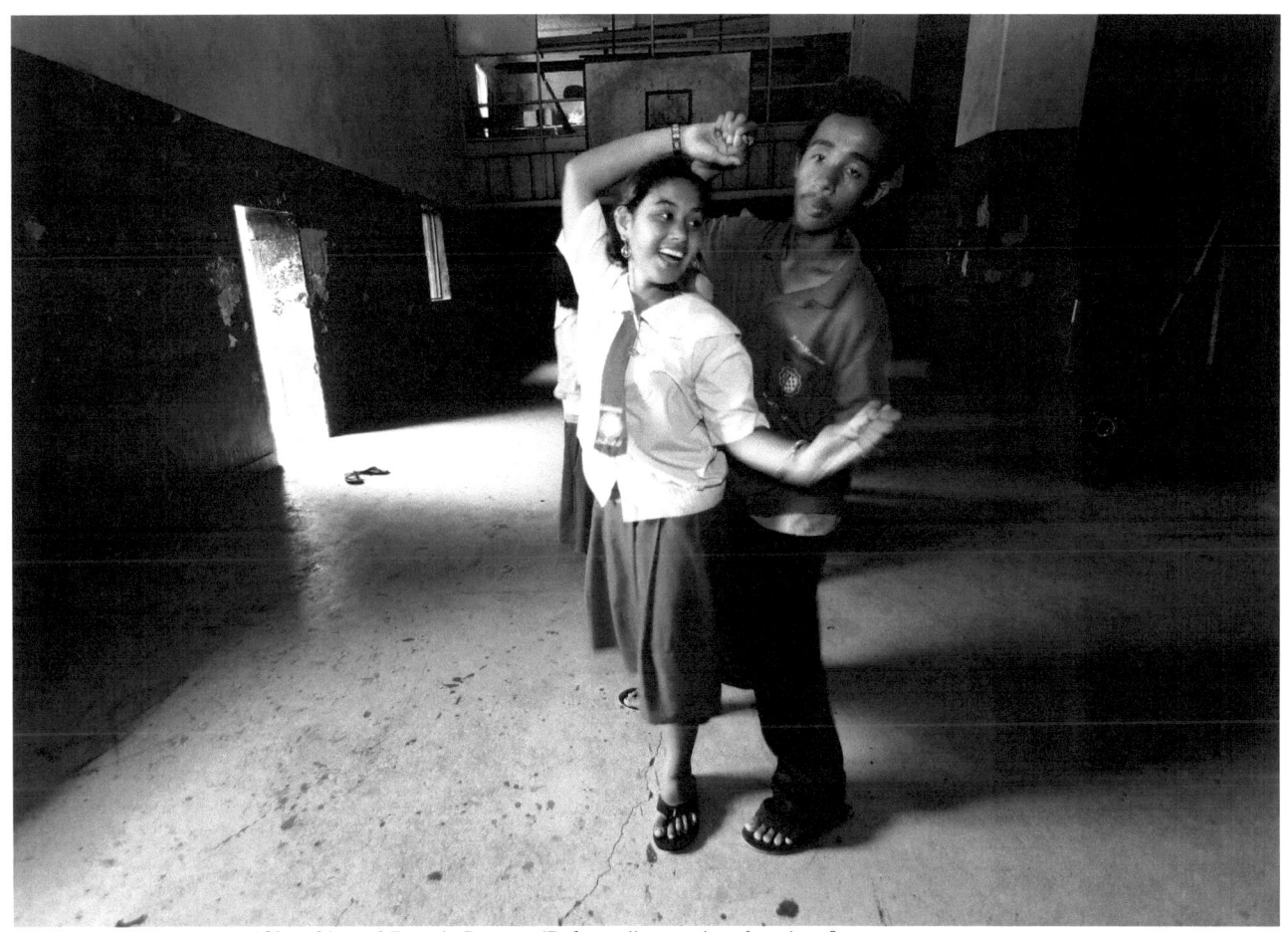

Freshmen Rolyn Esein (Chuuk) and Bernis Bemes (Pohnpei) practice dancing for a program.

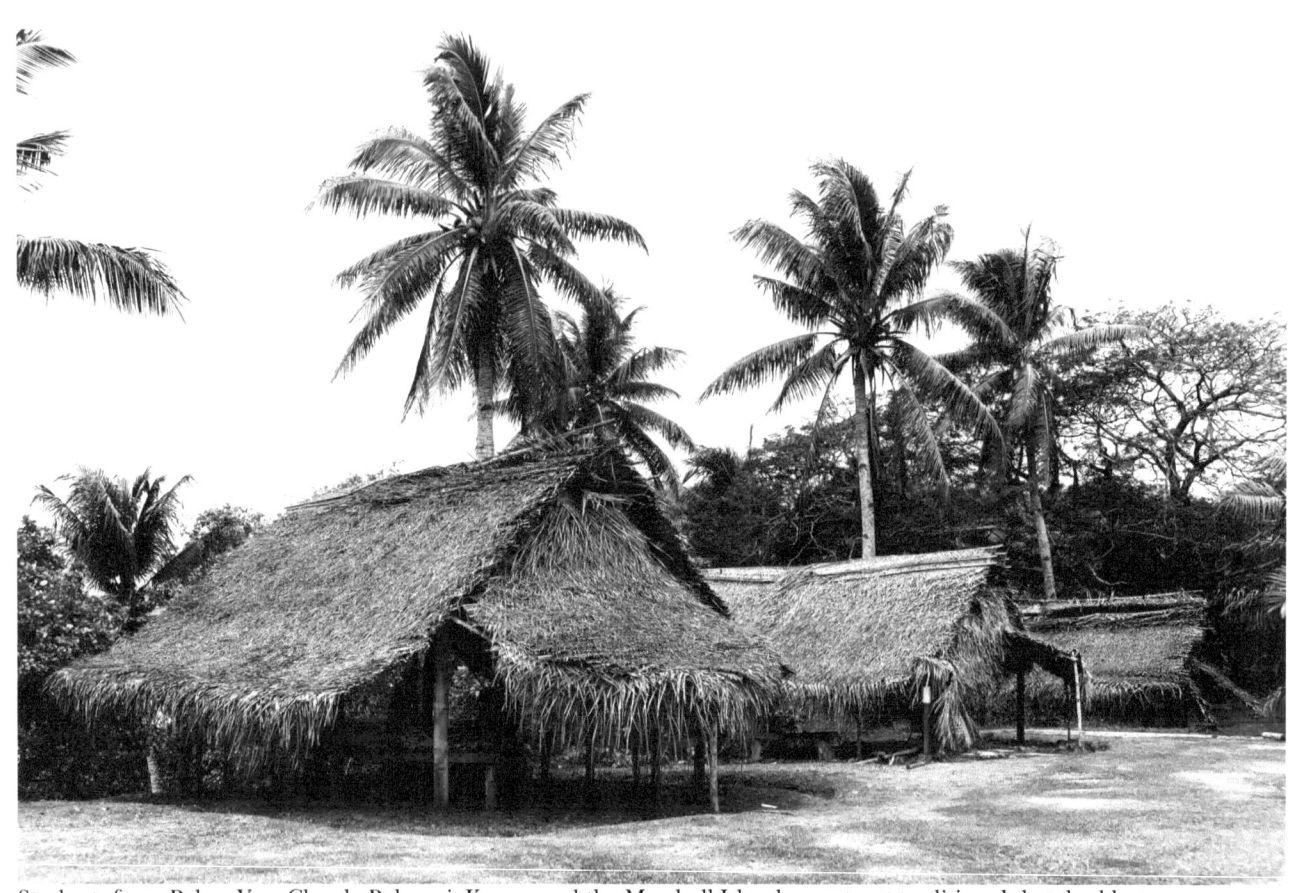

Students from Palau, Yap, Chuuk, Pohnpei, Kosrae and the Marshall Islands construct traditional thatched huts on campus.

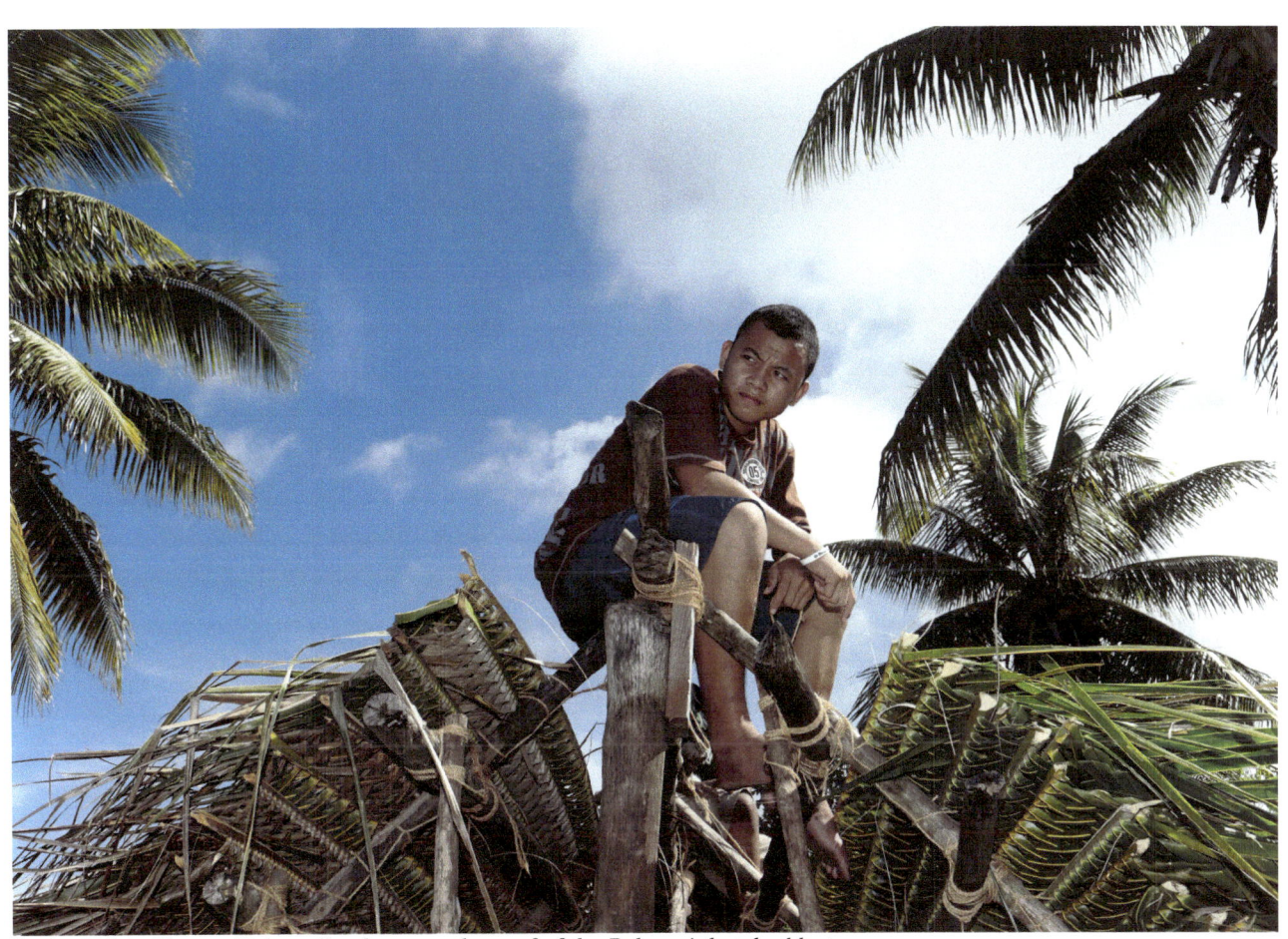

Junior Kalvin Ehmes (Pohnpei) relaxes on the roof of the Pohnpei thatched hut.

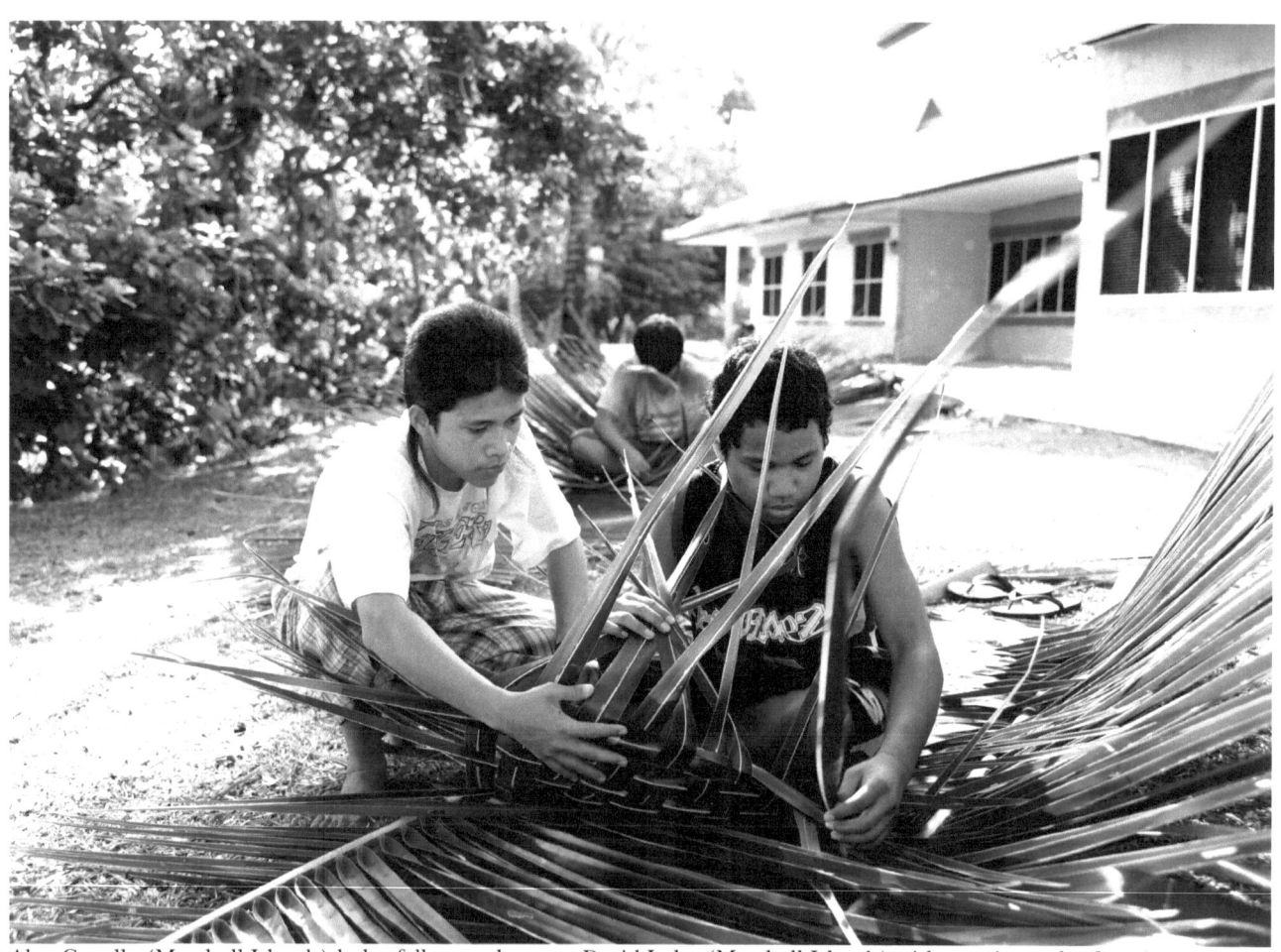

Alex Capelle (Marshall Islands) helps fellow sophomore David Lelet (Marshall Islands) with weaving palm fronds.

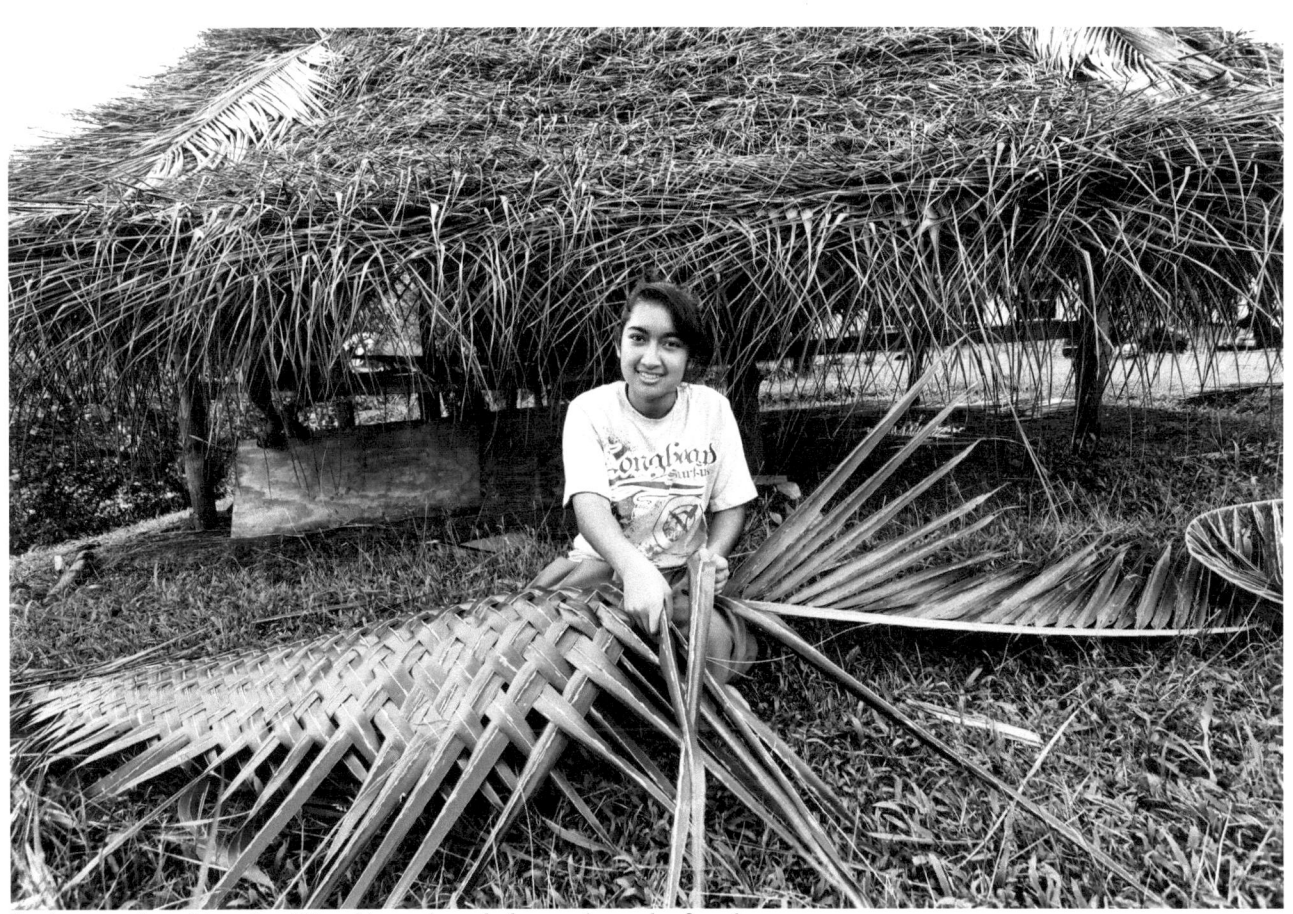

Sophomore Lyra Narruhn (Chuuk) needs no help weaving palm fronds.

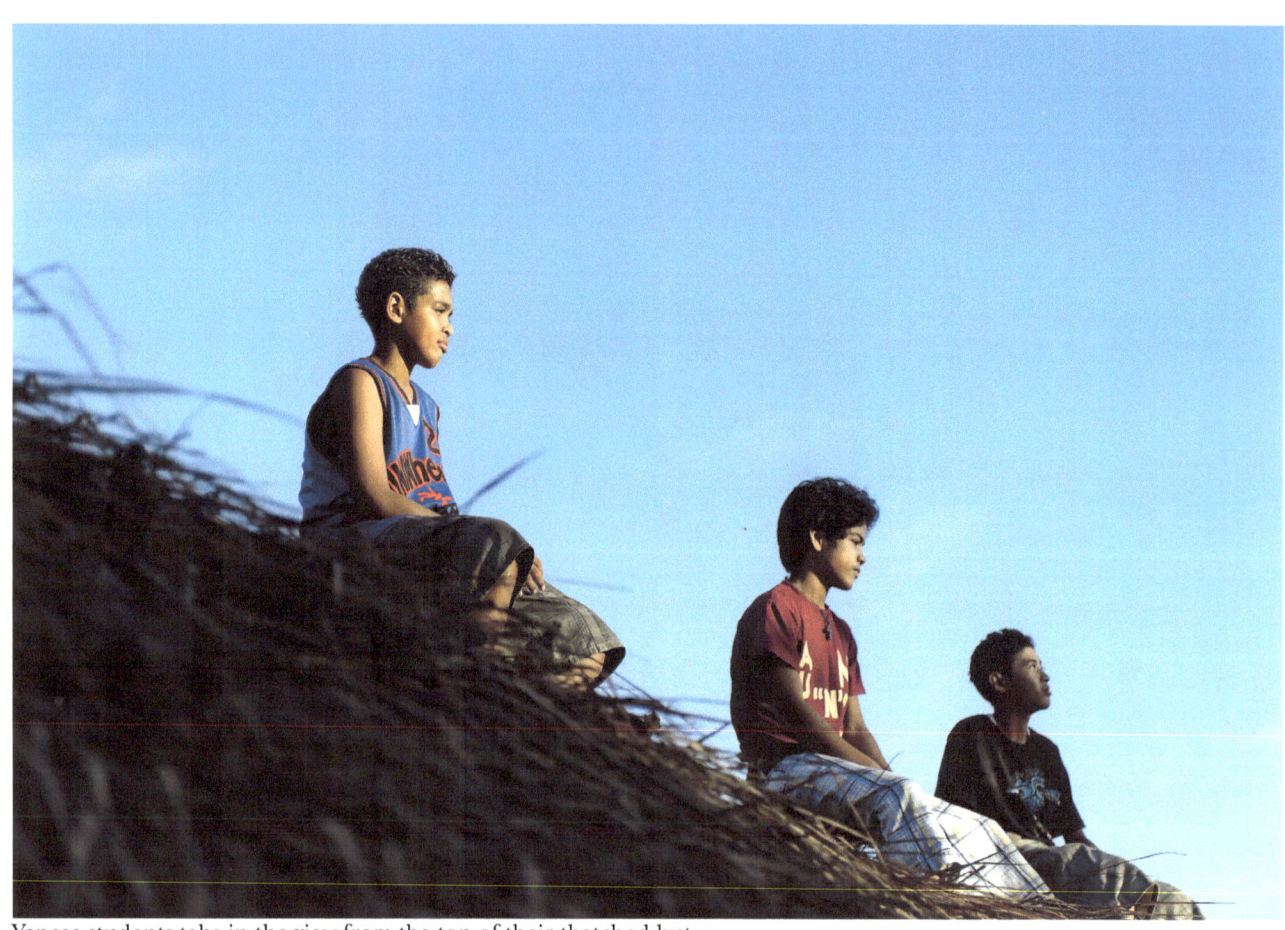

Yapese students take in the view from the top of their thatched hut.

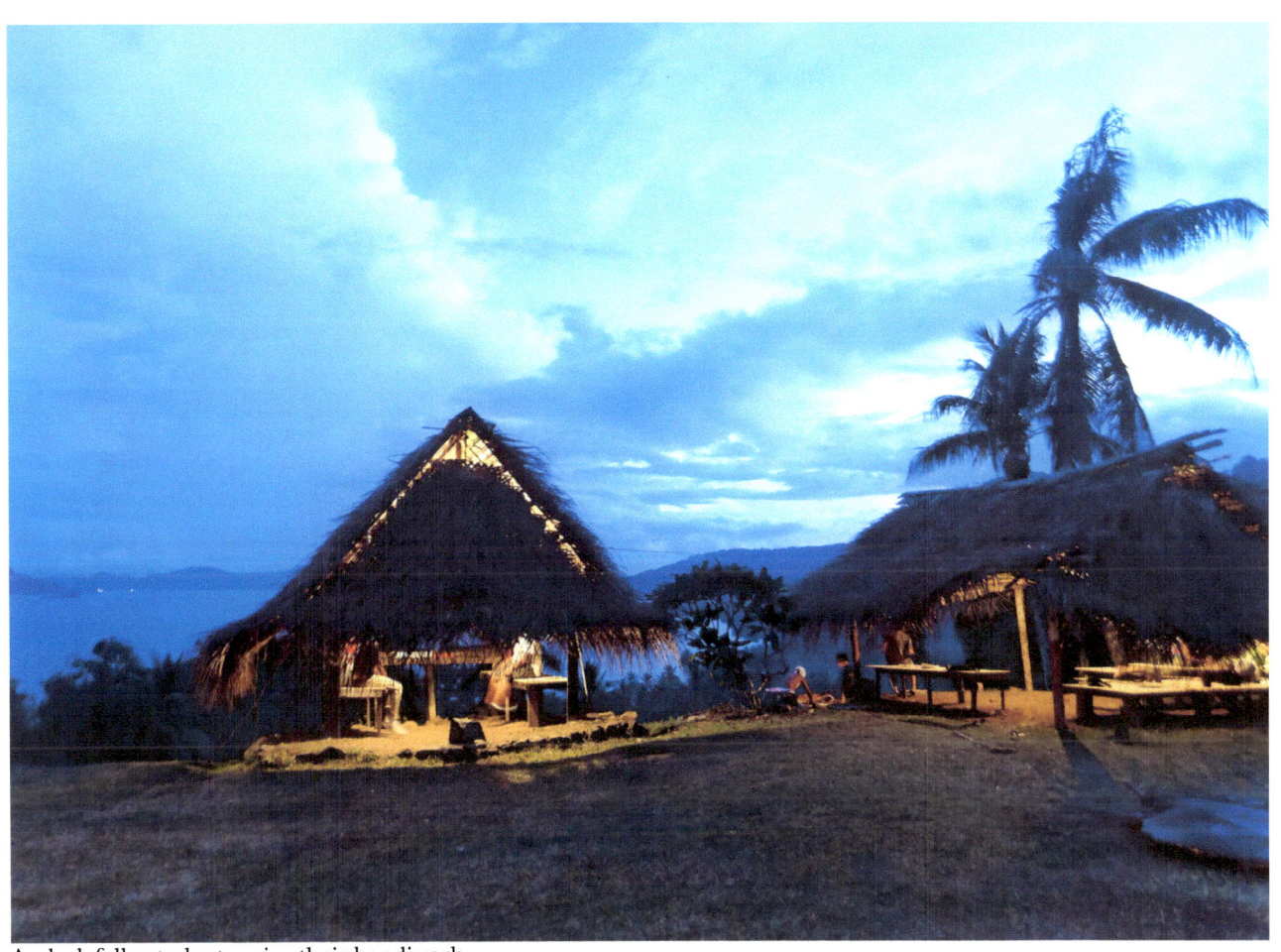

As dusk falls, students enjoy their handiwork.

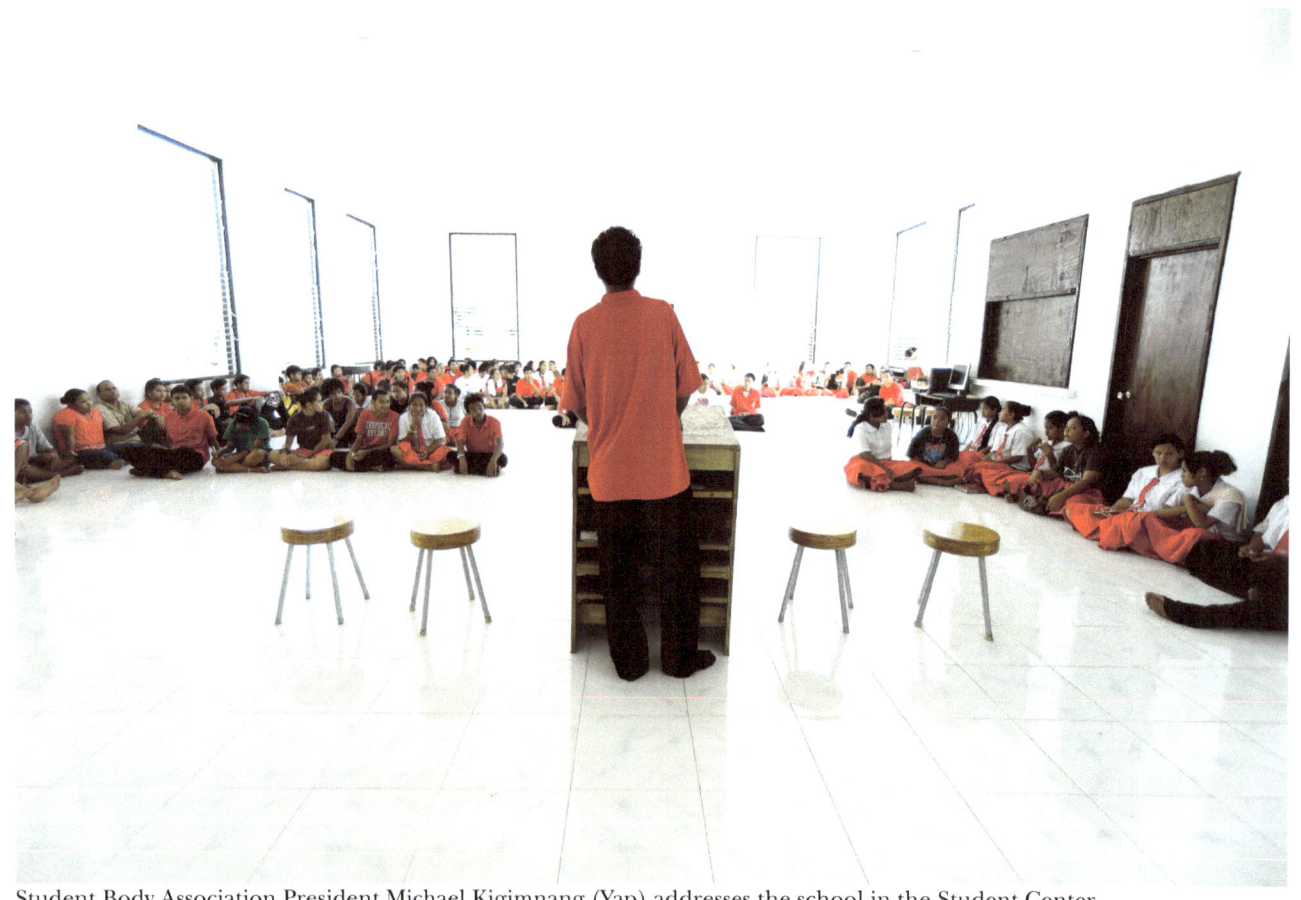

Student Body Association President Michael Kigimnang (Yap) addresses the school in the Student Center.

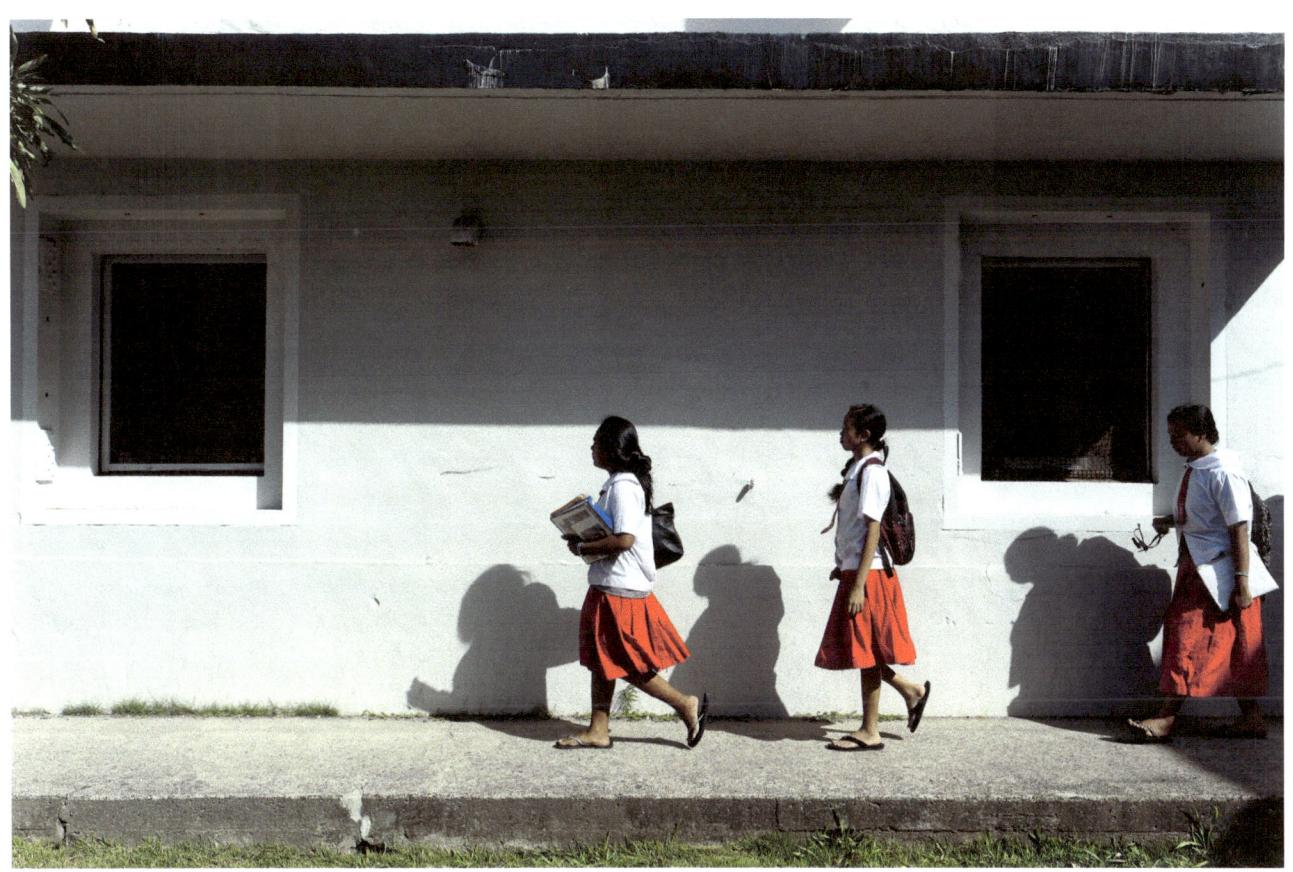

Students on their way to class.

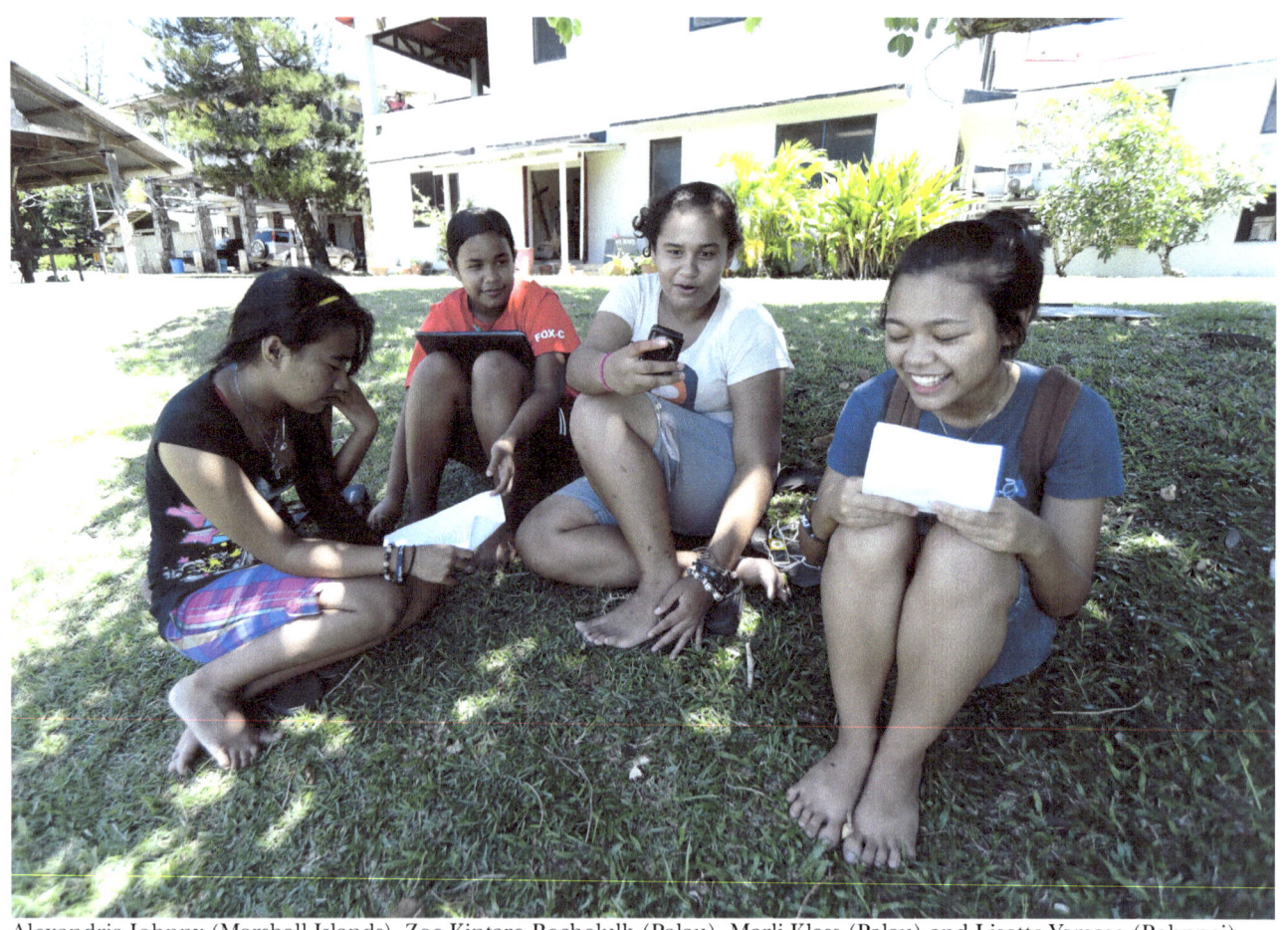

Alexandria Johnny (Marshall Islands), Zoe Kintaro Rechelulk (Palau), Marli Klass (Palau) and Lisette Yamase (Pohnpei).

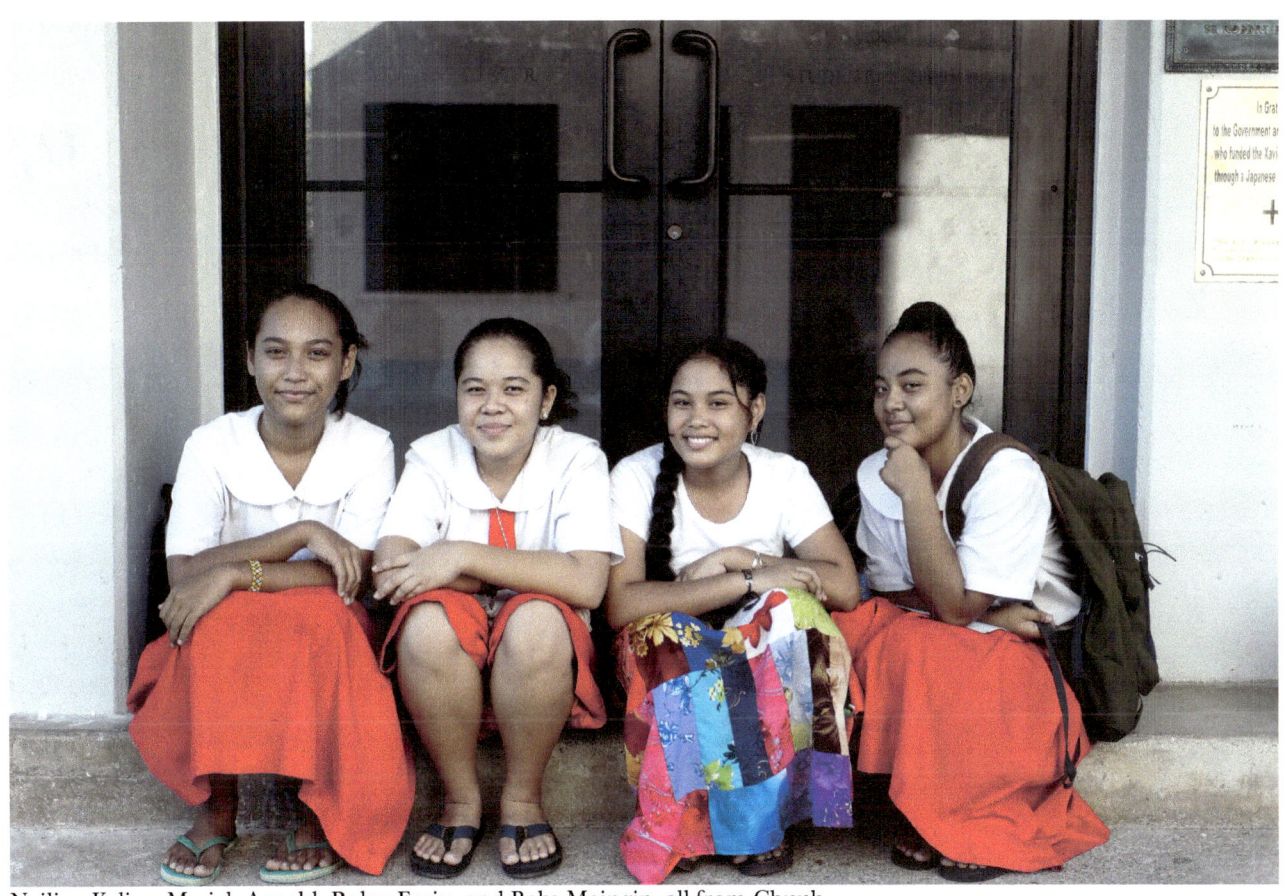

Neilien Kaliga, Mariah Arnold, Rolyn Esein, and Beka Meingin, all from Chuuk.

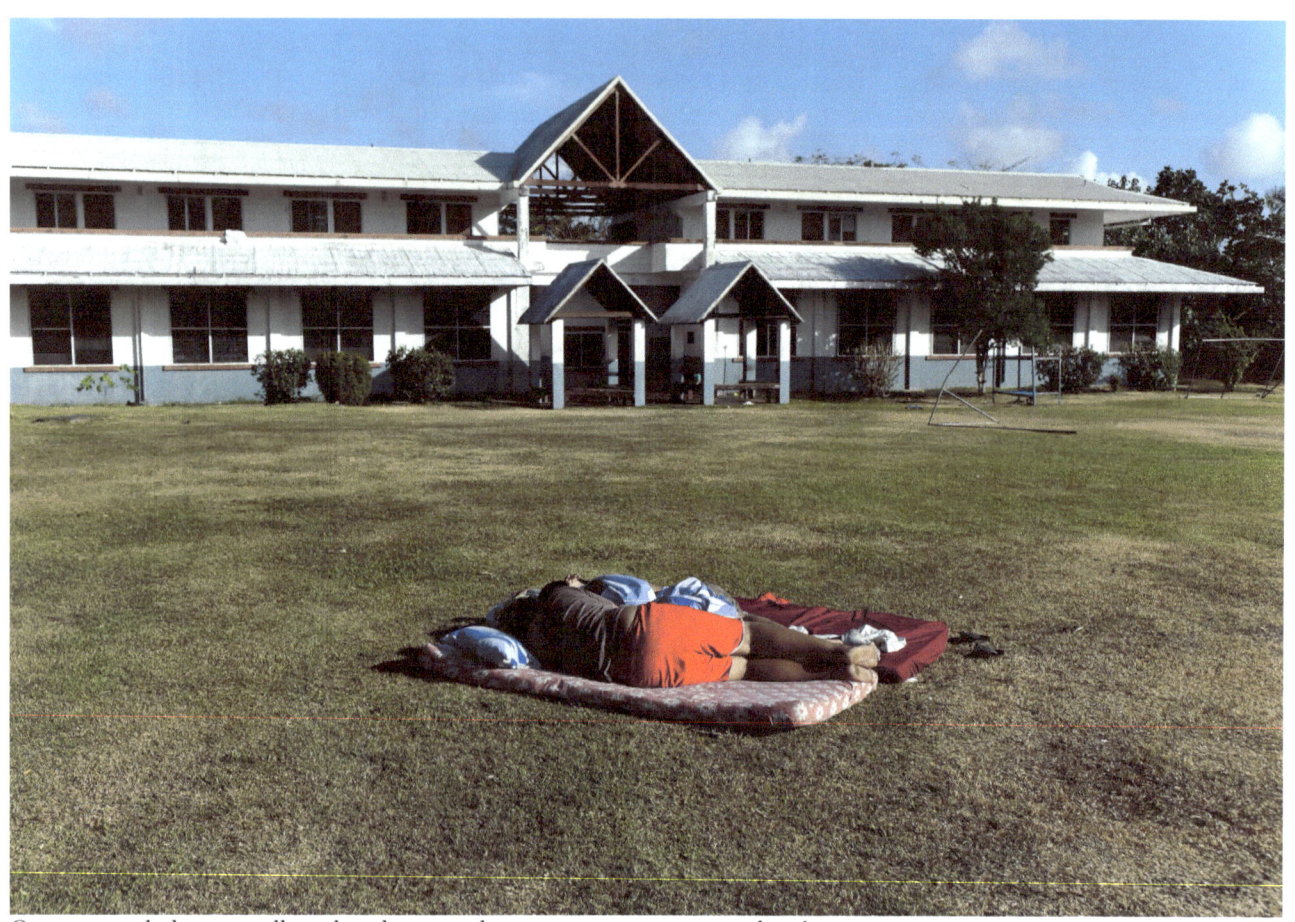

Once a month, boys are allowed to sleep anywhere on campus over a weekend.

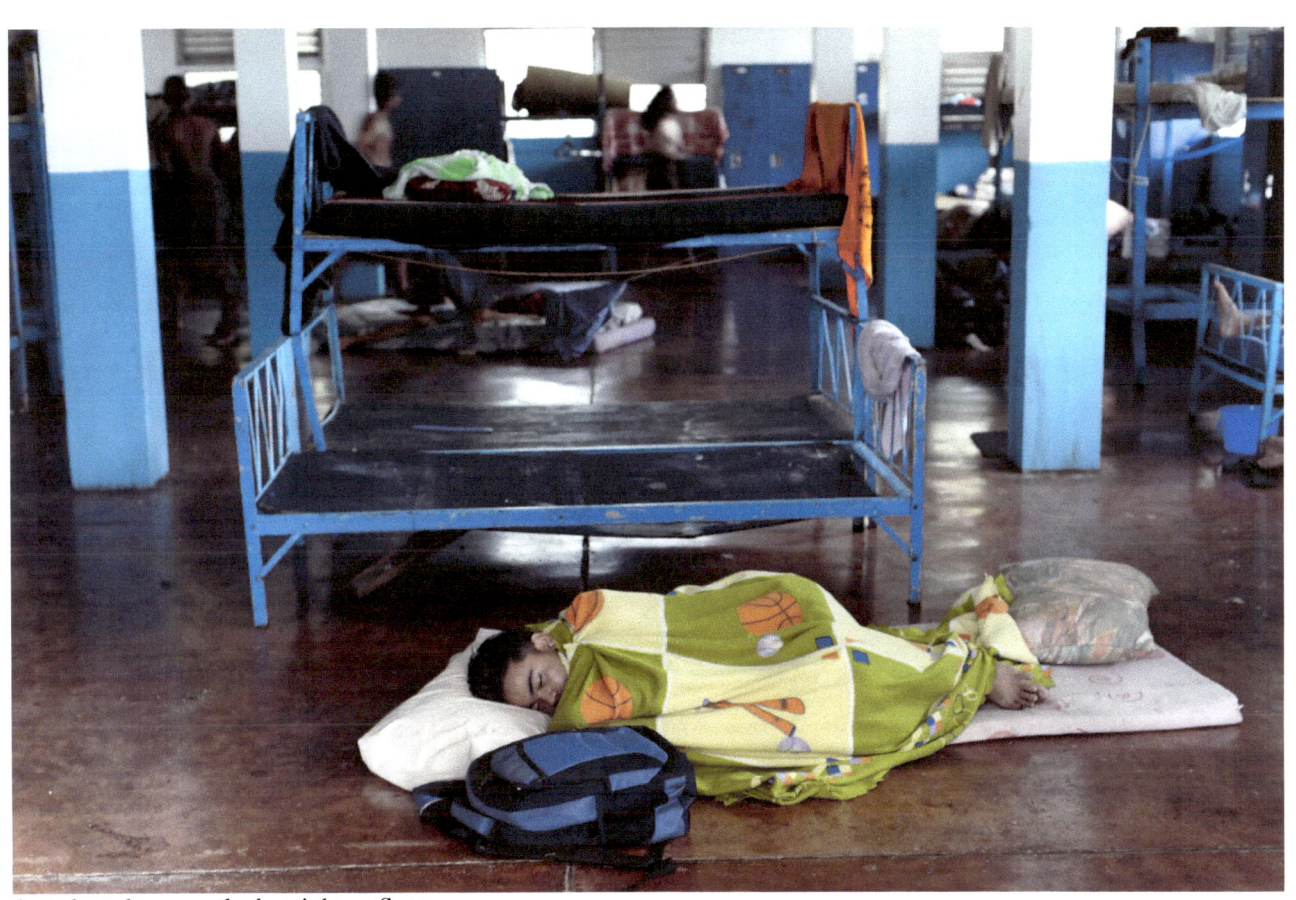

A student sleeps on the boys' dorm floor.

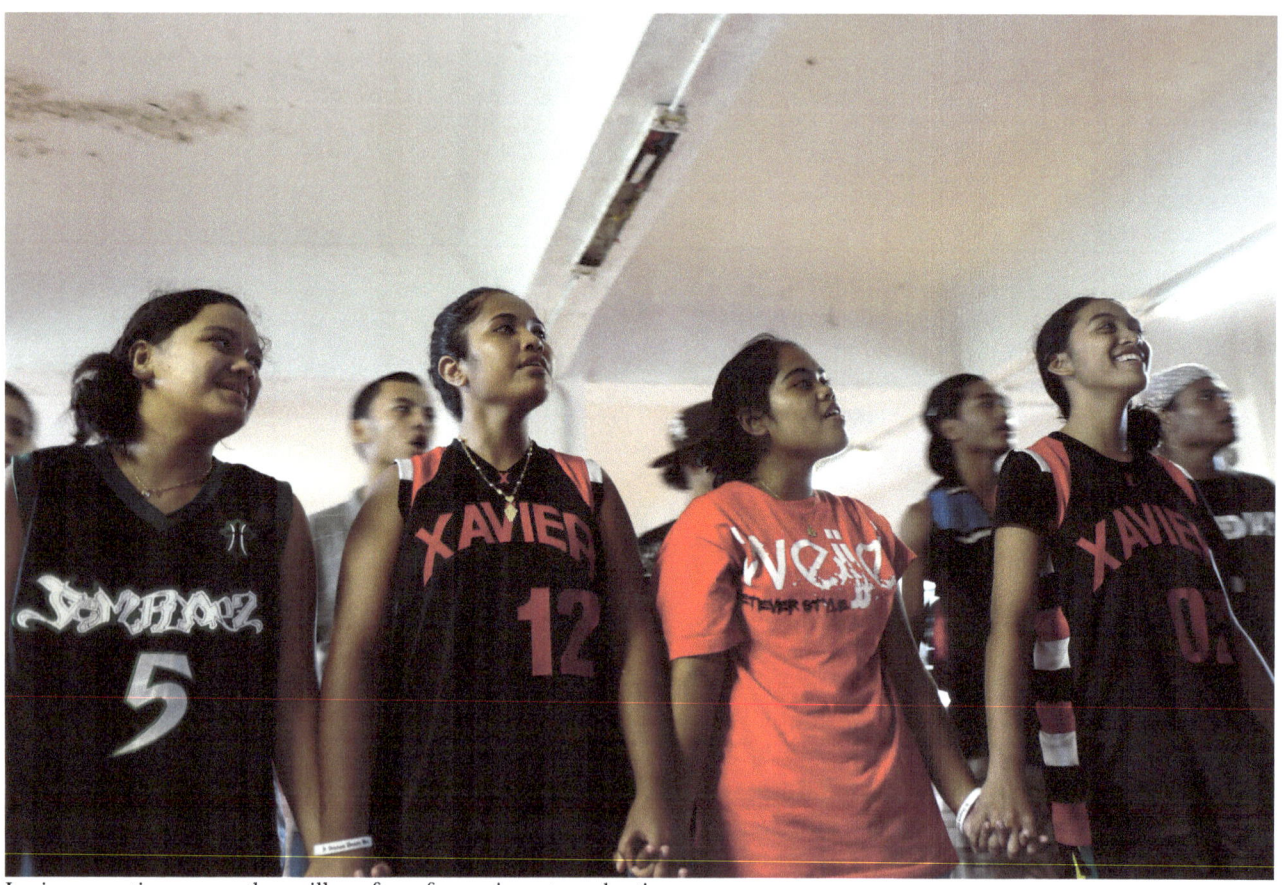

Juniors practice a song they will perform for seniors at graduation.

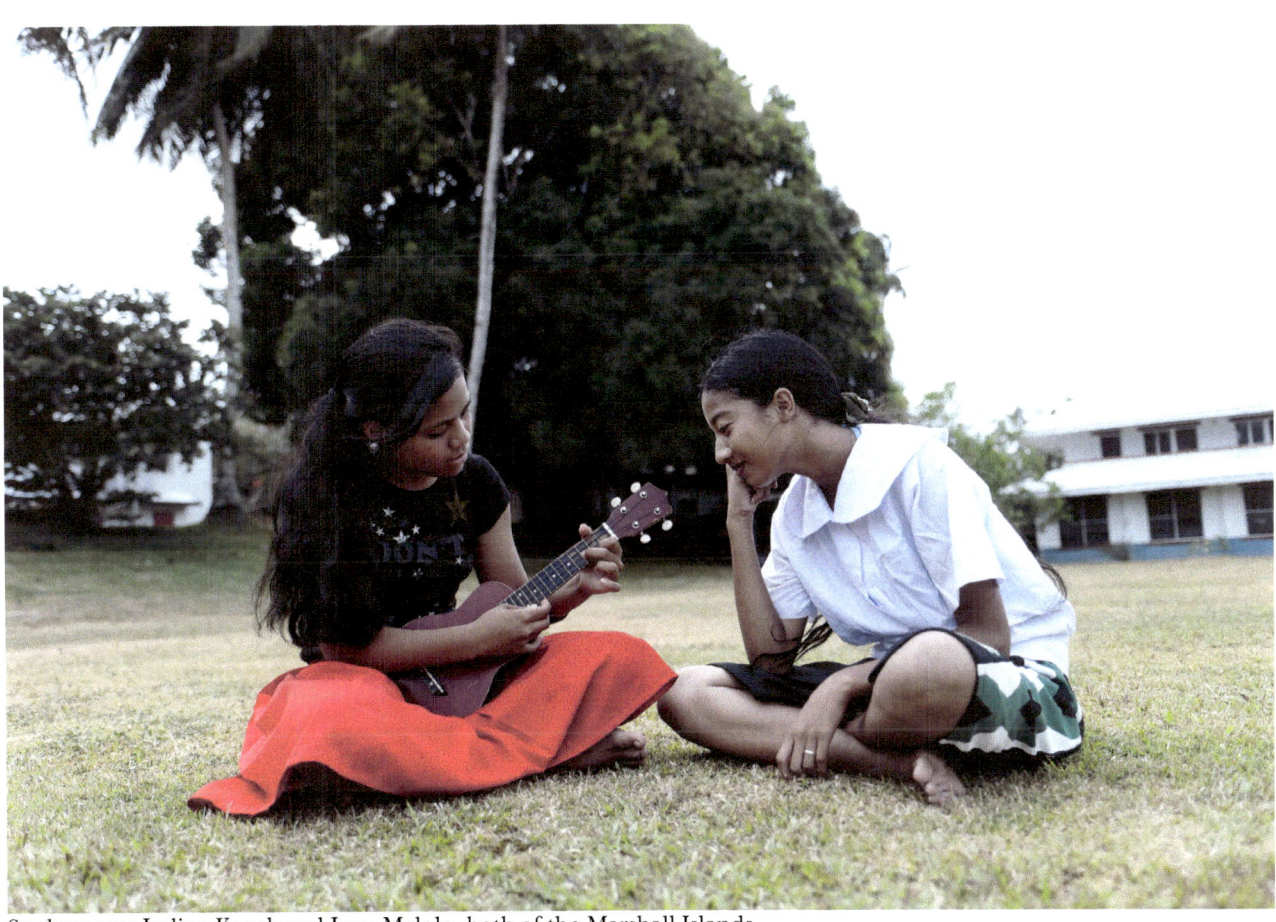

Sophomores Judina Korok and Jean Malolo, both of the Marshall Islands.

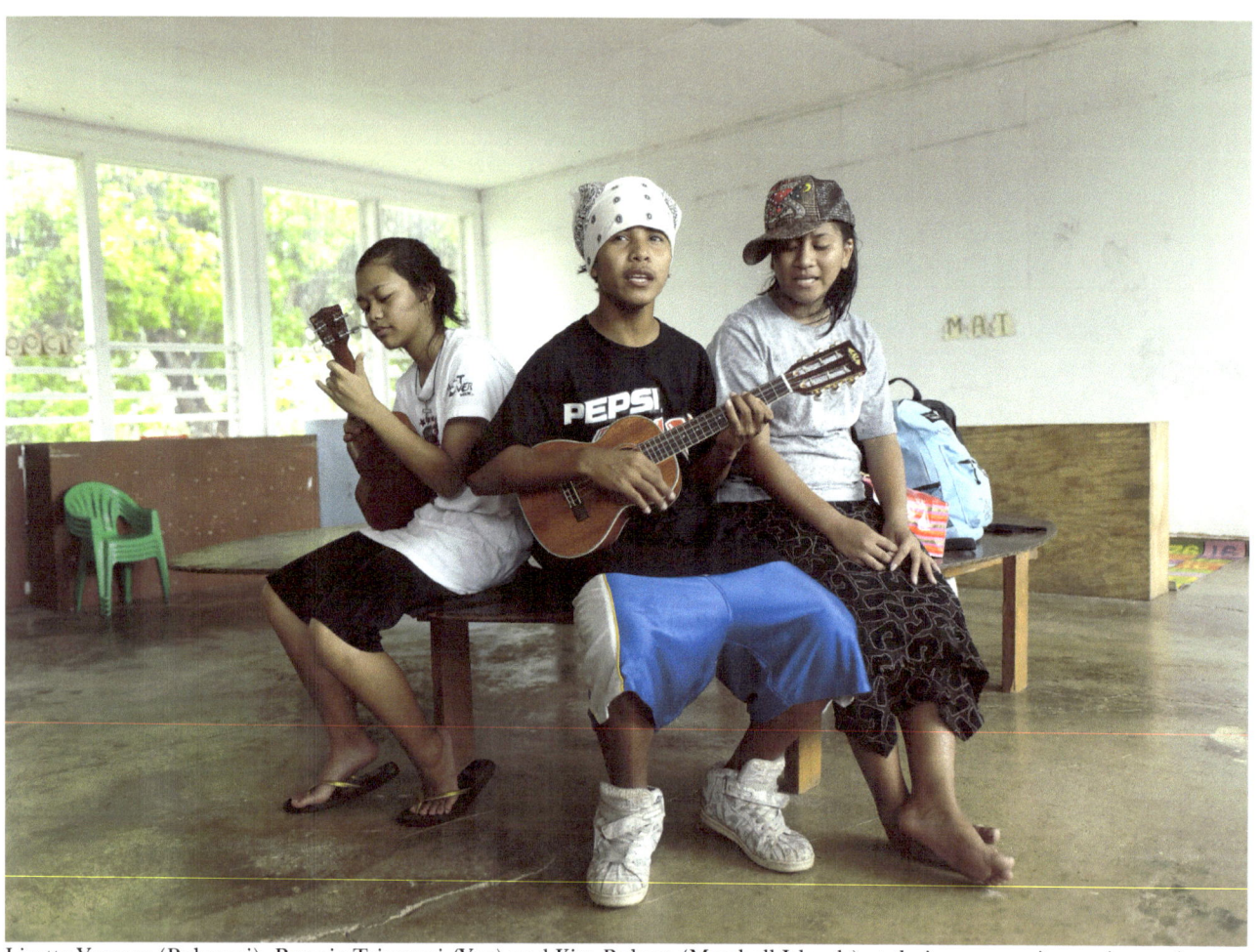

Lisette Yamase (Pohnpei), Rennie Taiugmai (Yap) and Kira Robert (Marshall Islands) at their community service project.

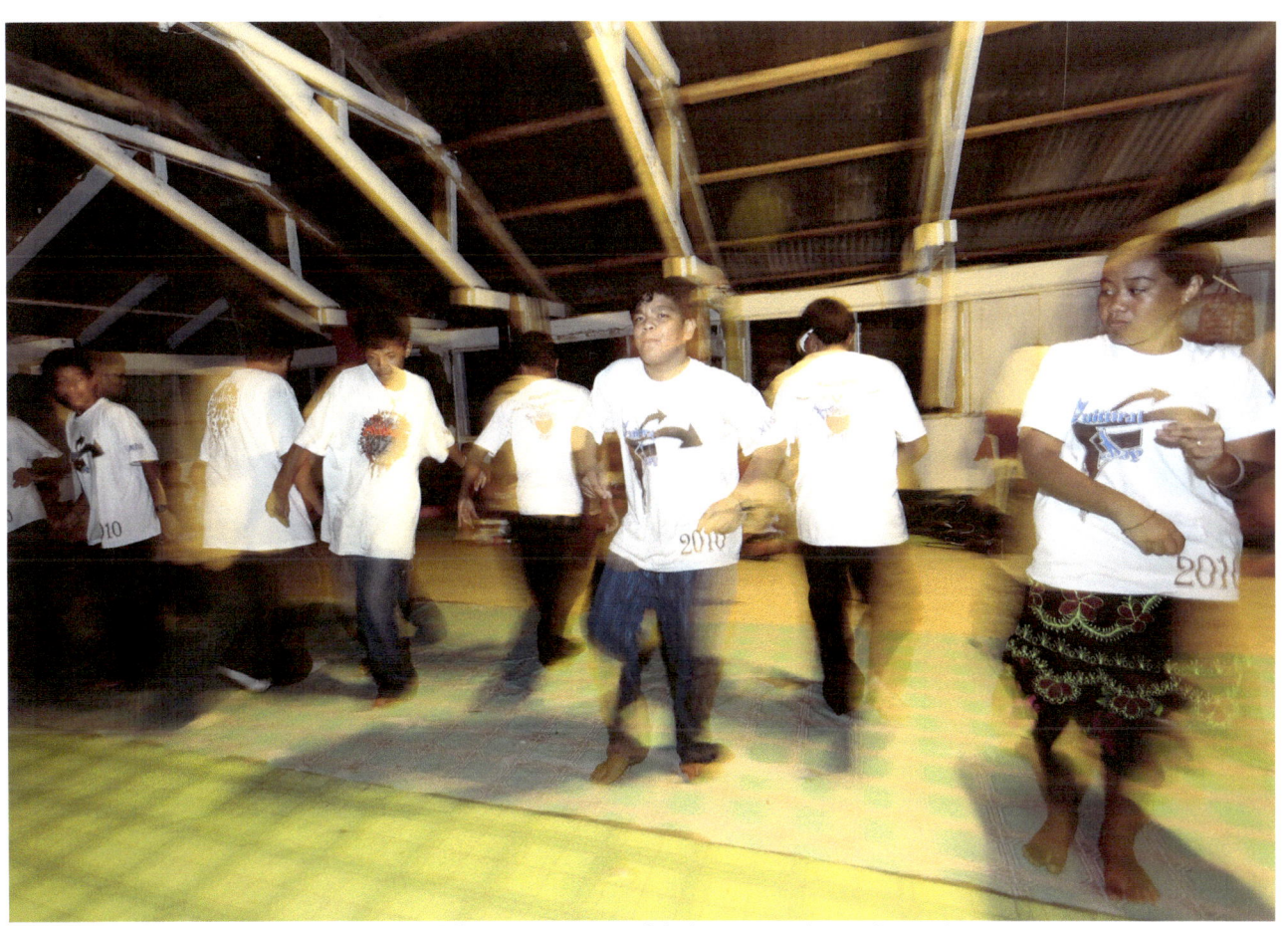

Freshmen perform a dance in the Sapuk Village center, part of their community service project.

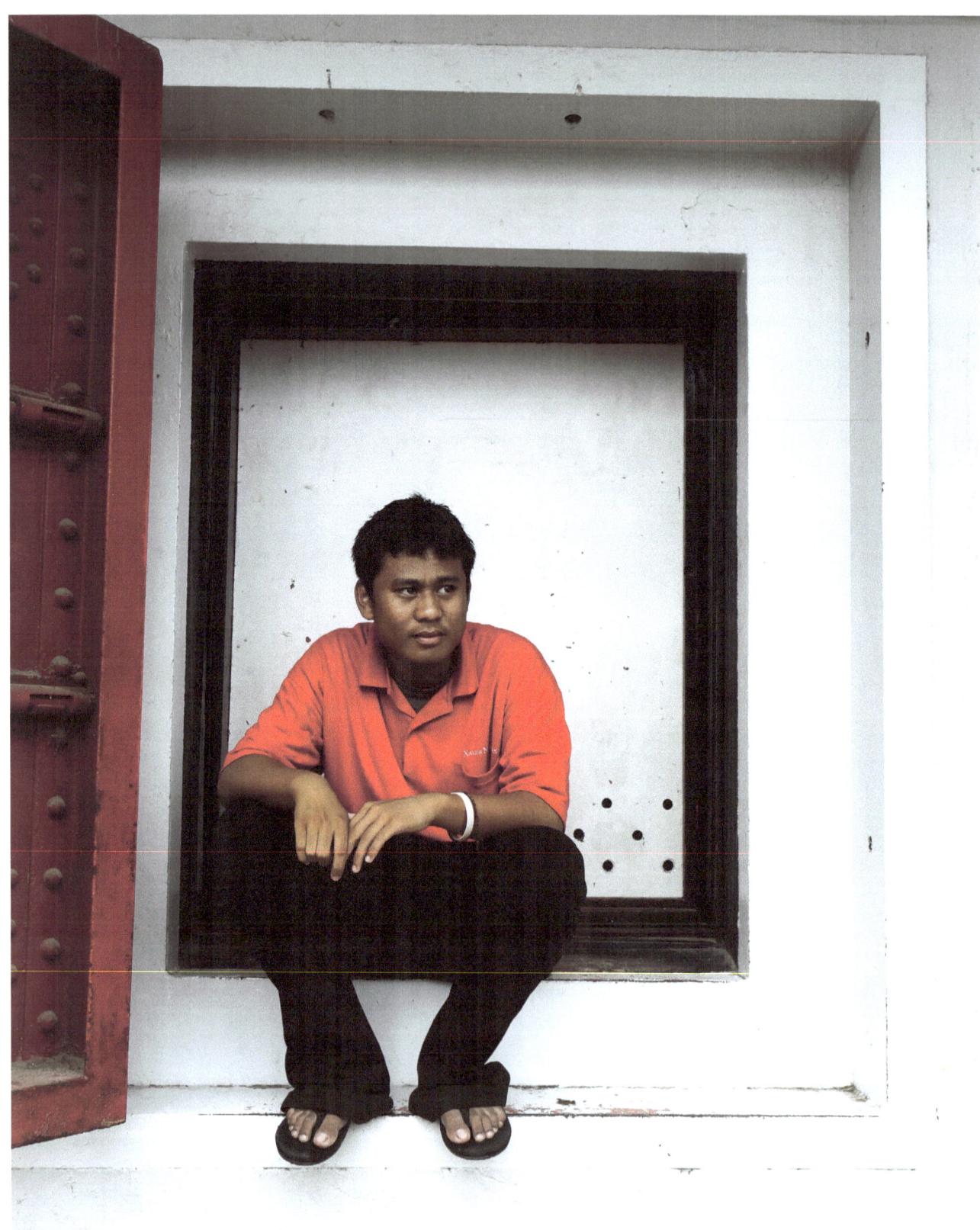

Sophomore Cody Chong-Gum (Marshall Islands).

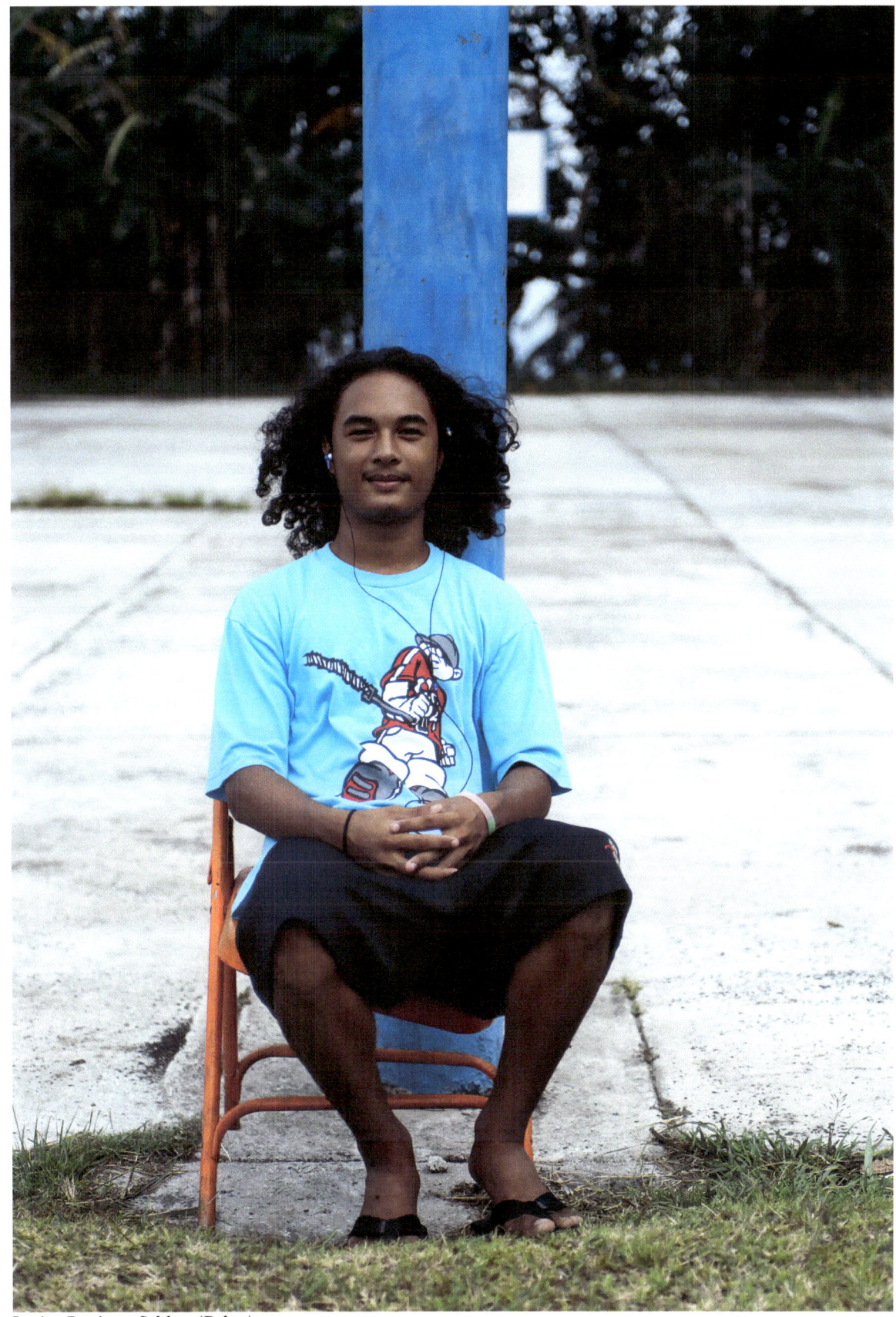

Junior Benigno Sablan (Palau).

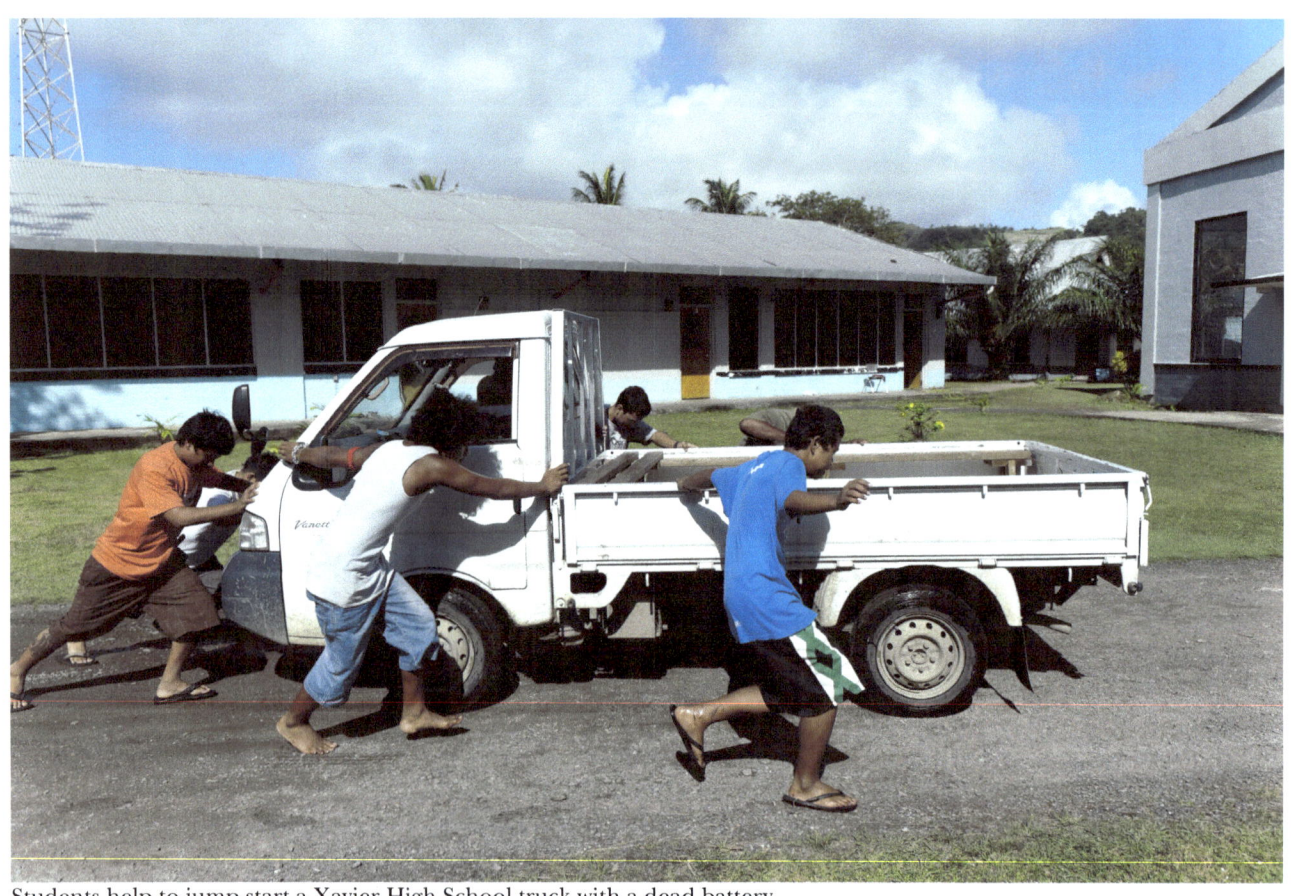

Students help to jump-start a Xavier High School truck with a dead battery.

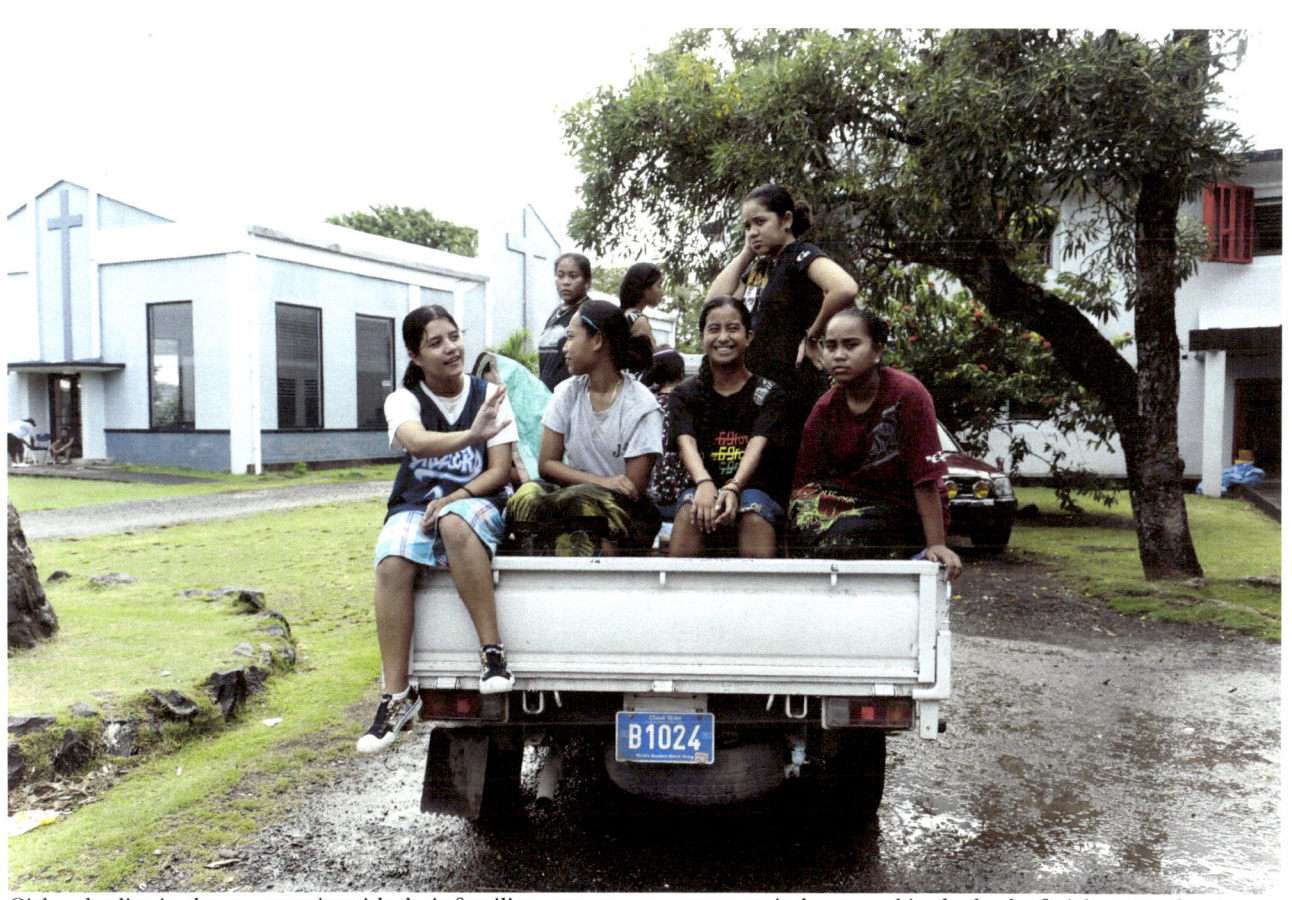

Girls, who live in the community with their families or sponsors, commute in buses and in the back of pick-up trucks.

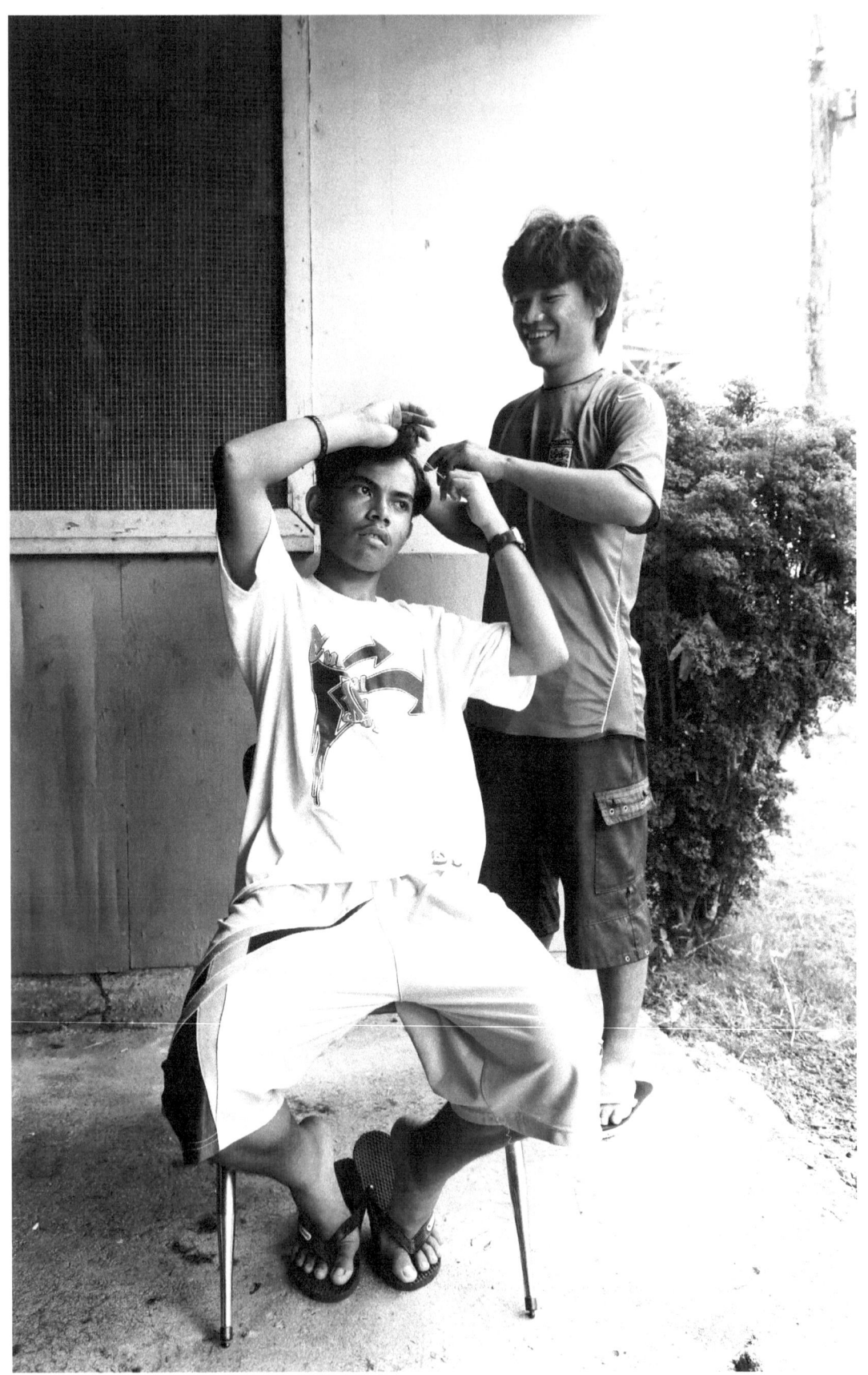

Brother Lin Yaw Mana, SJ, a religion teacher, cuts the hair of freshman Lee Lynch (Pohnpei).

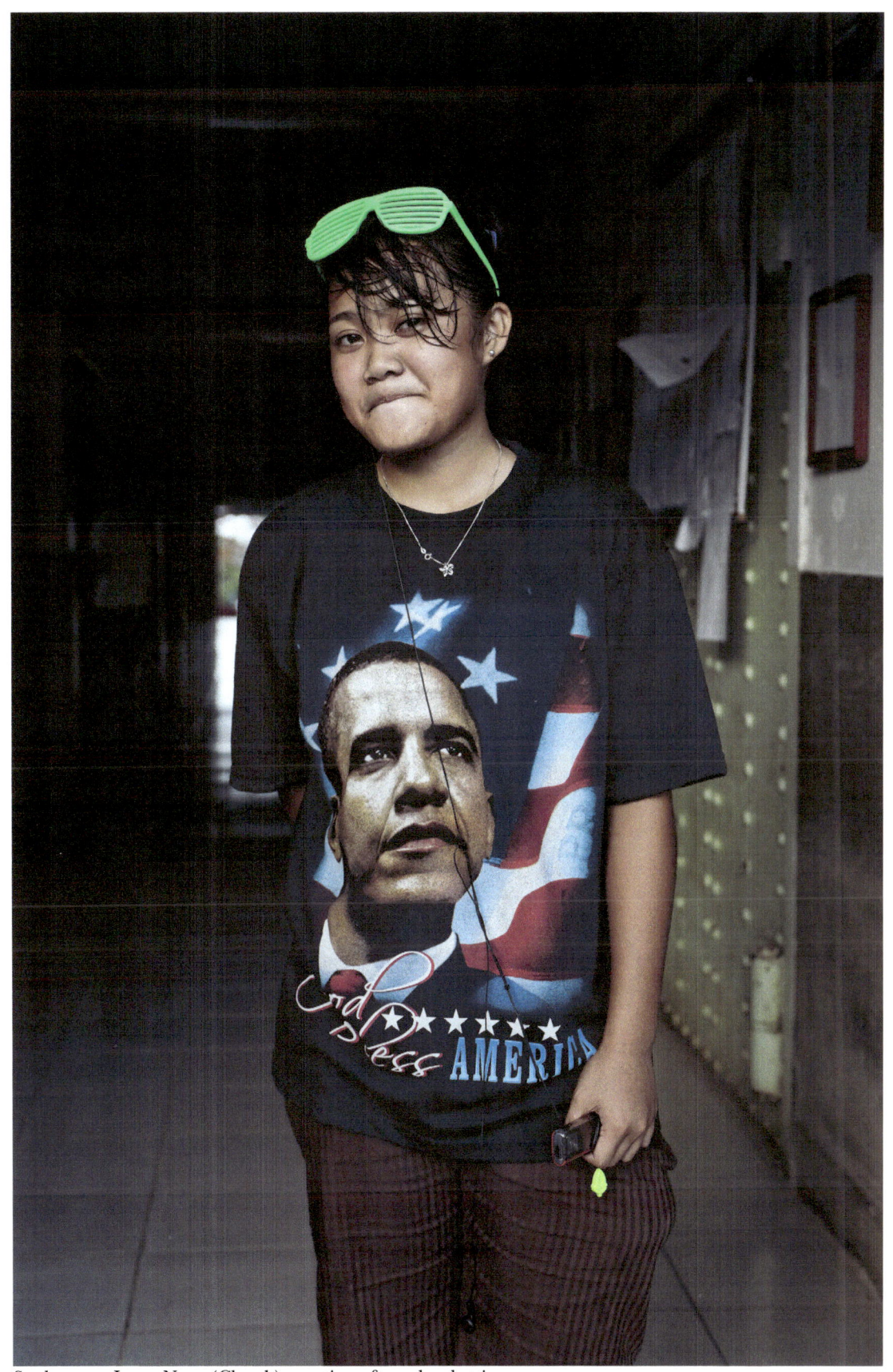

Sophomore Lyma Nero (Chuuk) sporting after-school attire on campus.

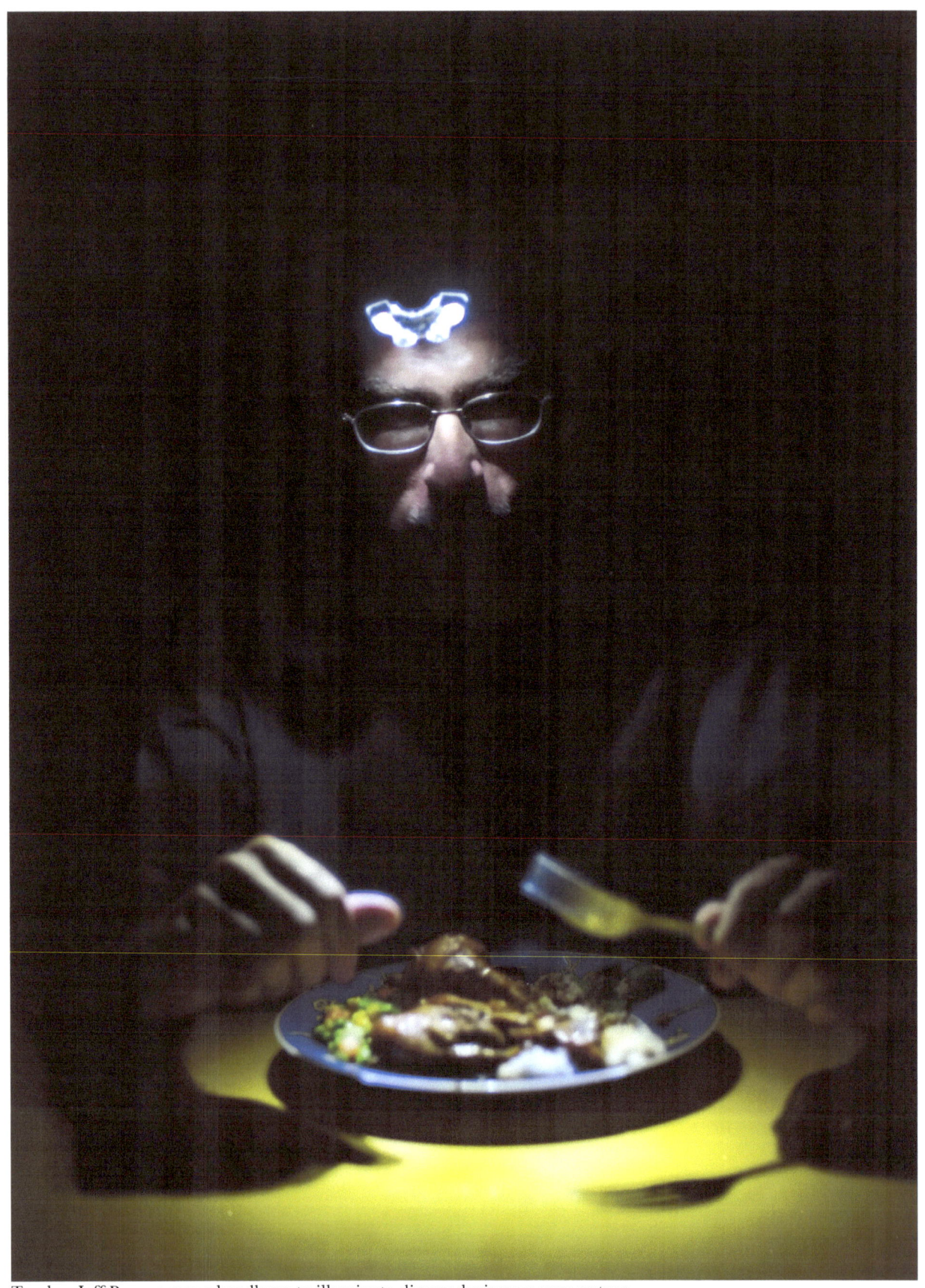

Teacher Jeff Pouzar uses a headlamp to illuminate dinner during a power outage.

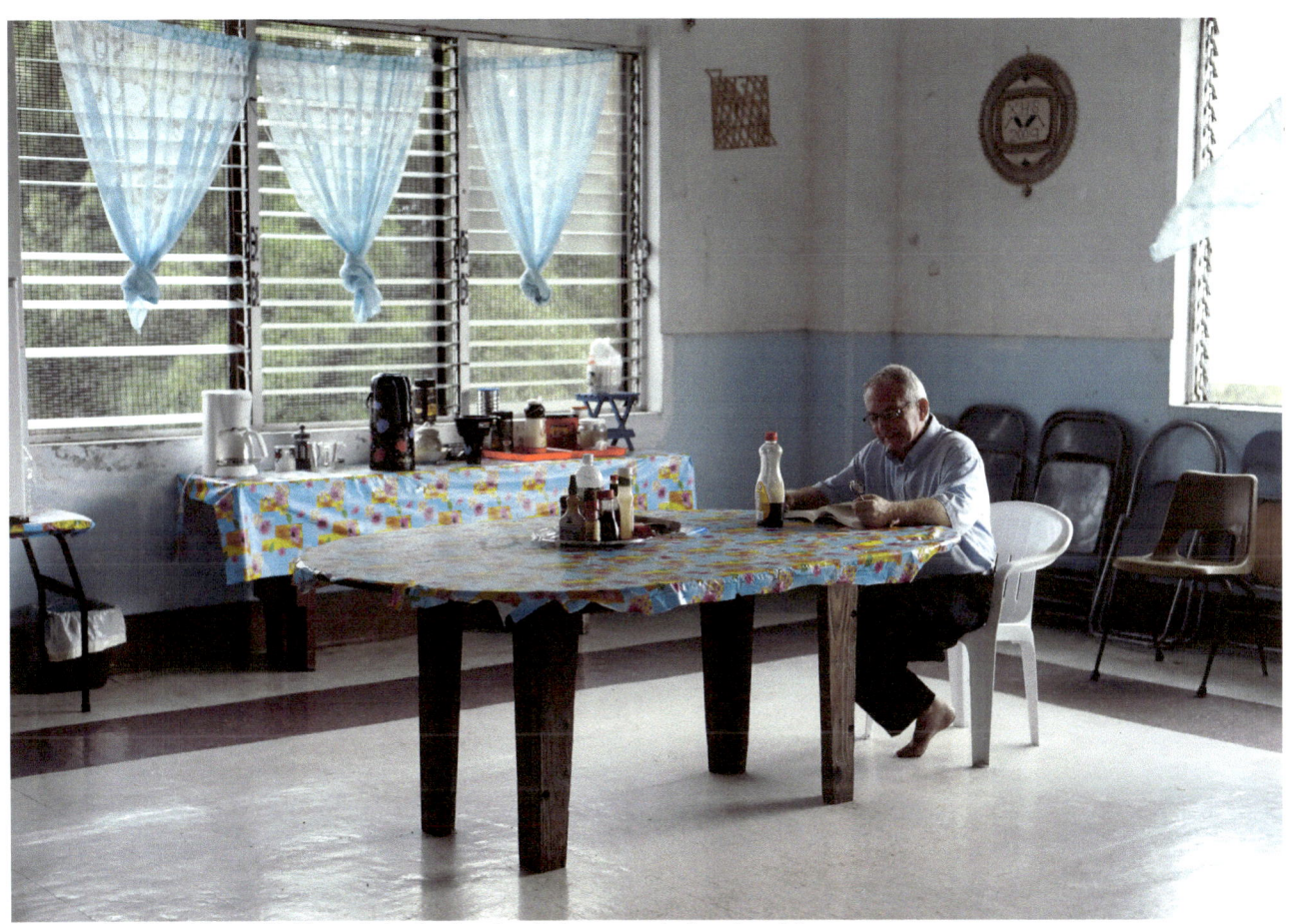

Director Fr. Rich McAuliff, SJ, reads in the faculty dining room before breakfast.

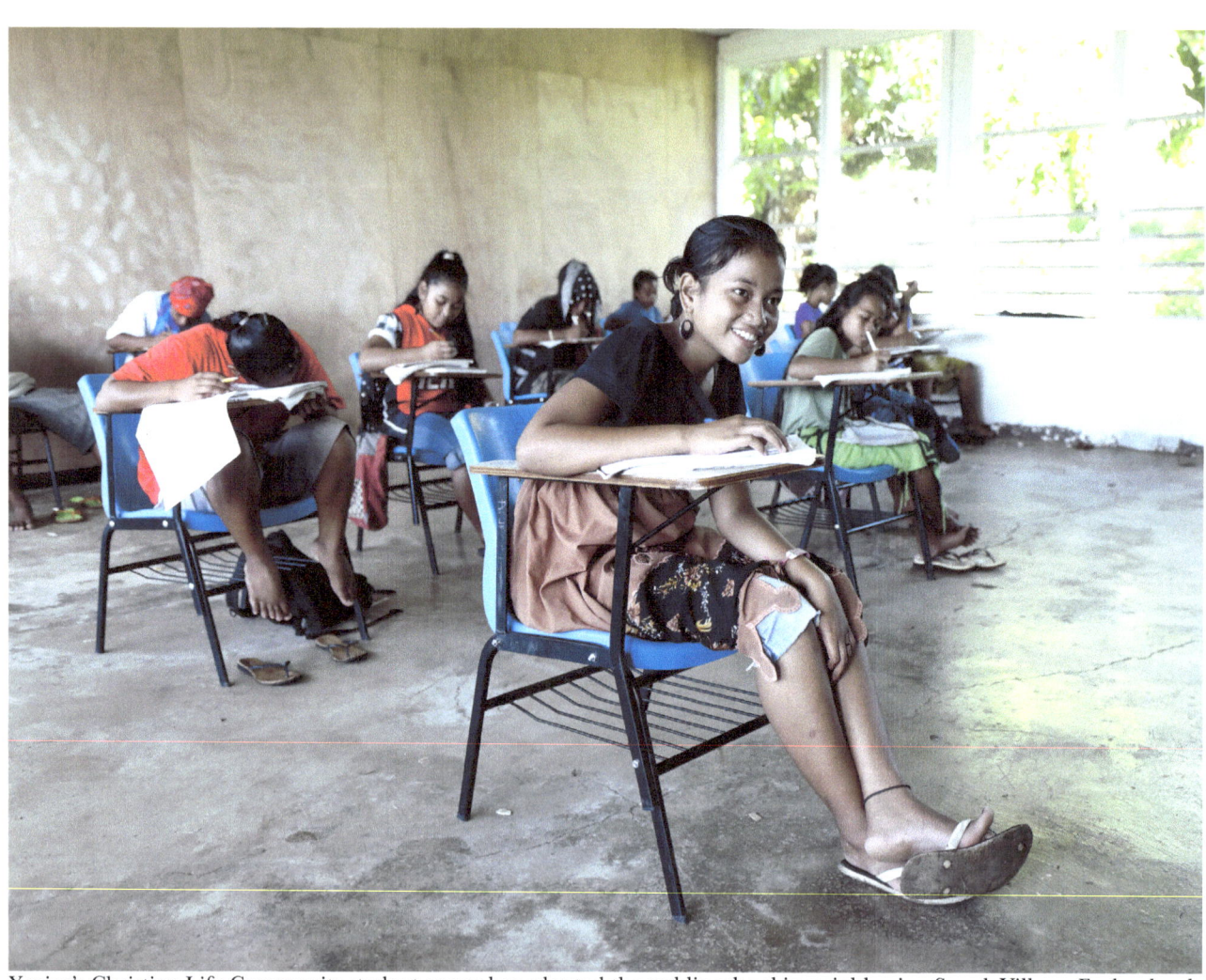

Xavier's Christian Life Community student group has adopted the public school in neighboring Sapuk Village. Each school day morning, 10 or so Xavierites go to Sapuk School to teach for an hour. The school has students from kindergarten to eighth grade. It is not unusual for the Xavier students to be the only faculty because regular teachers have not shown up for work. These youngsters are in the eighth grade classroom for a lesson on adjectives taught by Xavier students.

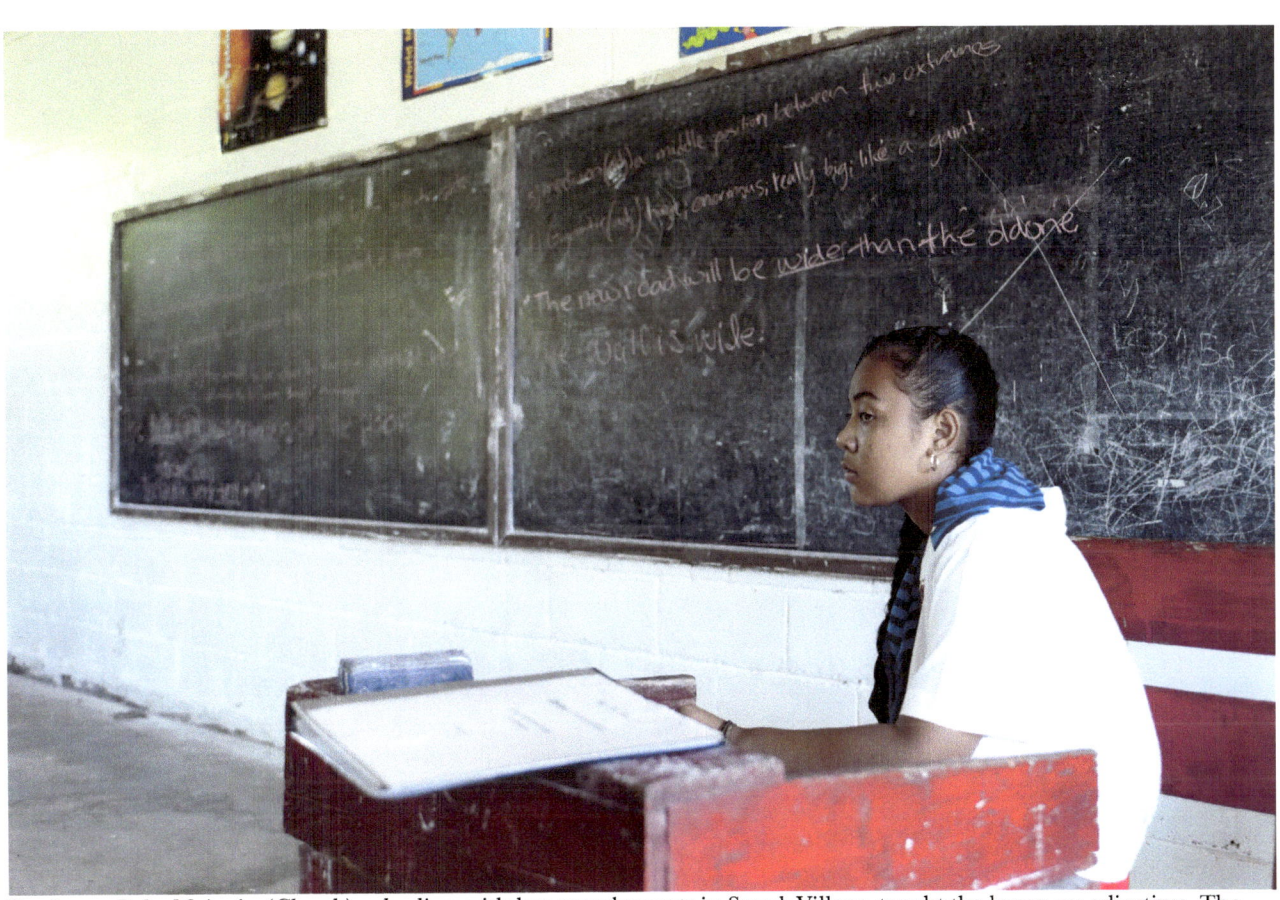

Freshman Beka Meingin (Chuuk), who lives with her grandparents in Sapuk Village, taught the lesson on adjectives. The Sapuk students had difficulty understanding adjectives, and how to use one in a sentence. I later asked Beka why she thought that was the case. She considered my question, and then said: "Yes, they were having trouble understanding adjectives. I think that is because they don't know what a noun is."

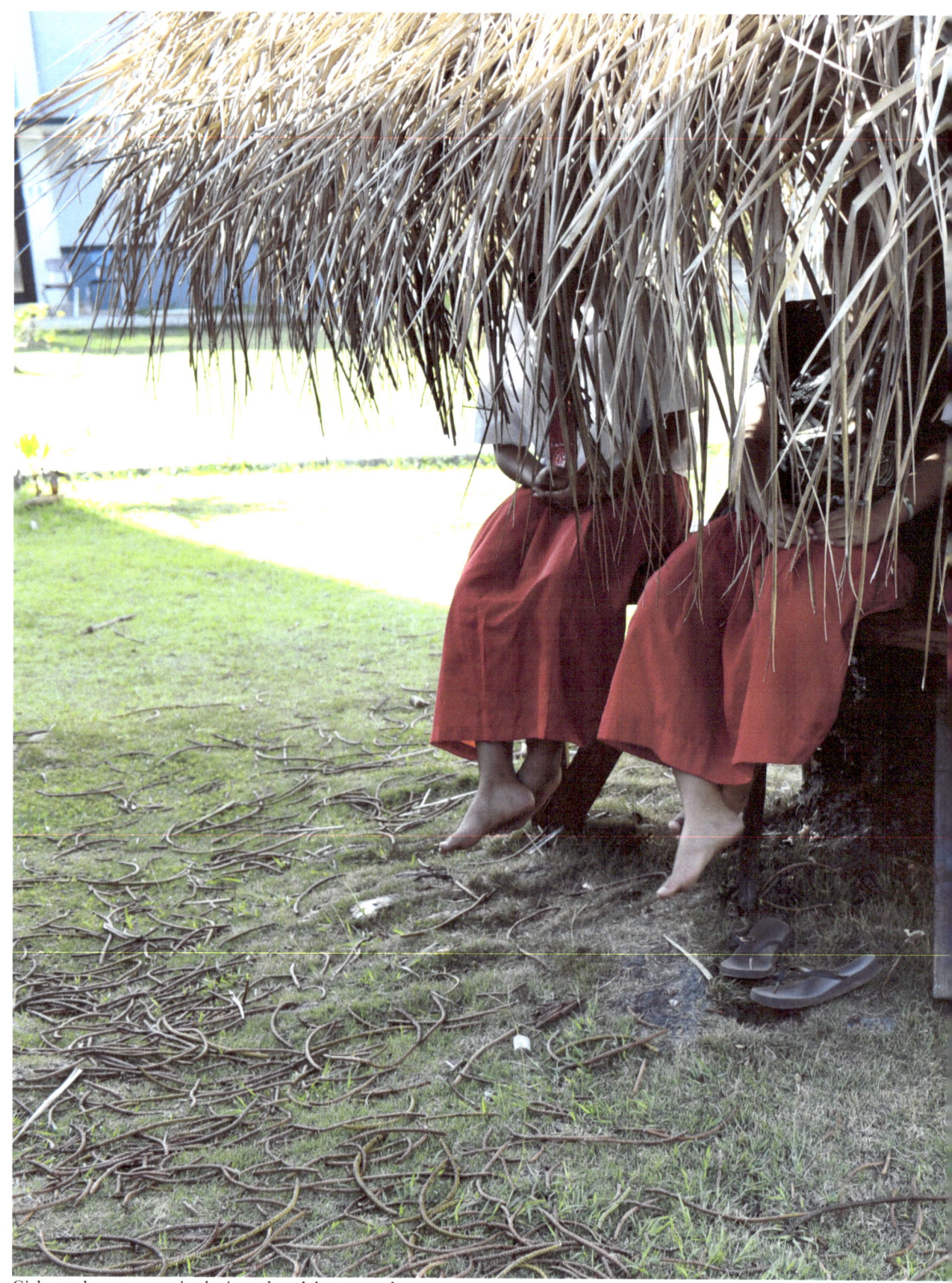

Girls catch up on gossip during a break between classes.

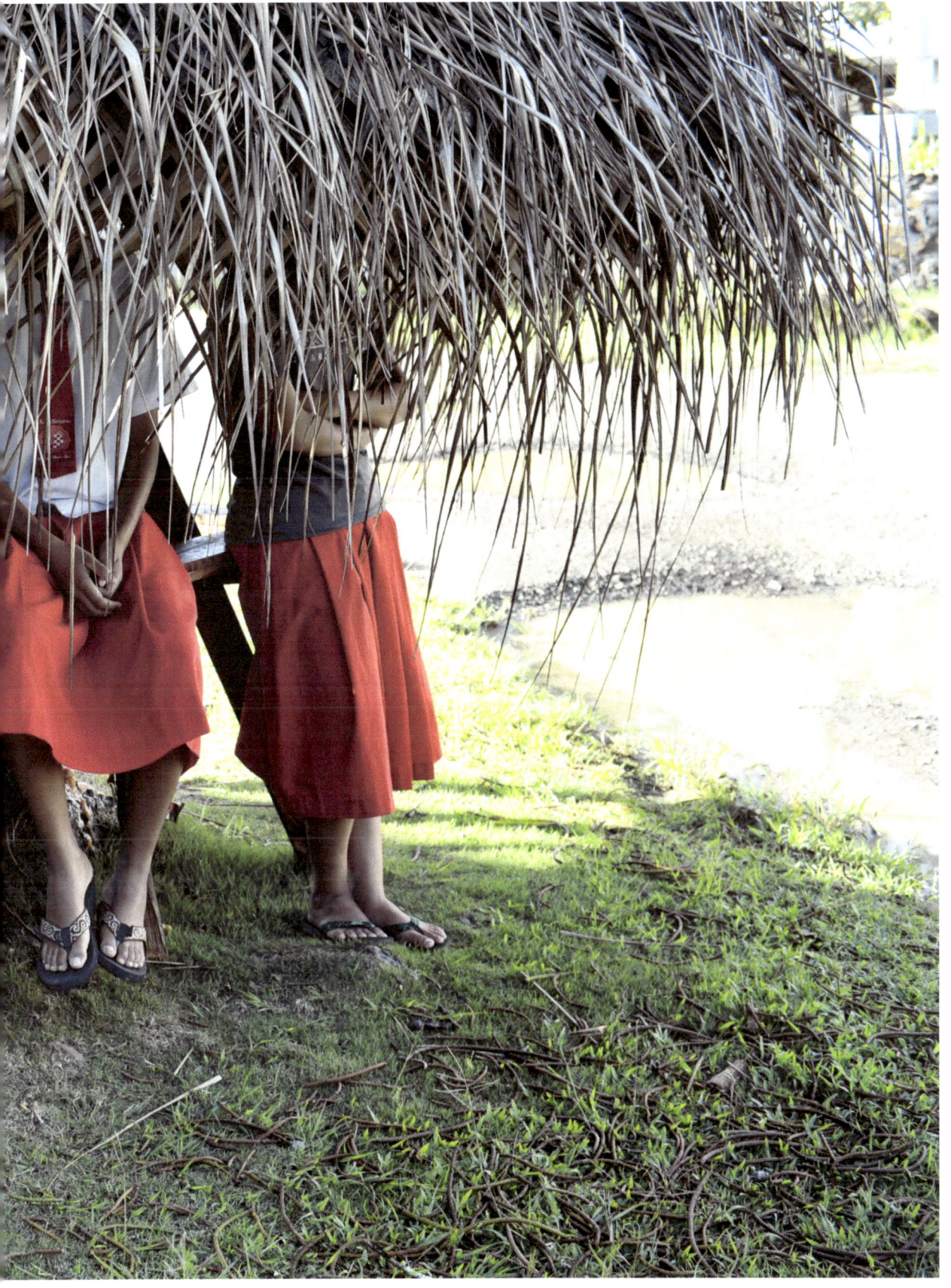

Body

Football may be king at most American high schools, but at Xavier High School in Micronesia, track is the measure by which schools determine their sports prowess. It is understandable why running is popular – you don't need special equipment, or even shoes; you don't have to be big; and, all you need is a road or a field to practice.

So at 4:30 a.m., the boys "marathon" team straggles onto the rutted road that connects Xavier with the rest of the island. They're training for what is in reality a half-marathon, but the race is called a "marathon" and so that's what it is. The squad will be back by about 7 a.m., having dodged dogs, traffic and navigated the steep, washed out road that will take them back to the top of Mabuchi hill.

Like athletes elsewhere, the Xavier runners (boys and girls) get some special privileges. On the early morning training days, they sleep in the school's main building, a two-story concrete bunker-like edifice built by the Japanese in the 1930s as an Imperial Navy communications center. For years, the building had a big hole in the roof caused by an American air attack in 1944.

Girls live off campus with families or sponsors, but the girls' track team also does sleepovers in the main building. Showers that are used on occasion by faculty are assigned to the girls. They sleep on mats in a room that is securely locked to keep away prying eyes.

On this morning, though, it is the boys' practice time. Most kept a good pace during the long run, but one, Travis Tamow of Yap, was a laggard that day. He walked onto the school's athletic field, where he had to run a last lap before cool-down exercises.

The school's Director, Fr. Rich McAuliff, SJ, is also the track coach. With stopwatch in hand, he yelled across the field to Travis to pick up his pace and run his last lap. When the admonition didn't result in more speed, Fr. Rich, barefoot, took off across the field. Travis, seeing the priest headed his way at speed, dug deep and found the energy to pick up his pace. He finished his last lap with Fr. Rich only steps behind him.

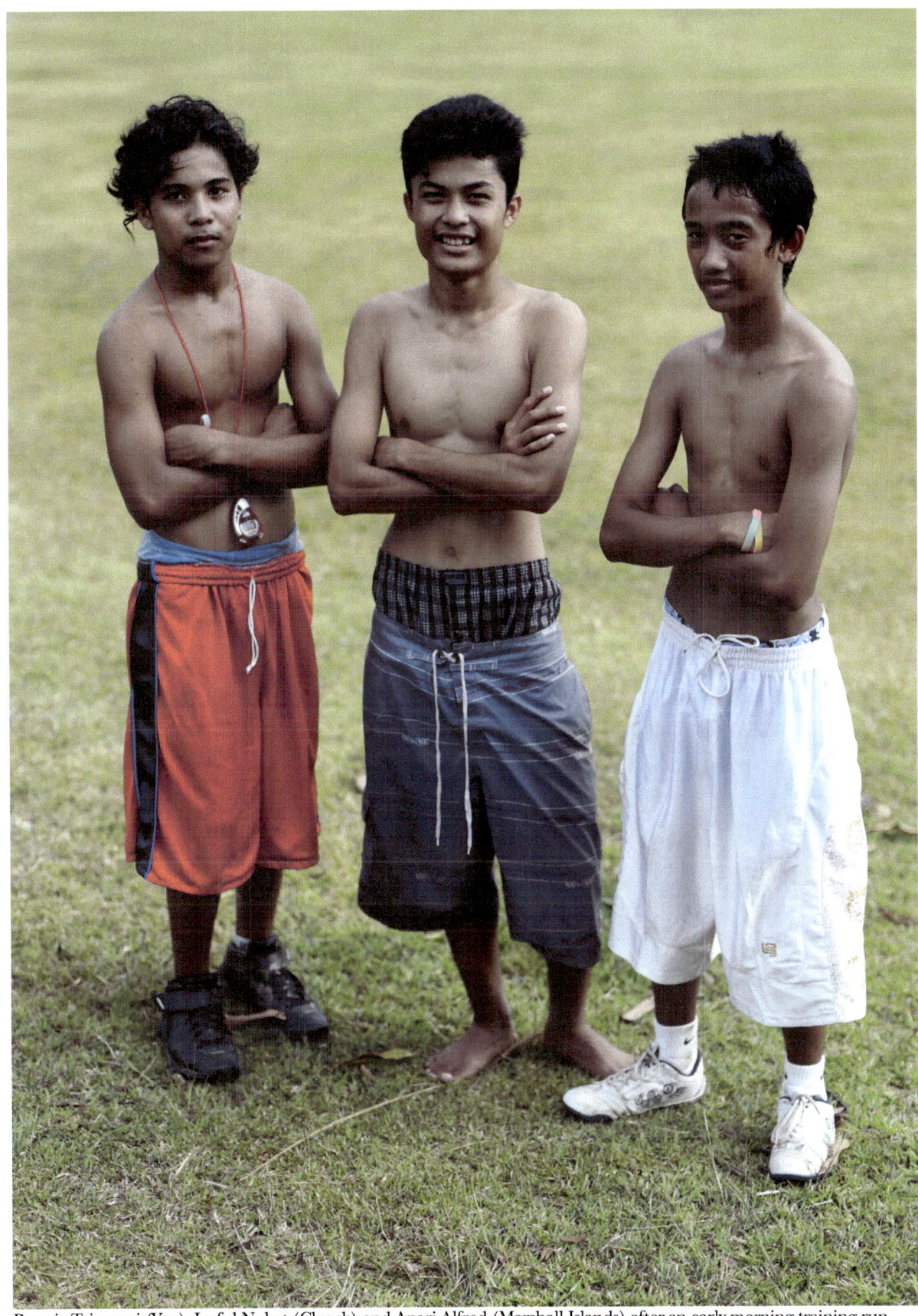

Rennie Taiugmai (Yap), Joyful Noket (Chuuk) and Anari Alfred (Marshall Islands) after an early morning training run. **103**

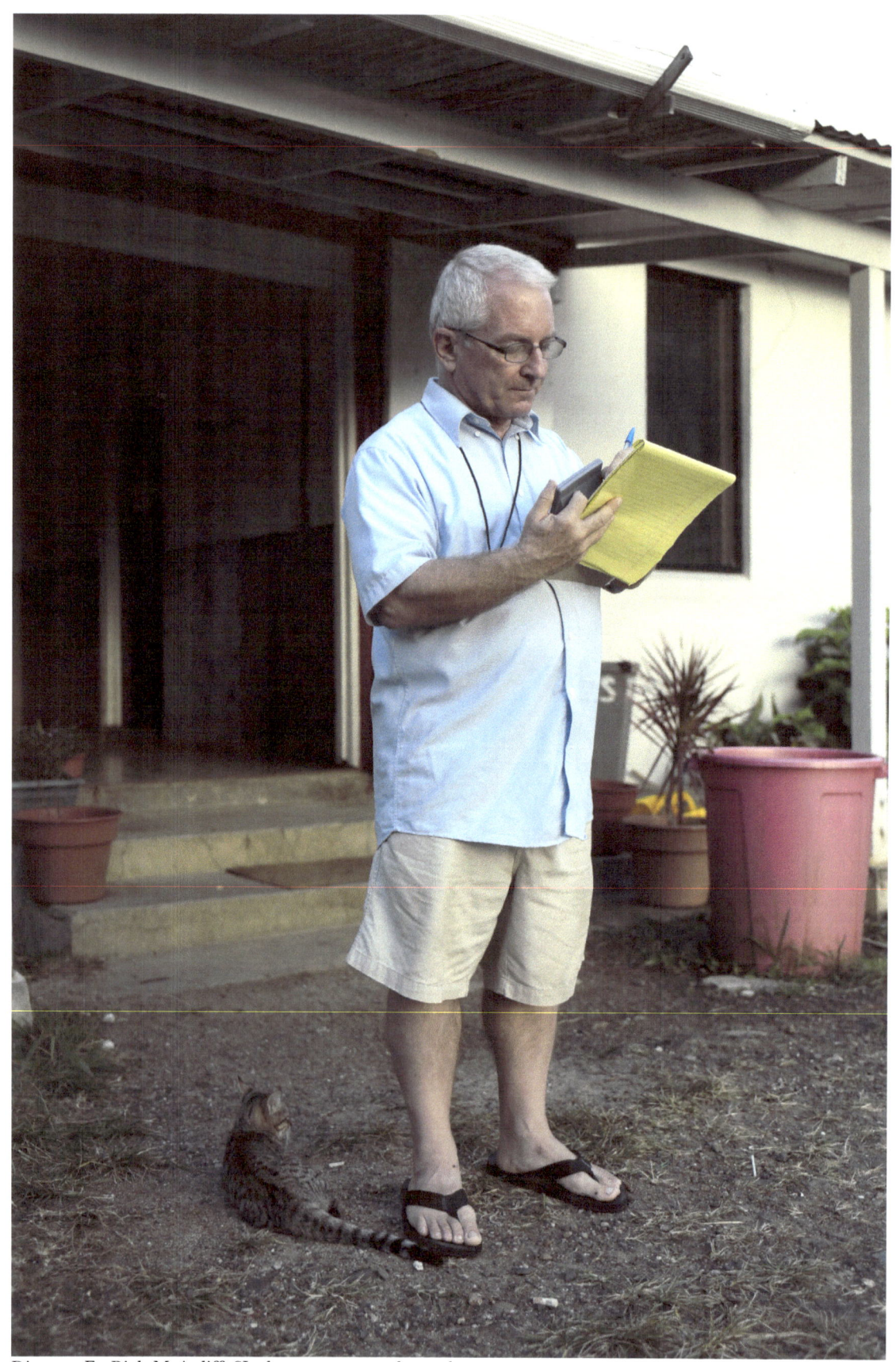

Director Fr. Rich McAuliff, SJ, also serves as track coach.

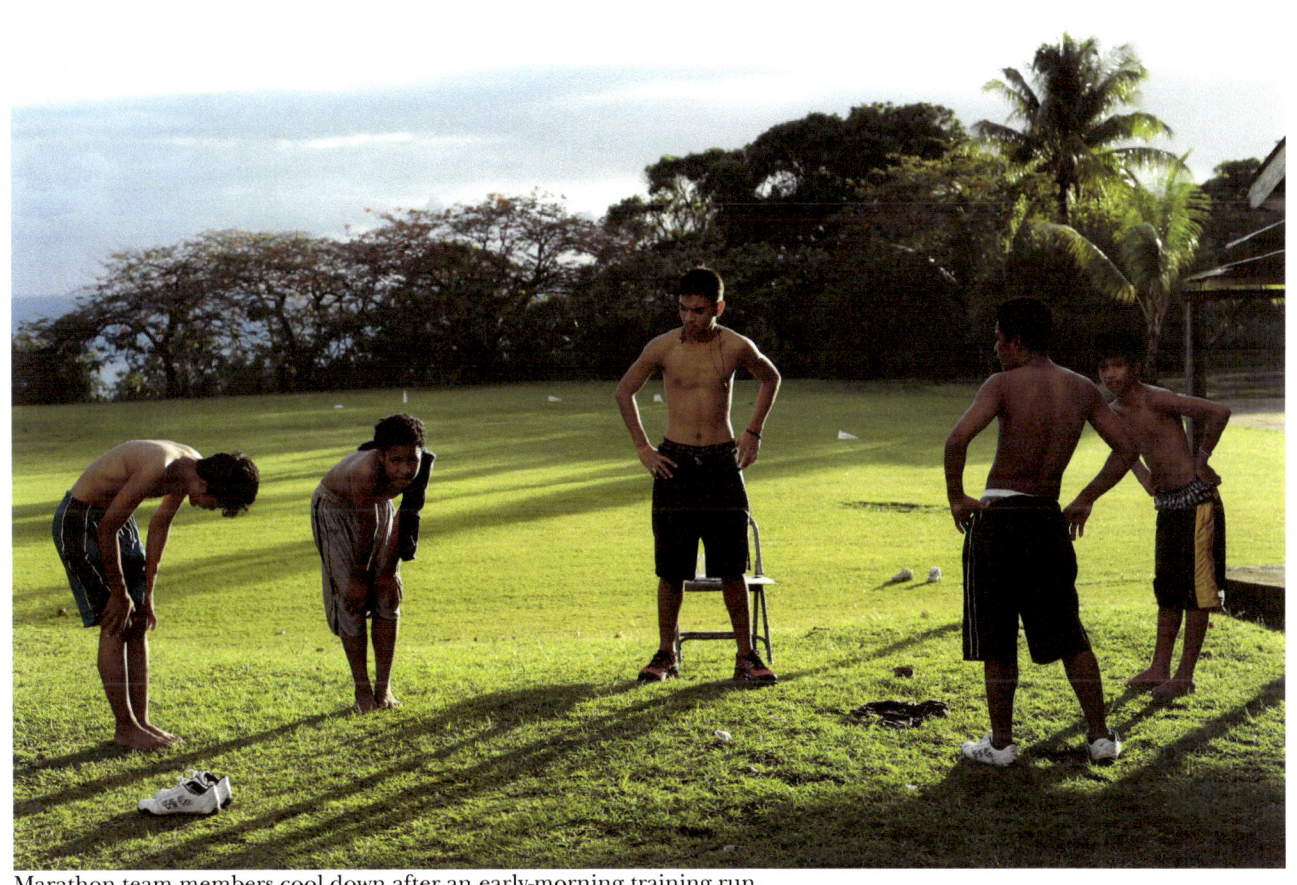

Marathon team members cool down after an early-morning training run.

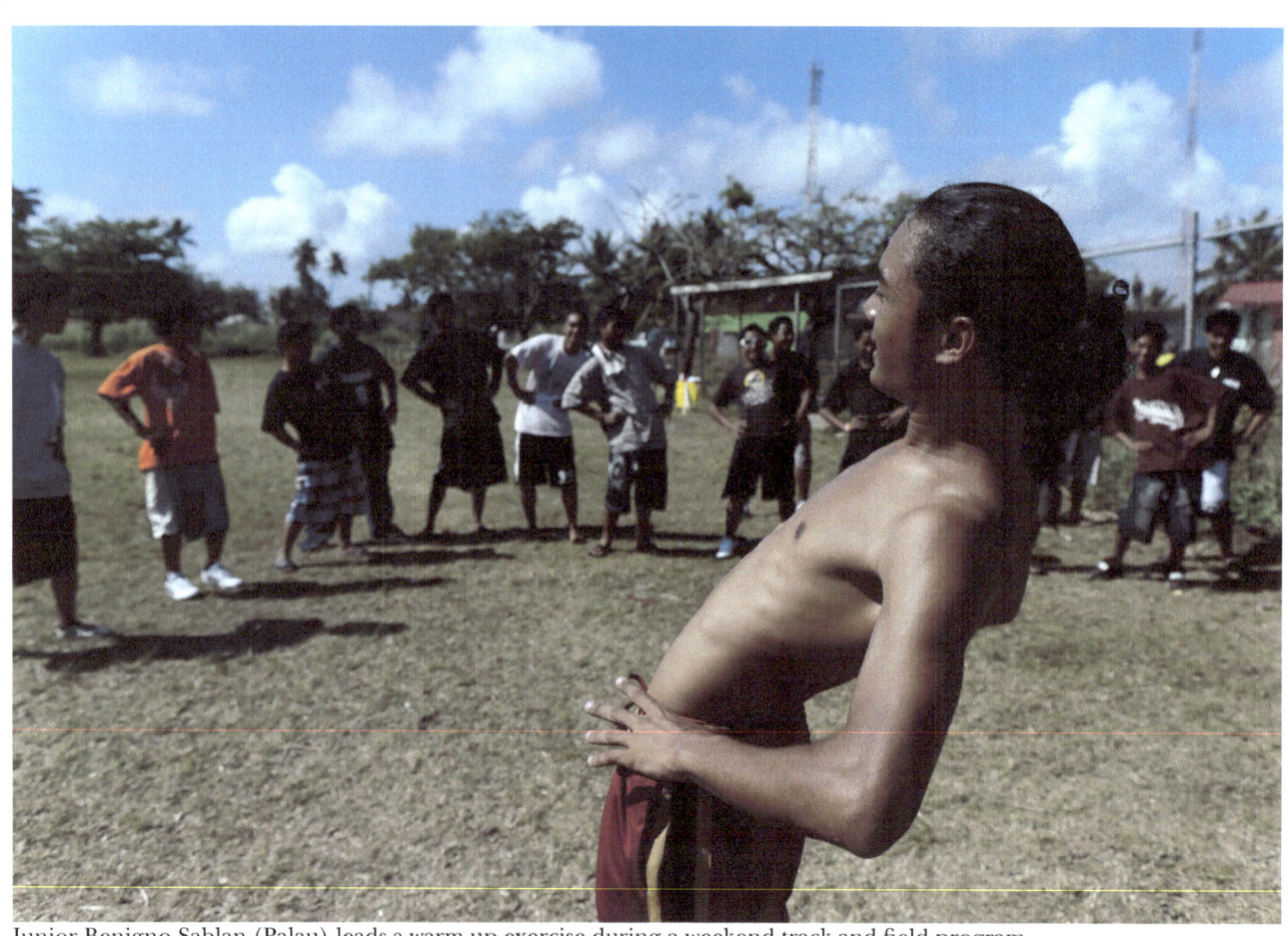

Junior Benigno Sablan (Palau) leads a warm-up exercise during a weekend track-and-field program.

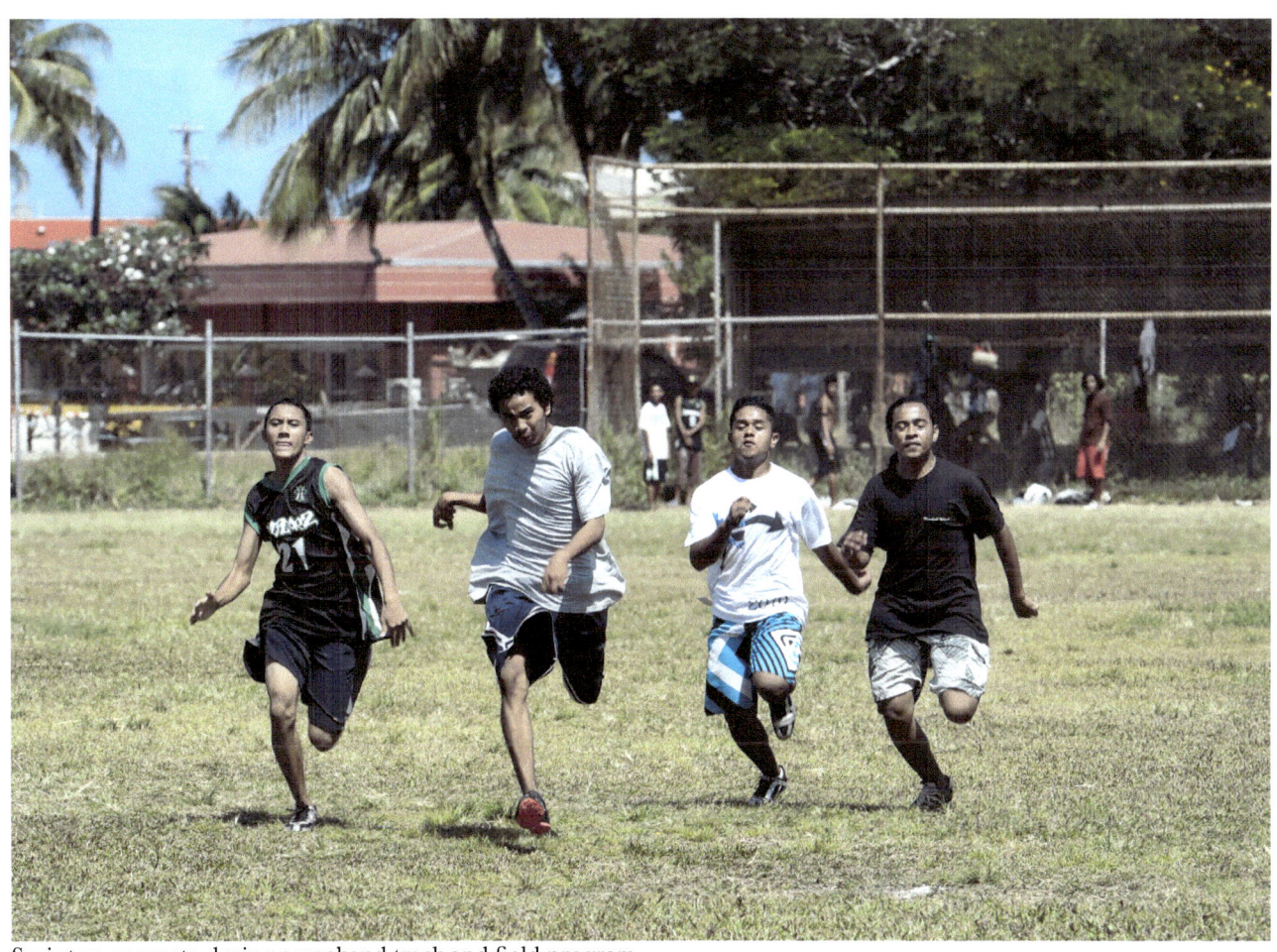
Sprinters compete during a weekend track-and-field program.

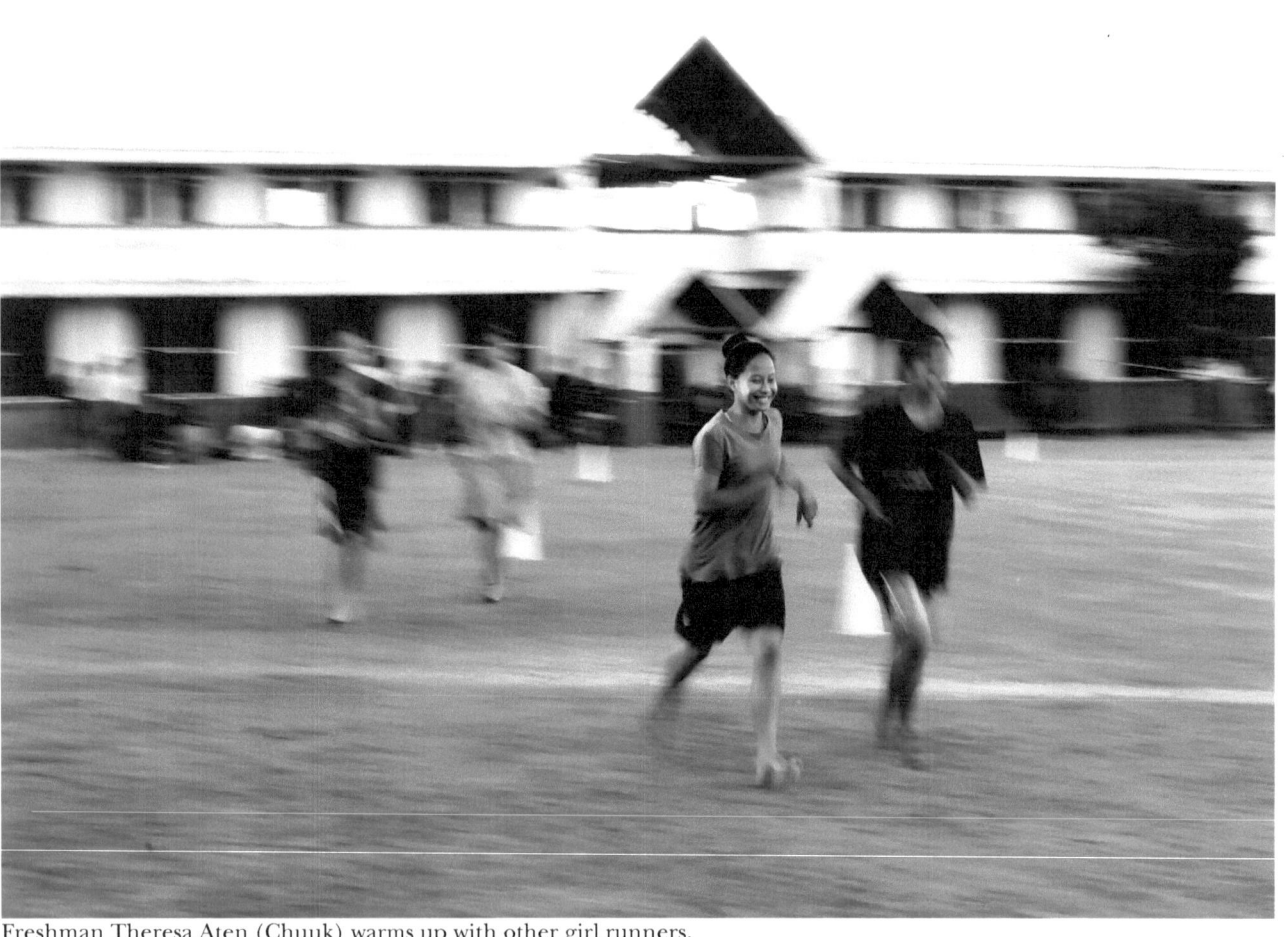

Freshman Theresa Aten (Chuuk) warms up with other girl runners.

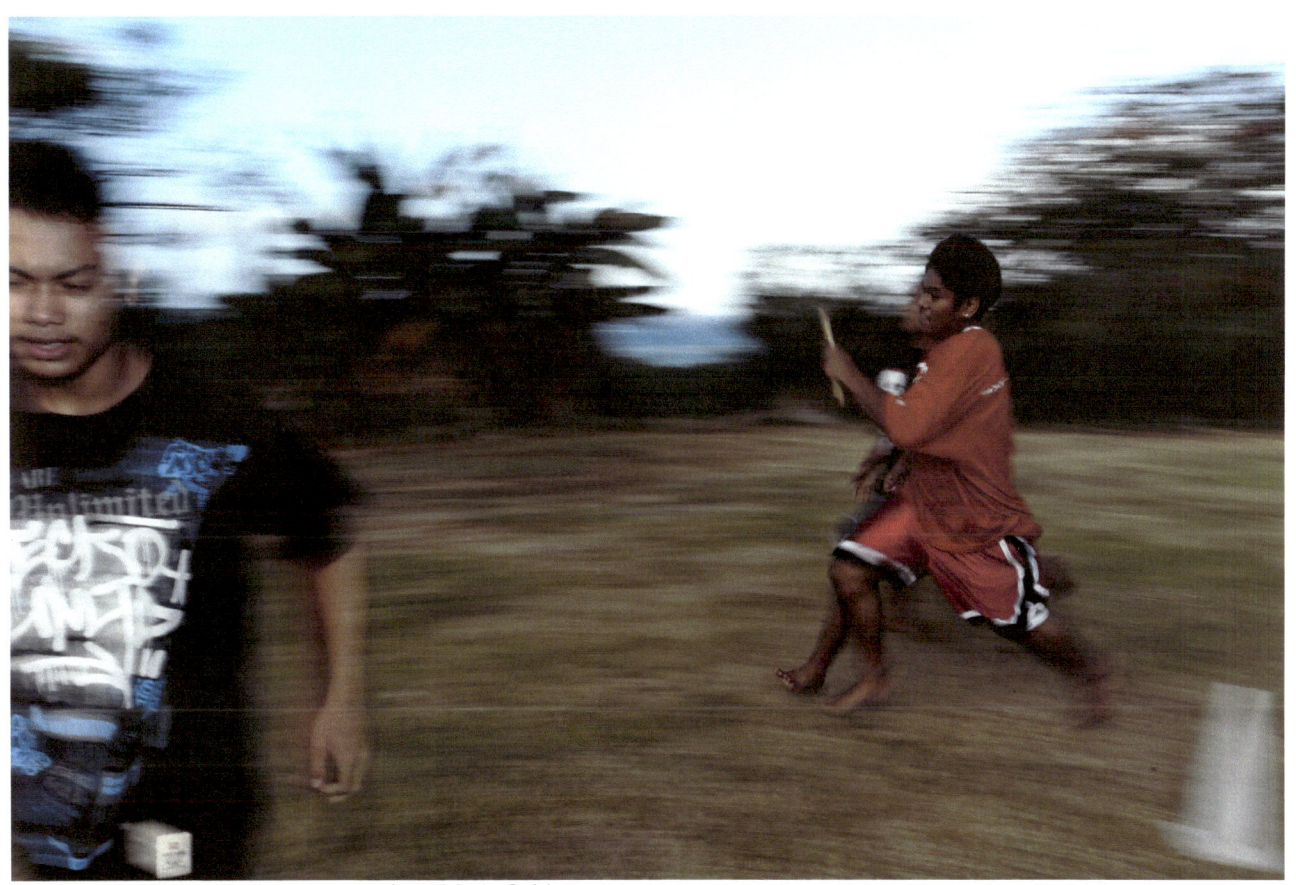

Boys hold intramural relay races on the athletic field.

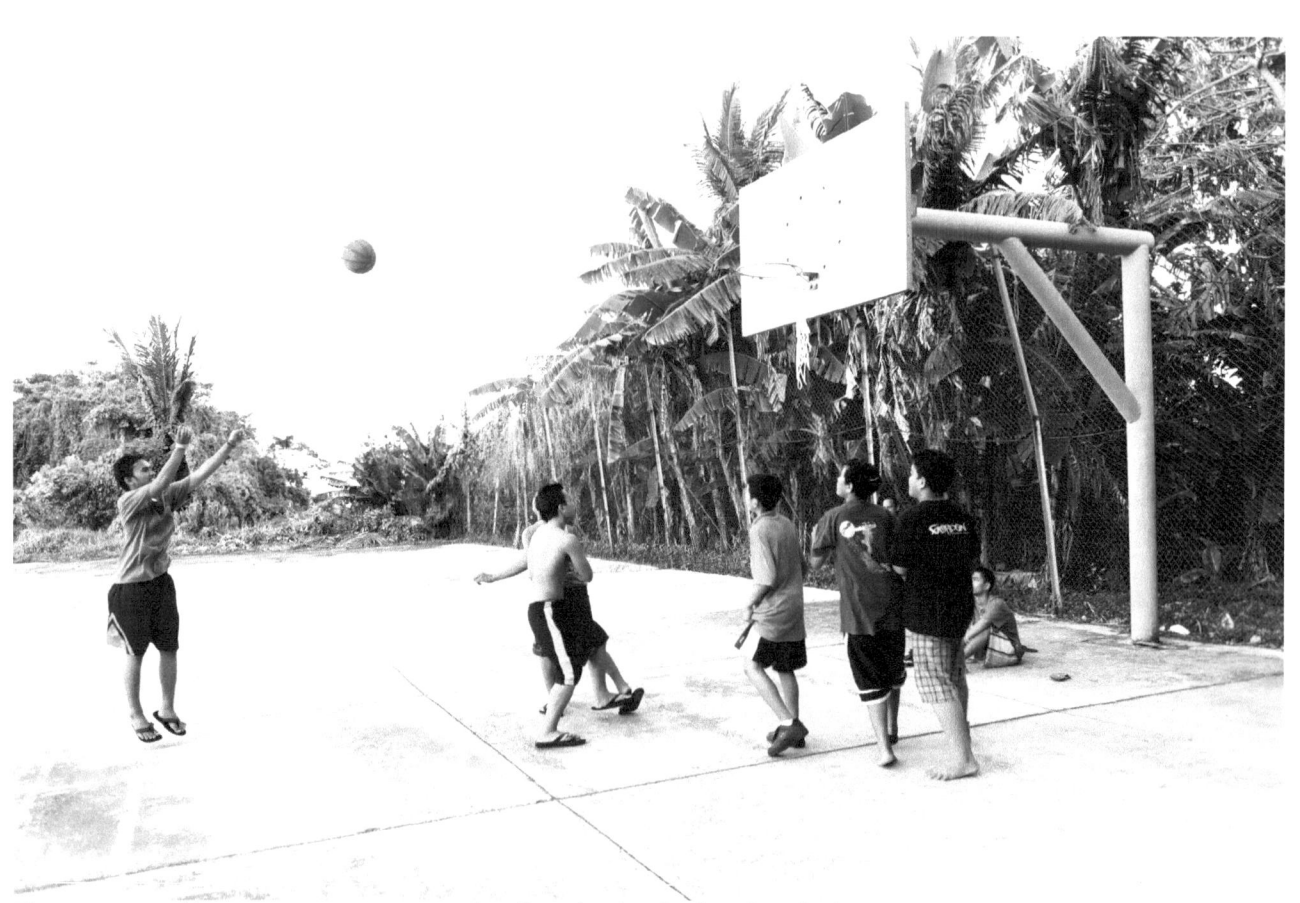

The campus multi-purpose courts are a popular after-school gathering place for boys.

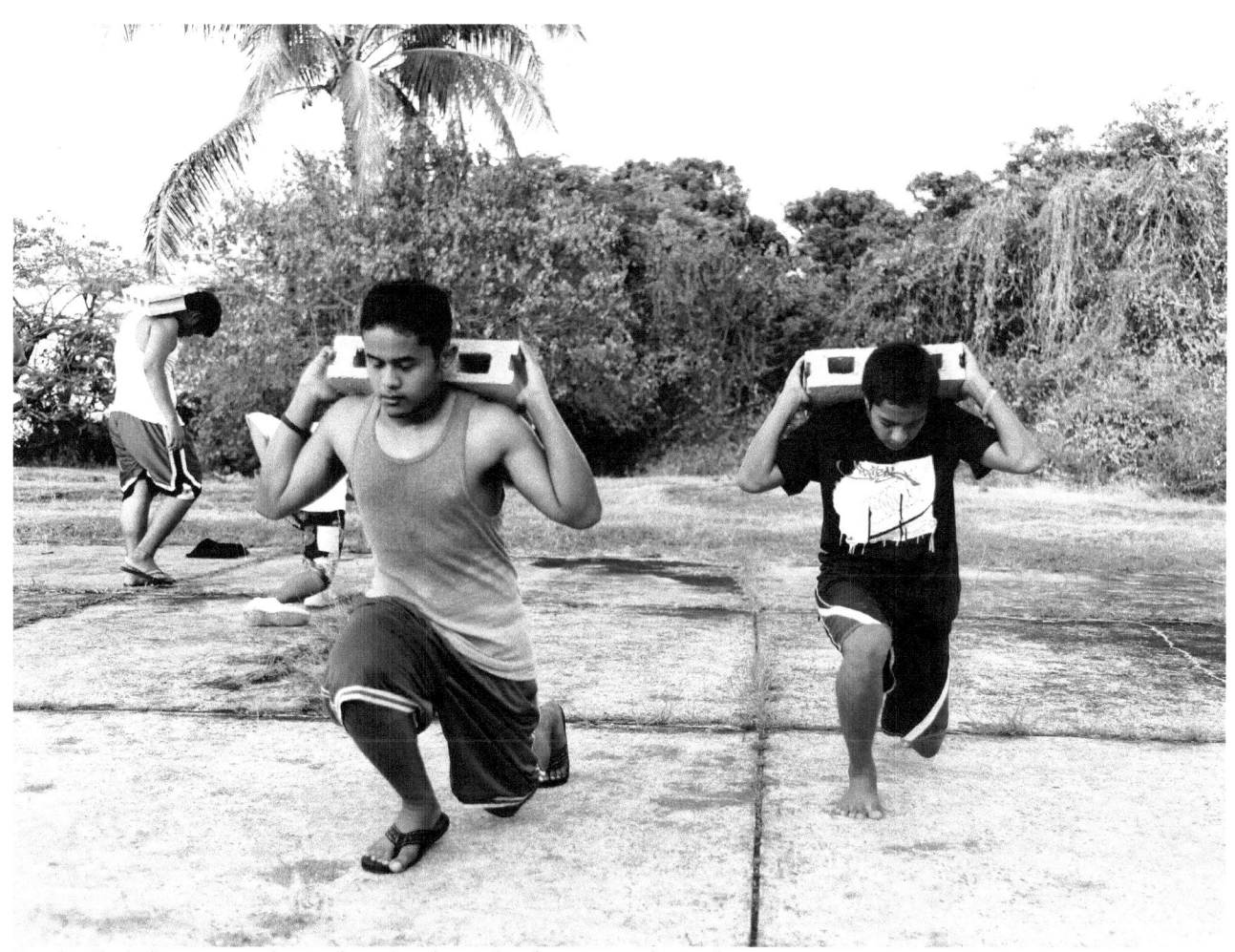

Boys' volleyball team members, who missed practice, have a penalty workout.

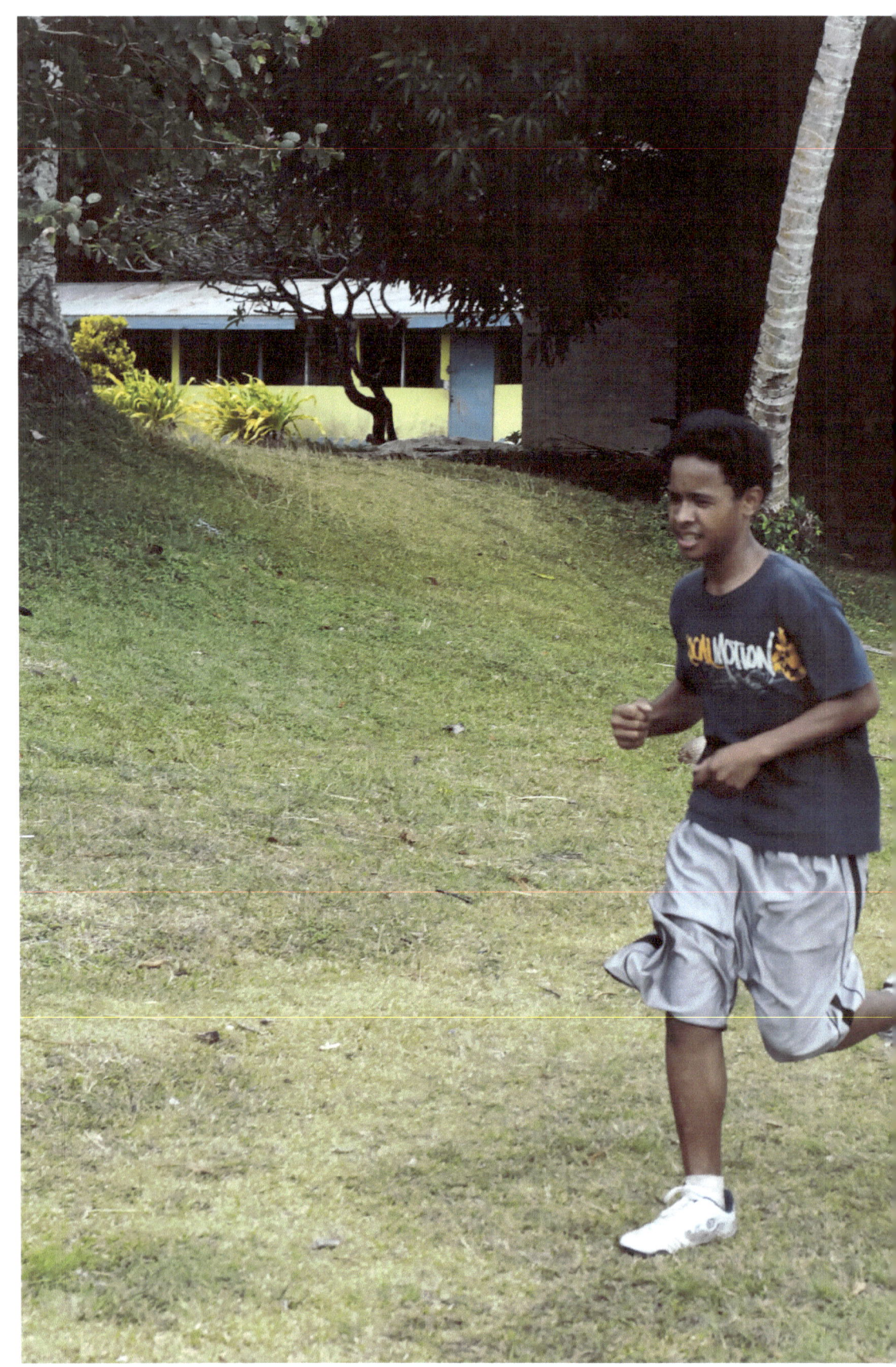

Fr. Rich McAuliff, SJ, chases freshman runner Travis Tamow (Yap).

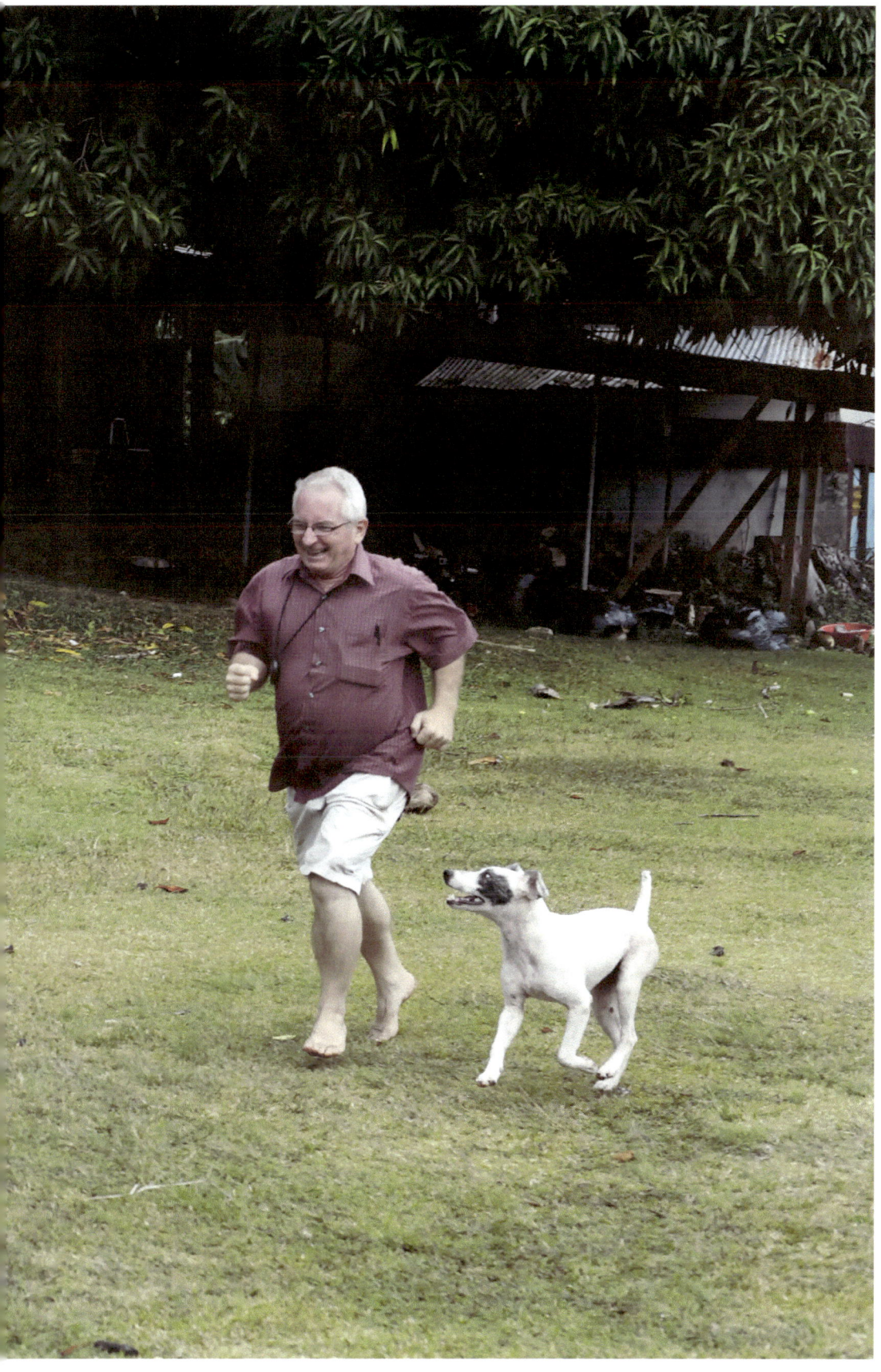

Faces

Ethnic diversity doesn't begin to describe the student body at Xavier High School. It goes beyond noting who are Palauan, Marshallese, Pohnpeian, Kosraean, Chuukese and Yapese. There are some students who are part-Gilbertese from what is now Kiribati. Others have a foreign parent. And a few students have parents and ancestors who come from different parts of Micronesia.

The Micronesian region was, from 1919 until 1944, administered by Japan. That heritage is evident in many student faces and names. There have even been Japanese nationals who have studied at Xavier, along with students from Southeast Asia and the Philippines.

How to show the school's remarkable diversity? For a photographer, the answer is a portrait. So I set up a small studio in the student center. Students were invited to drop by to have their portraits taken; many did, some more than once!

There were also opportunities to take portraits around the Xavier campus. The study hall turned out to have beautiful morning light. An open-sided shed behind the main building had soft, gentle afternoon light, reflected off a bare cement floor, that made skin glow.

The diversity is evident in the faces of the small sampling of students portrayed here. But so is their beauty. Whether their skin is dark brown or mocha, whether their eyes are Asian- or island-influenced, these are young people who are clearly blessed by having been born "Micronesian."

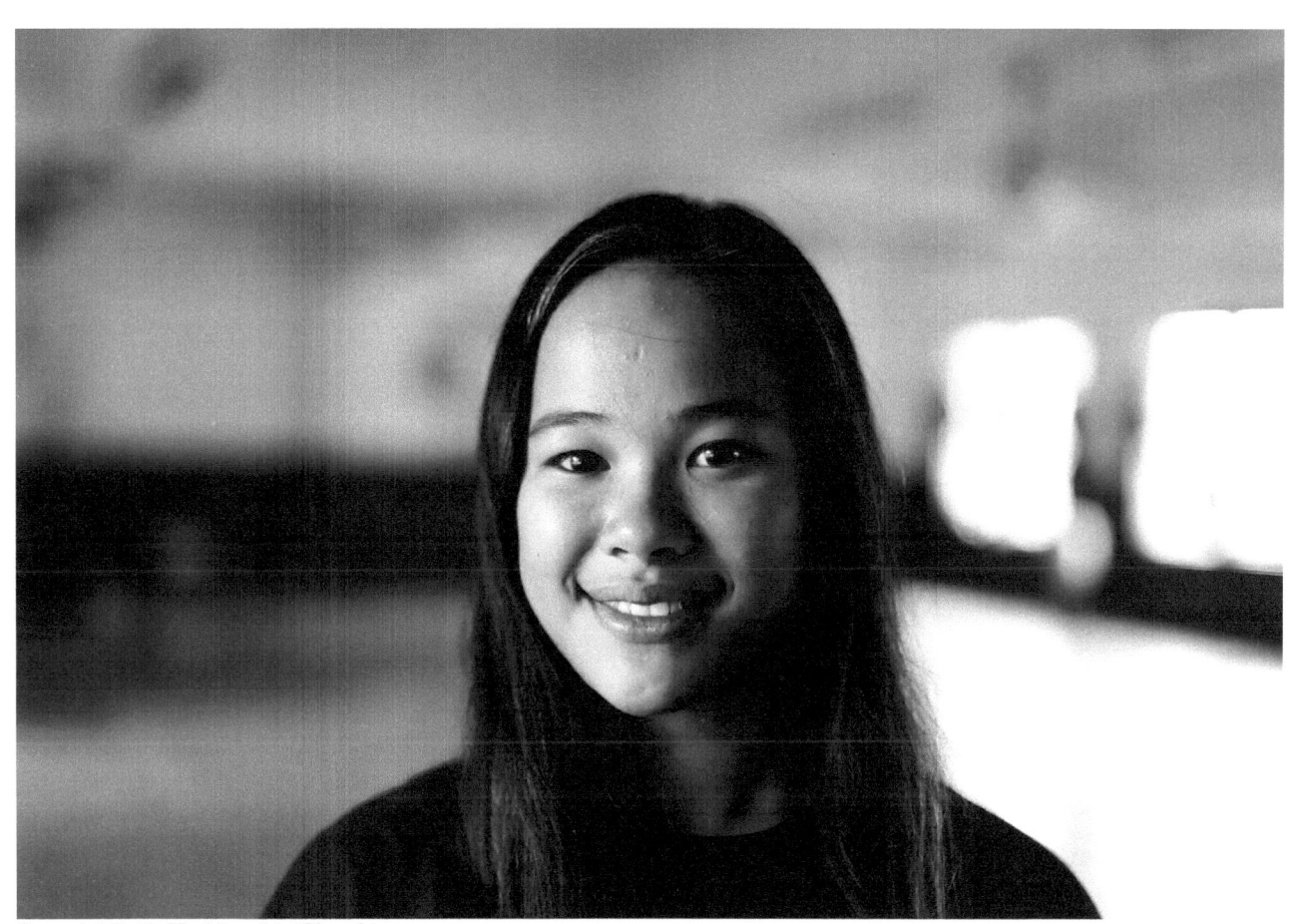

Shanalei Setik Hashiguchi (Chuuk)

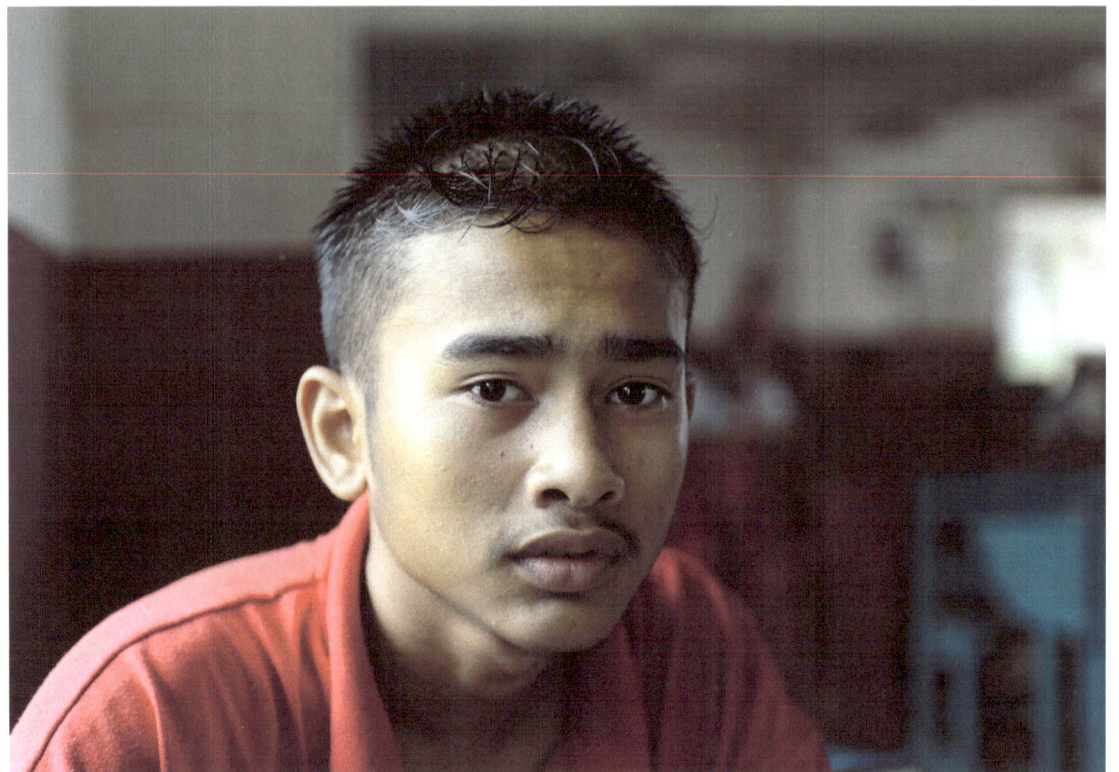

Jimmy Eldridge, Jr. (Pohnpei)

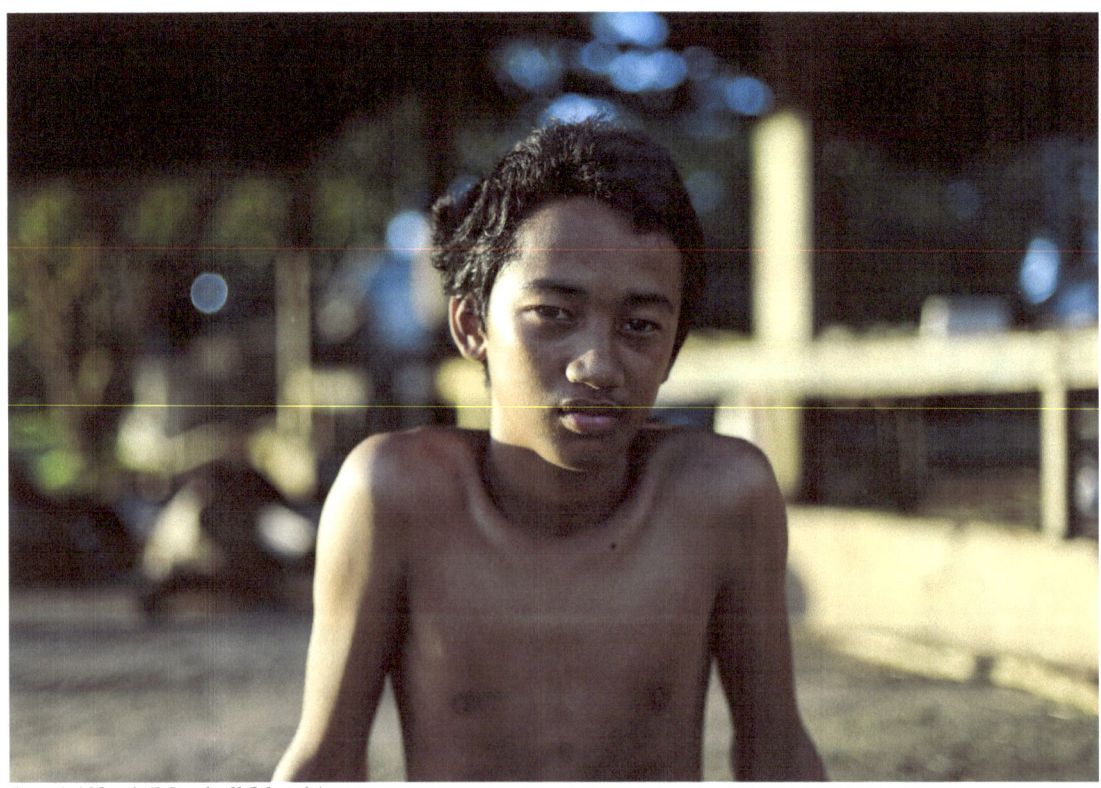

Anari Alfred (Marshall Islands)

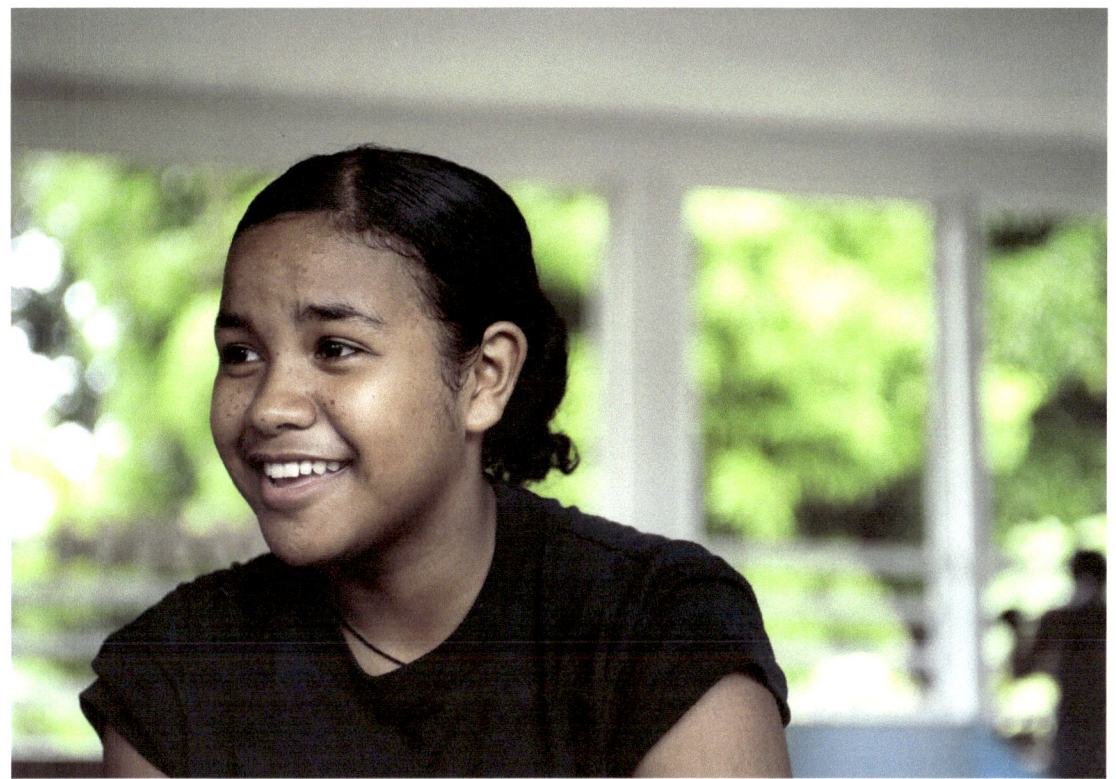

Zoe Kintaro Rechelulk (Palau)

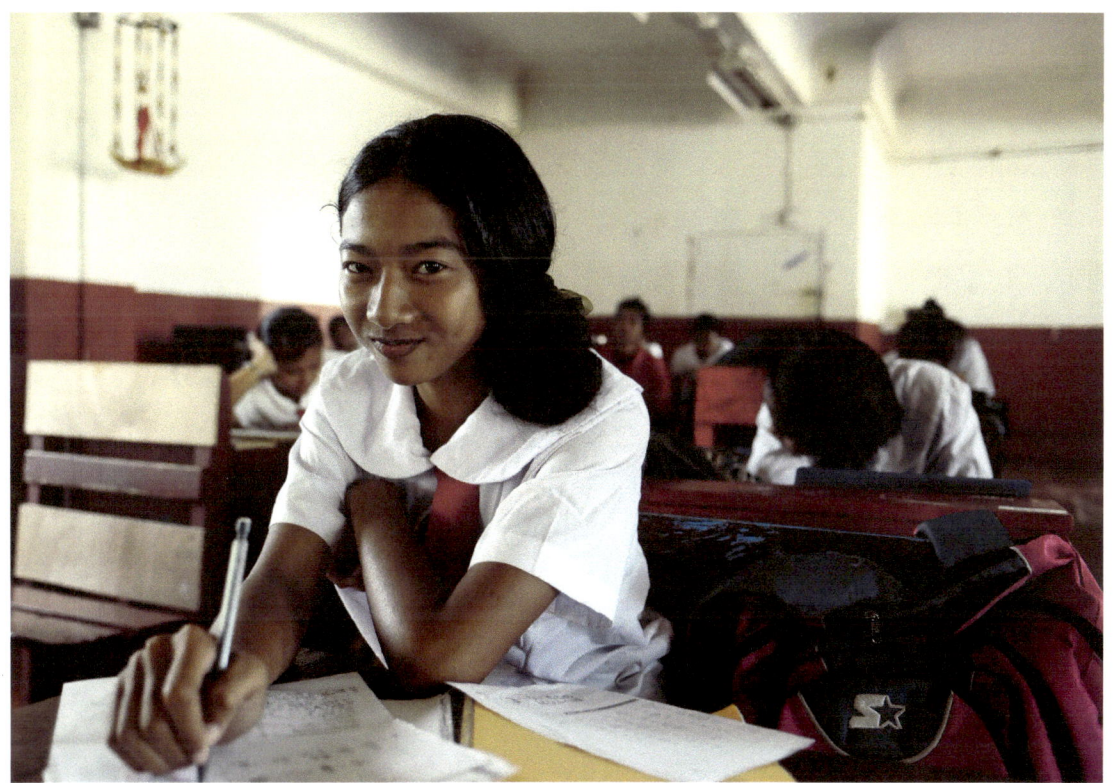

Jean Malolo (Marshall Islands)

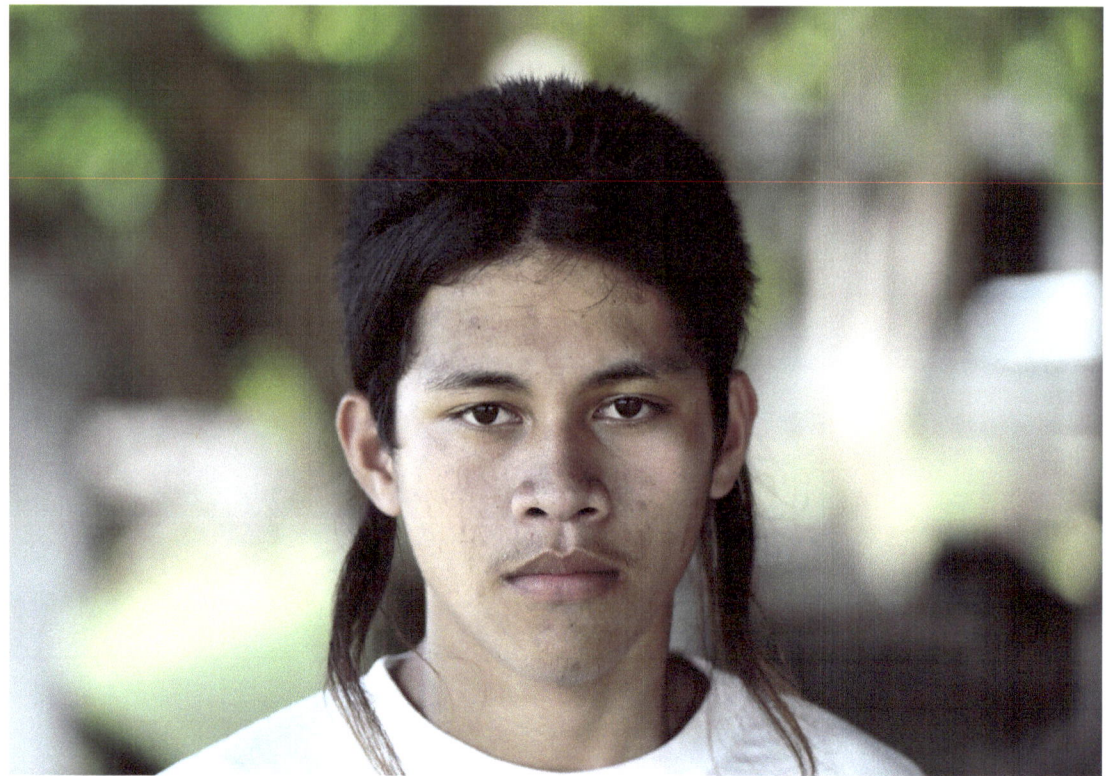

Alex Capelle (Marshall Islands)

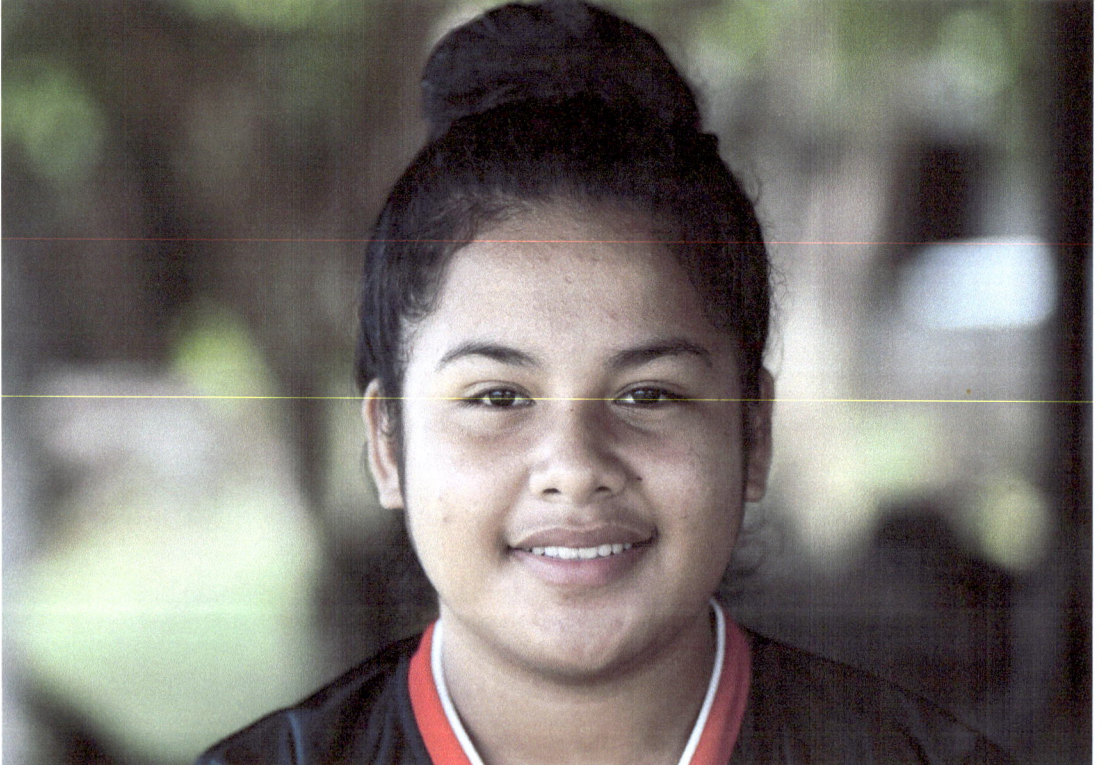

Myova Nedelec (Chuuk)

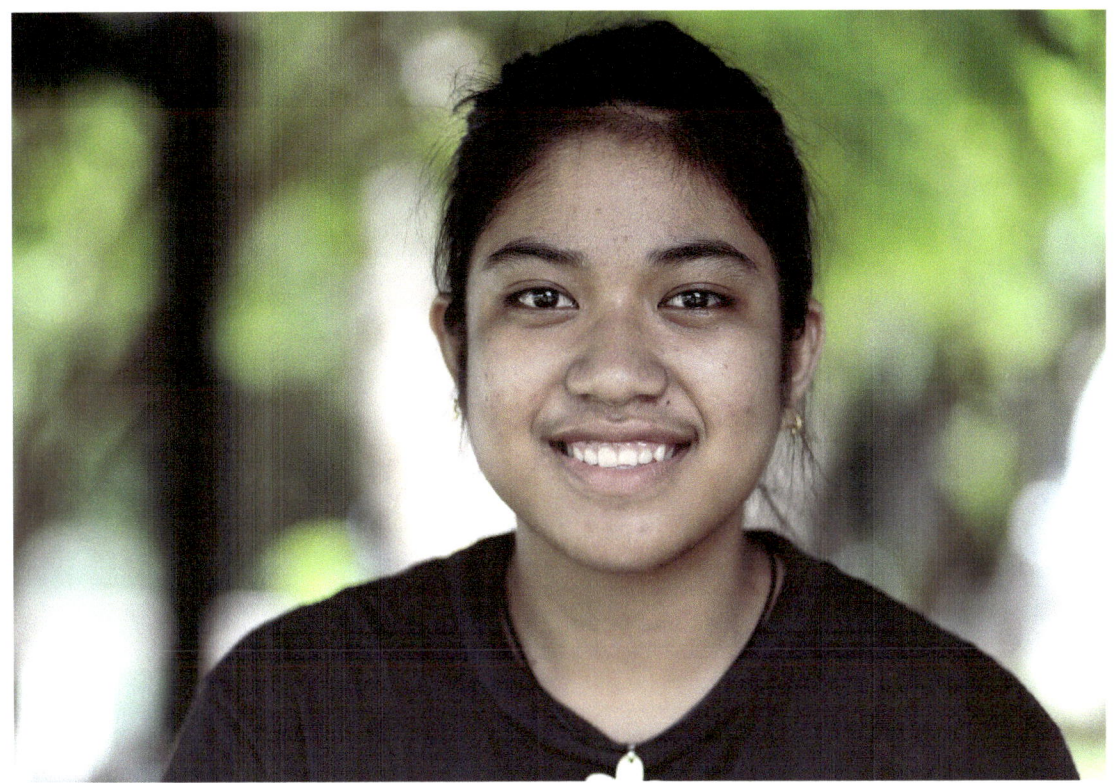

Pearl Asugar (Chuuk)

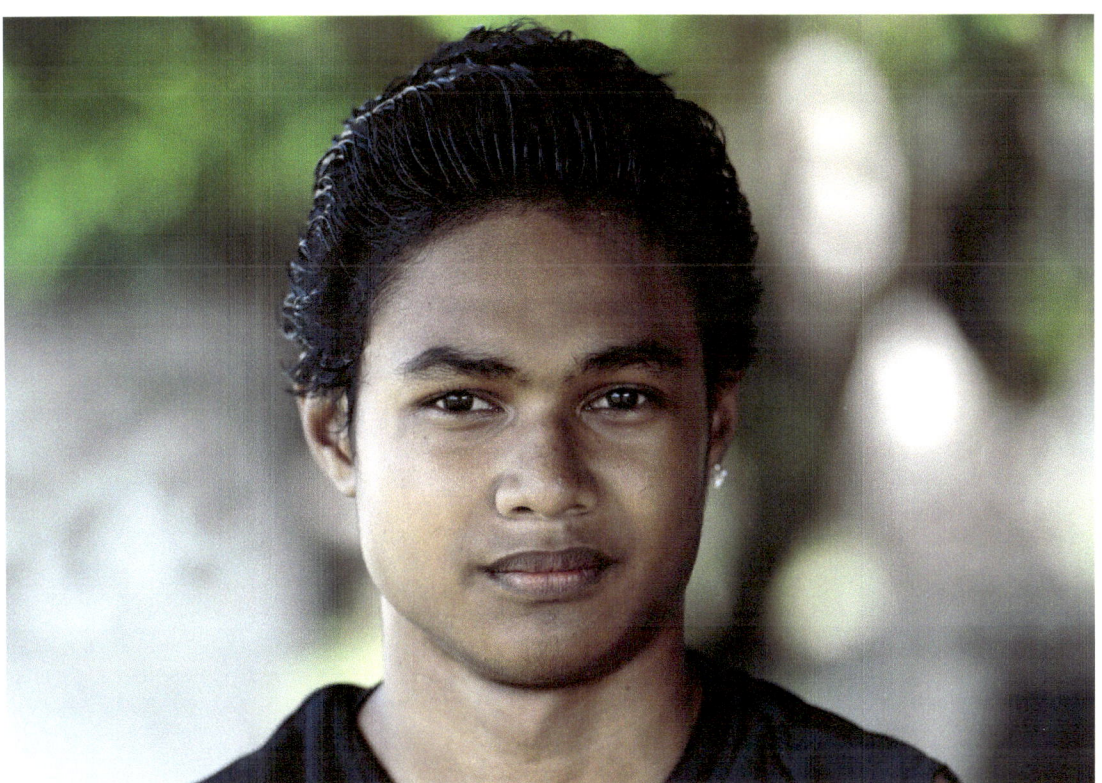

Joshua Bmaw (Yap)

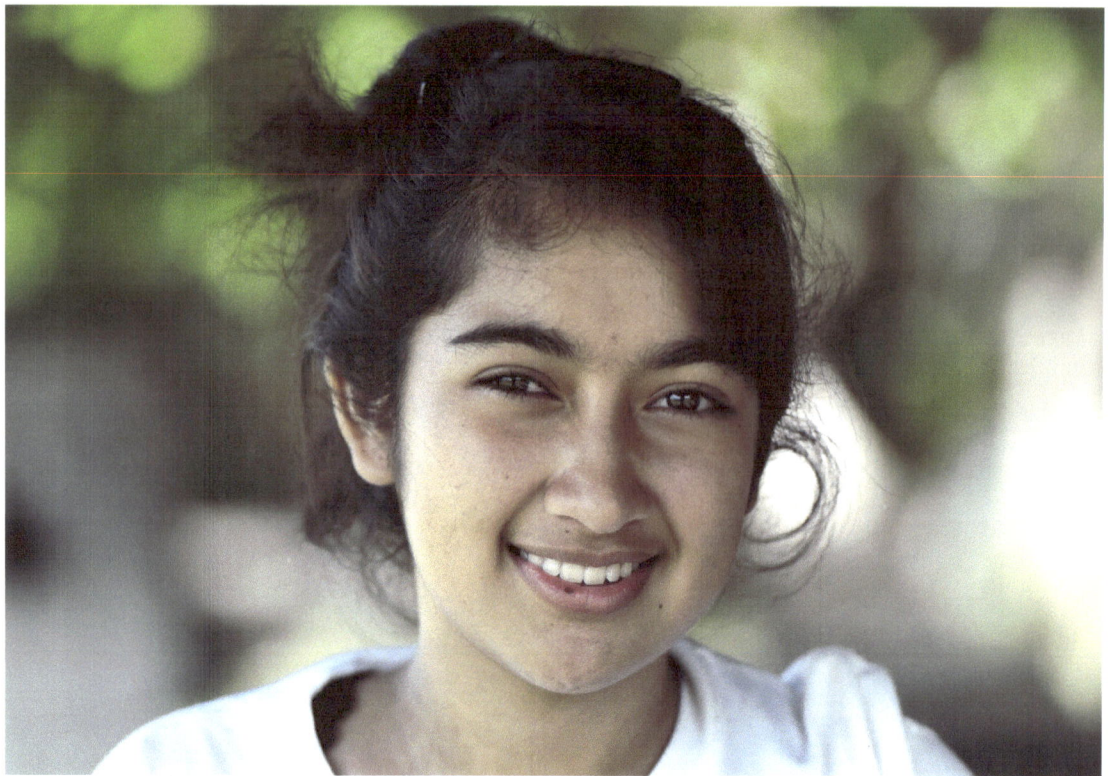

Lyra Narruhn (Chuuk)

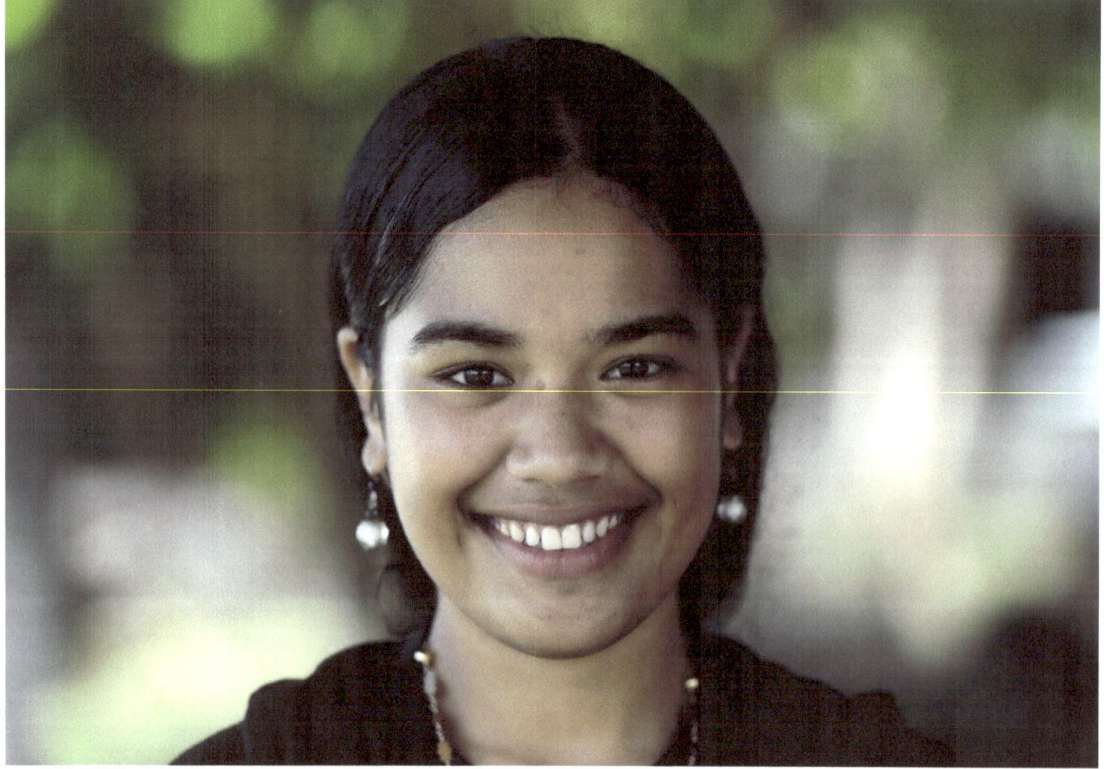

Laura Korwan (Marshall Islands)

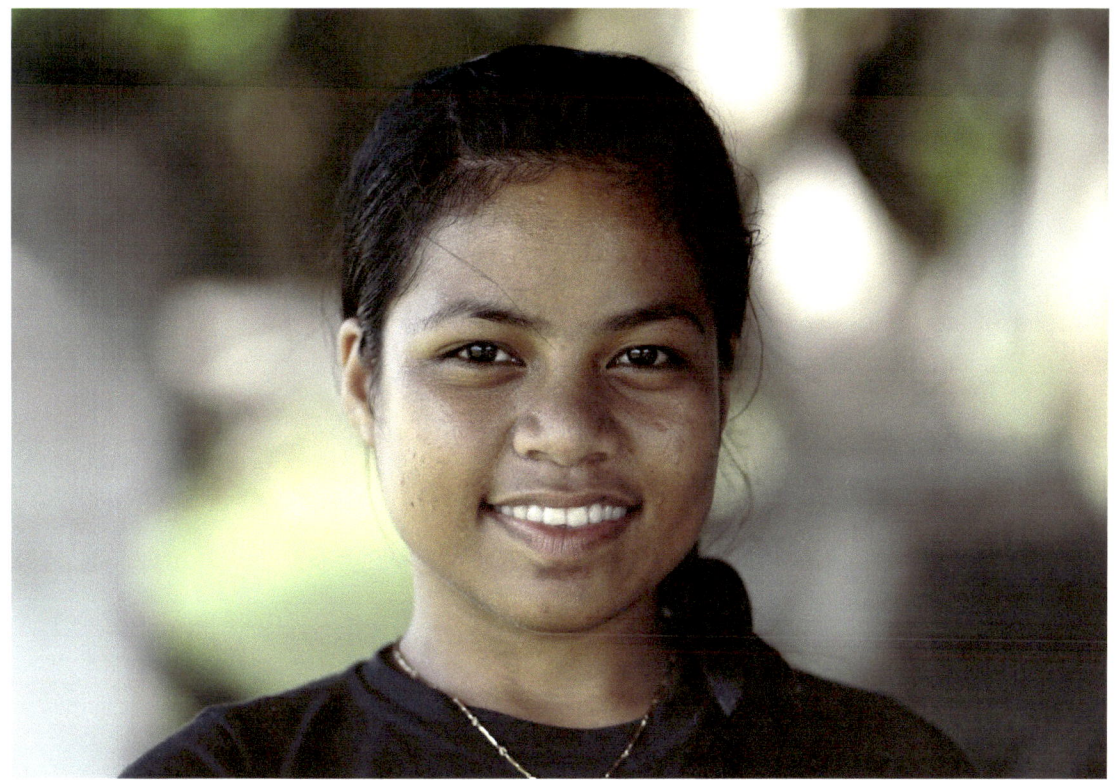

Judina Korok (Marshall Islands)

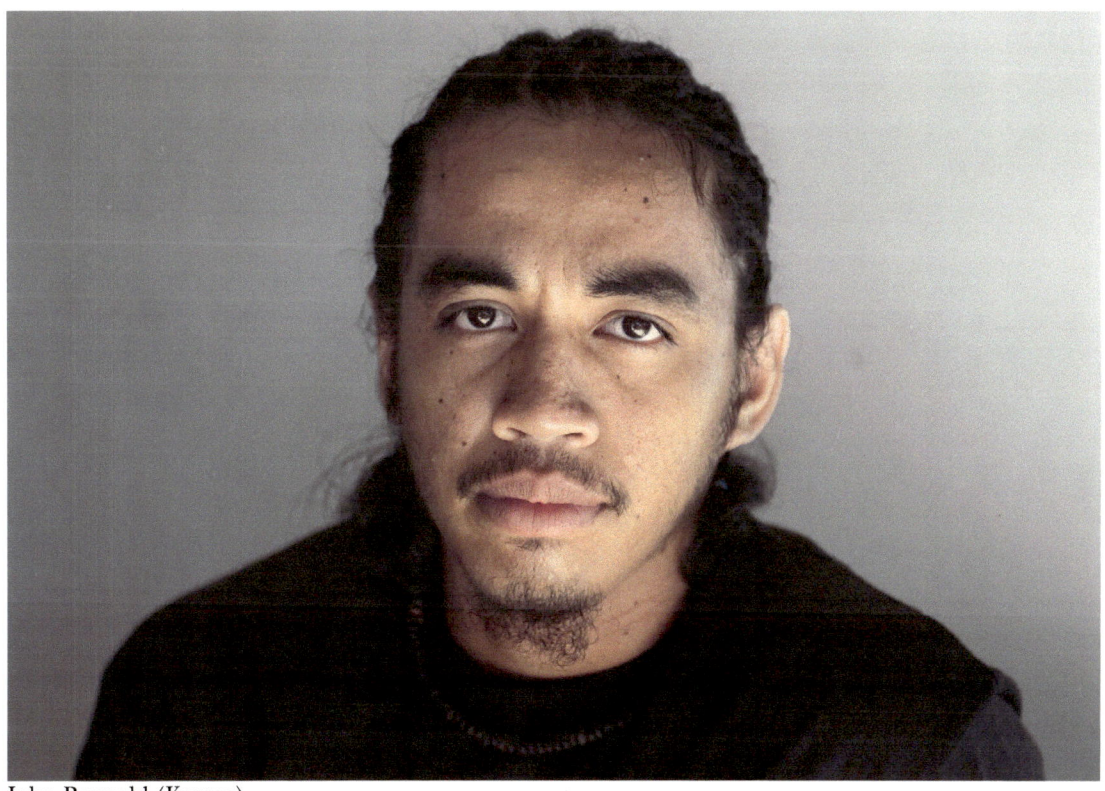

John Reynold (Kosrae)

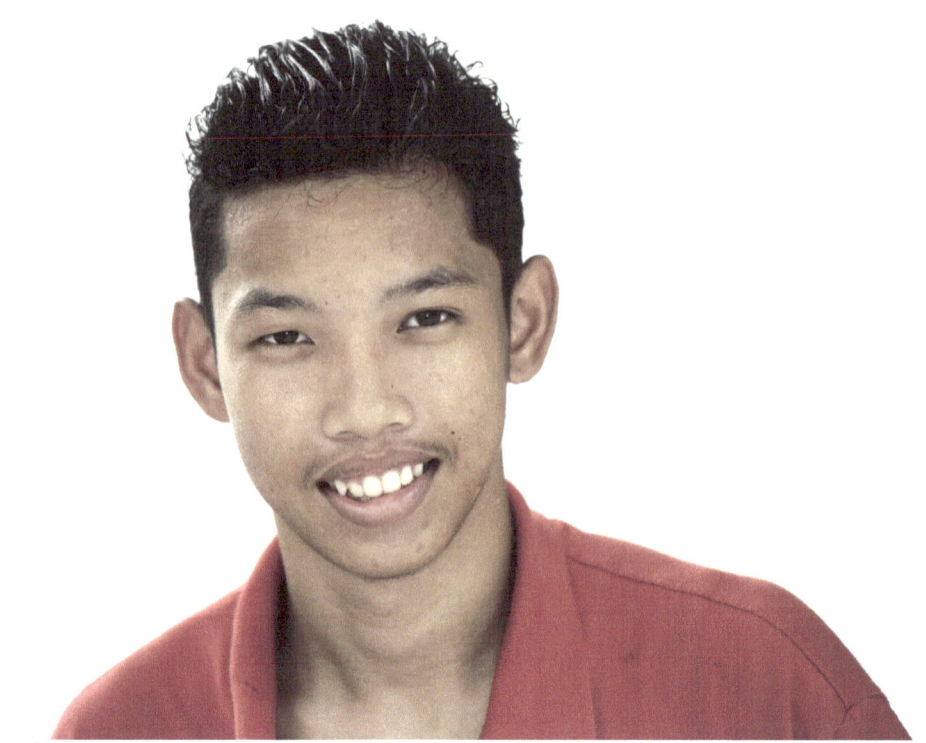

Eric Cano (Chuuk)

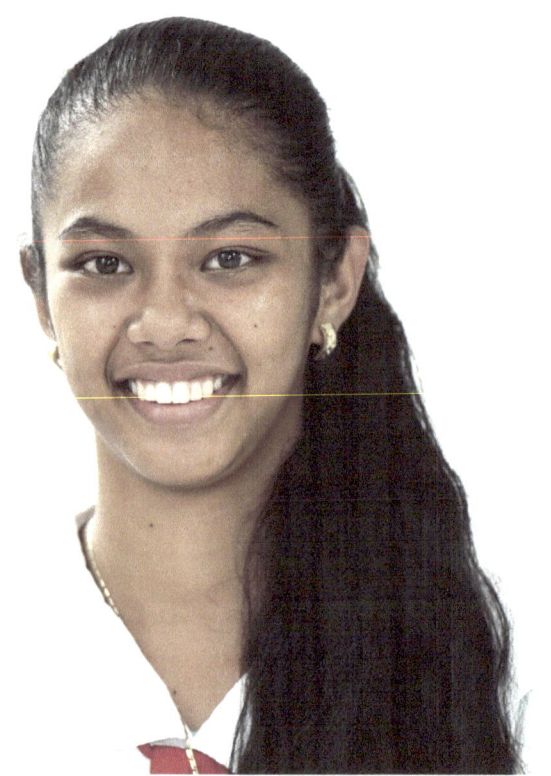

Naiomy Lohn (Pohnpei)

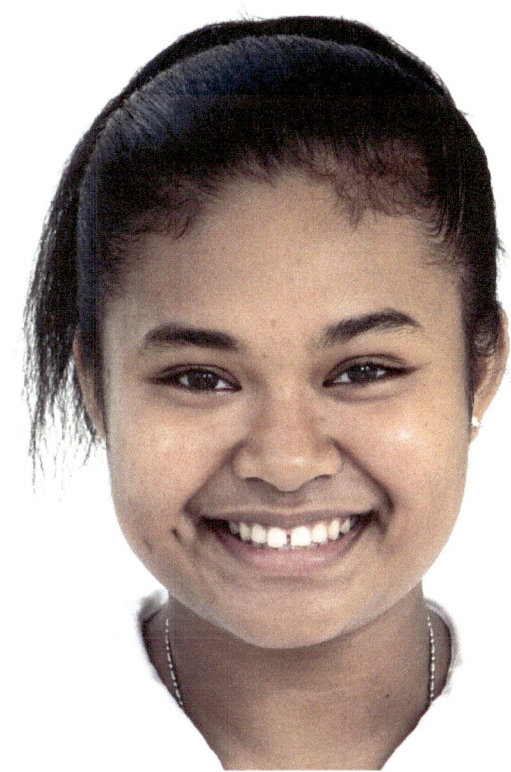

Polita Dil'Ungil Asanuma (Palau)

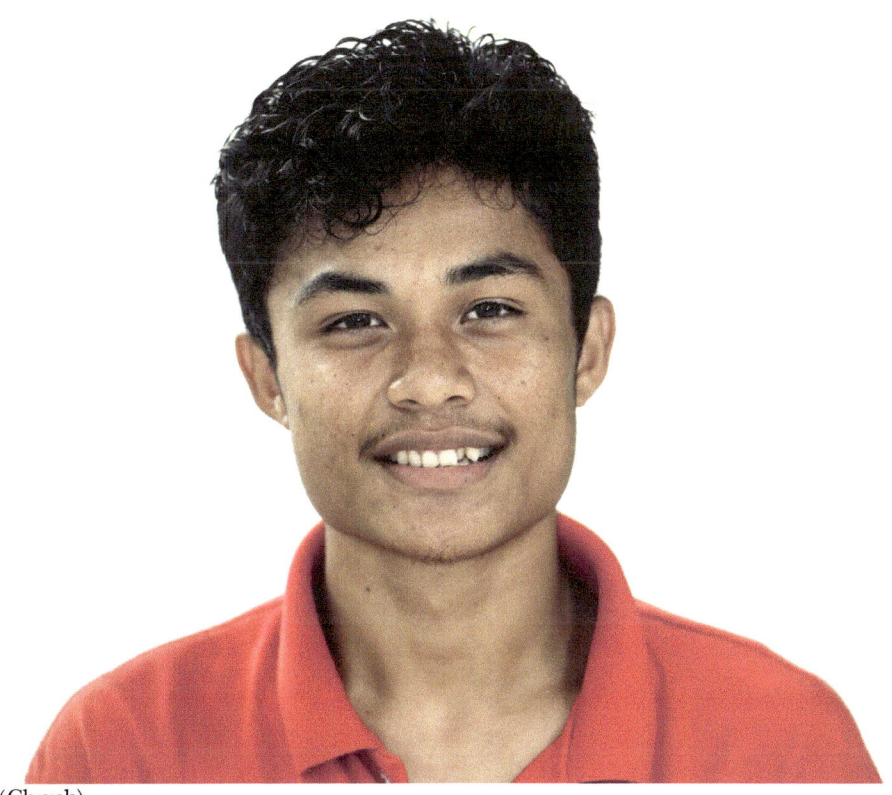

Joyful Noket (Chuuk)

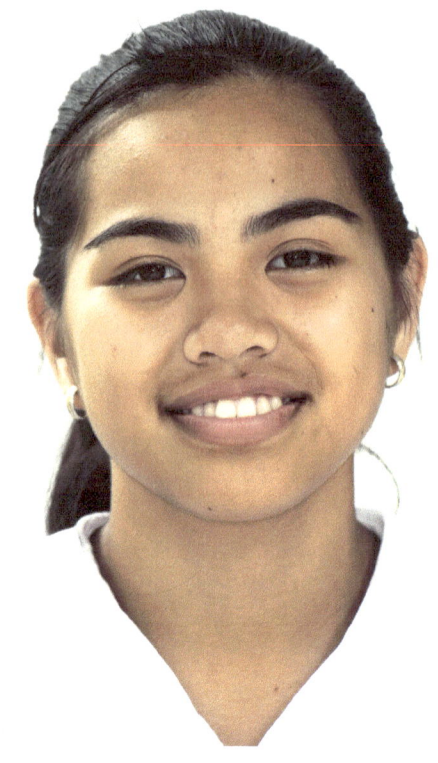

Camcam Irons (Chuuk)

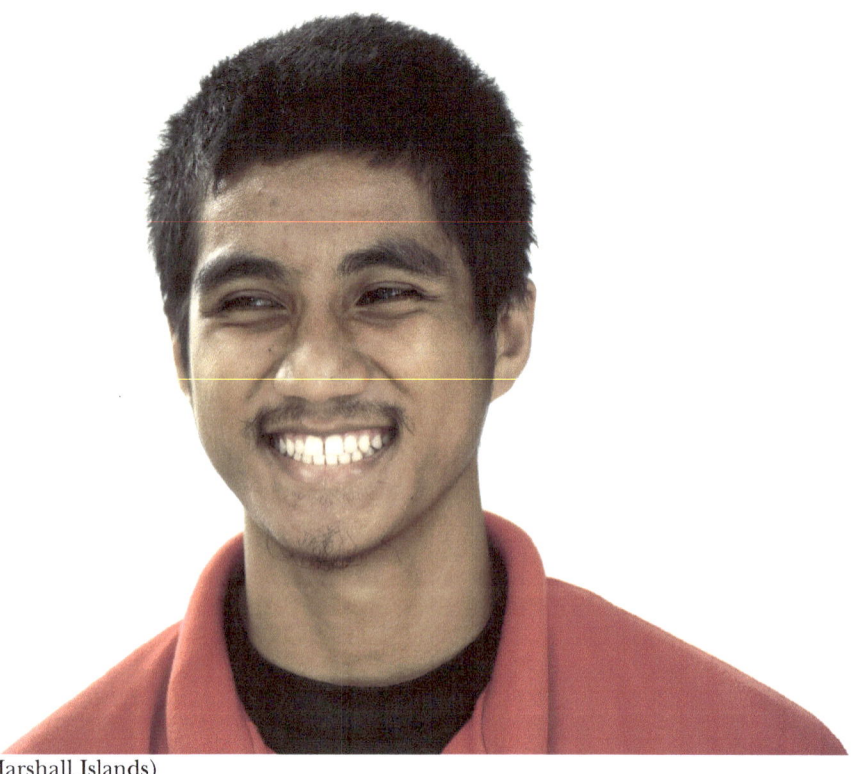

Keanu Reimers (Marshall Islands)

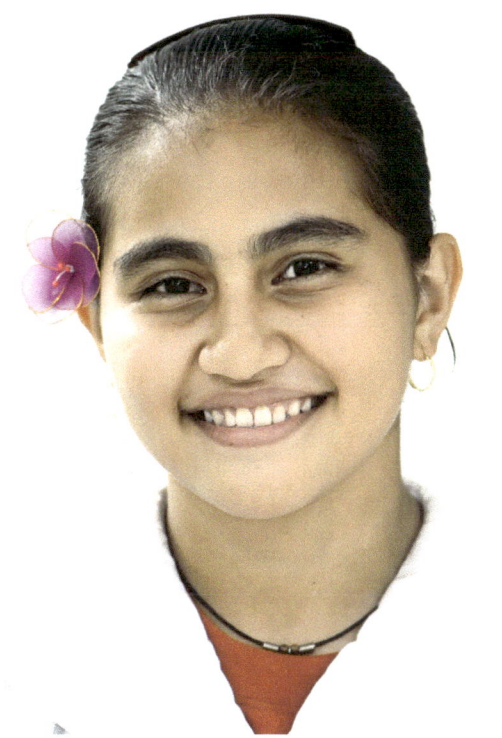

Melissa Mulalap (Yap)

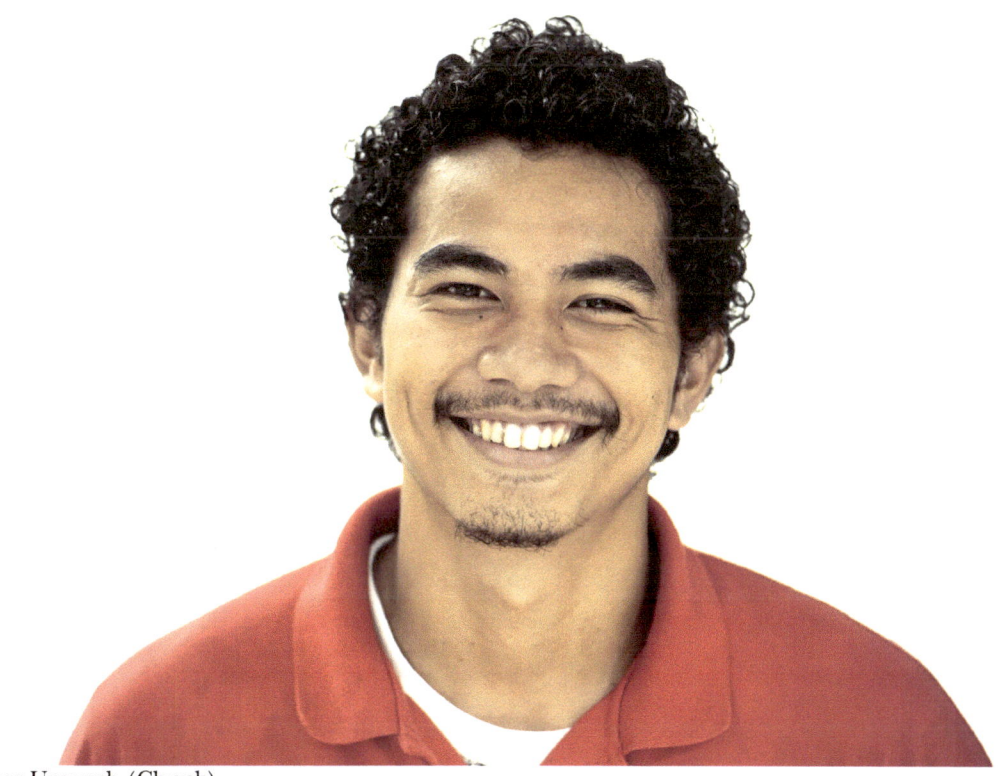

Eleisor Umwech (Chuuk)

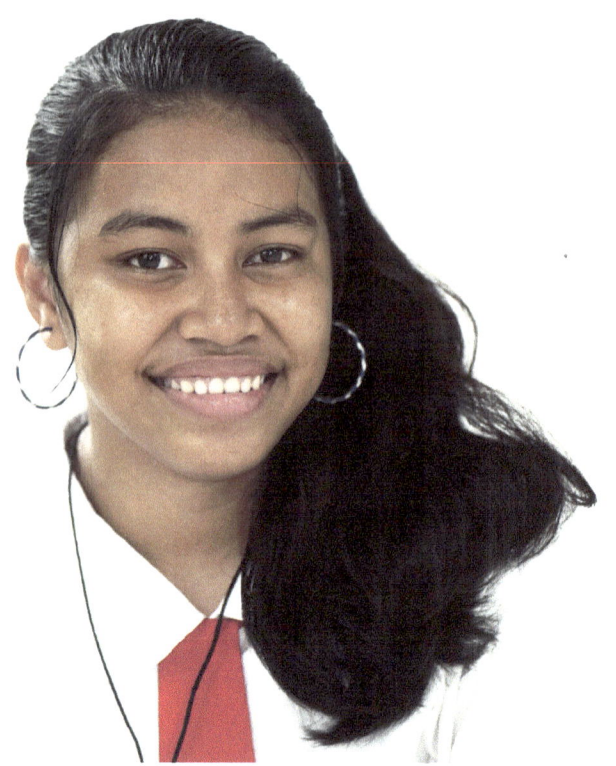

Lerina Nena (Kosrae)

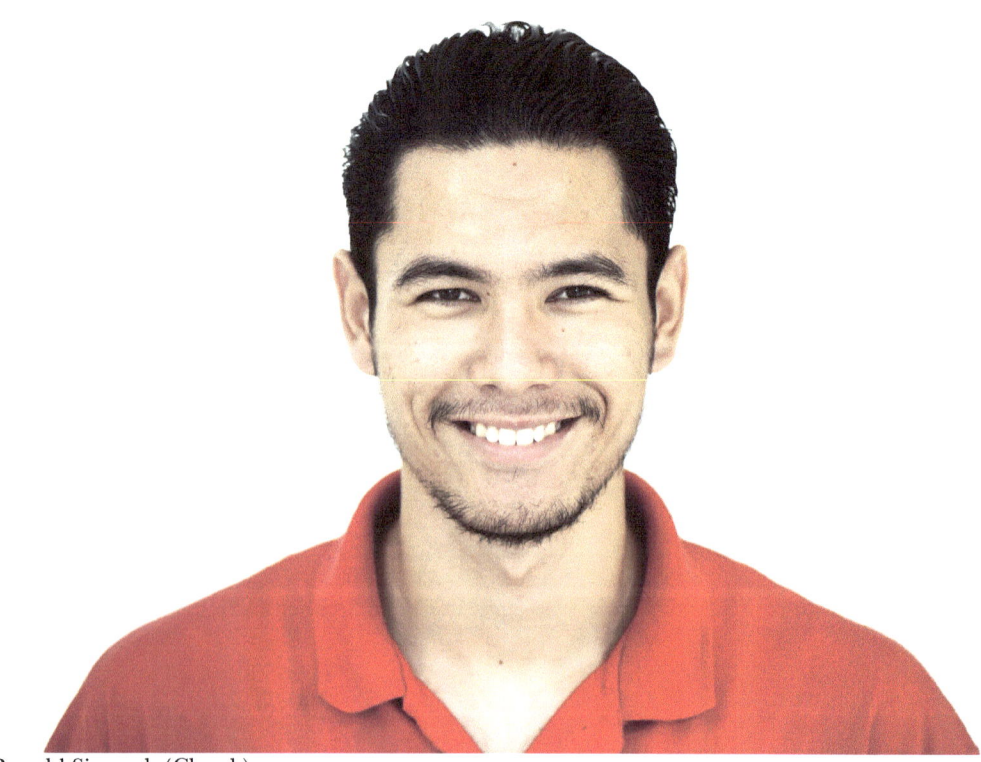

Ronald Sipenuk (Chuuk)

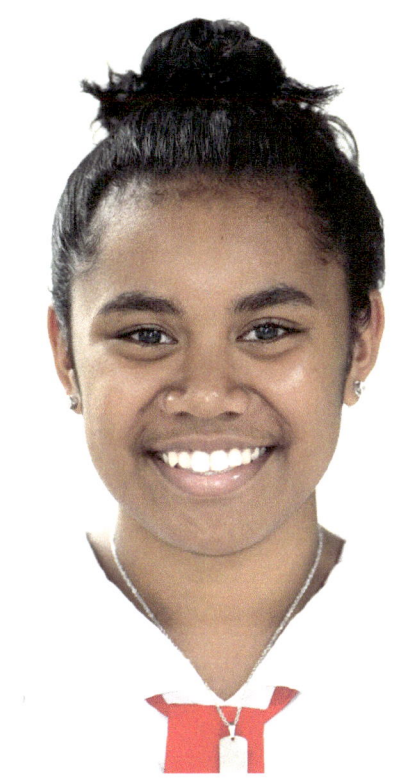

Eleanor Titimil (Palau)

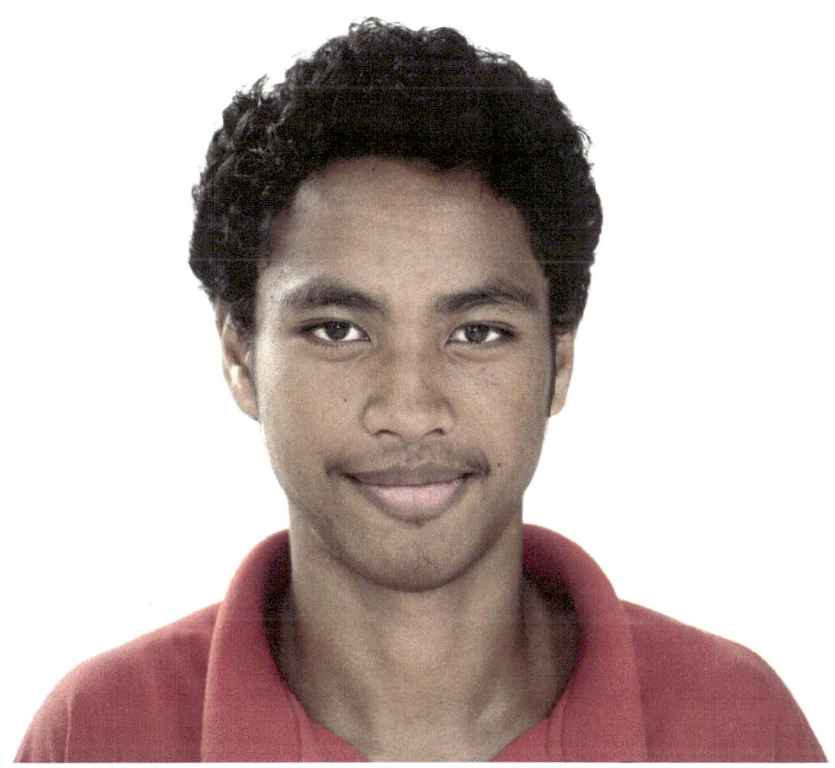

Michael Kigimnang (Yap)

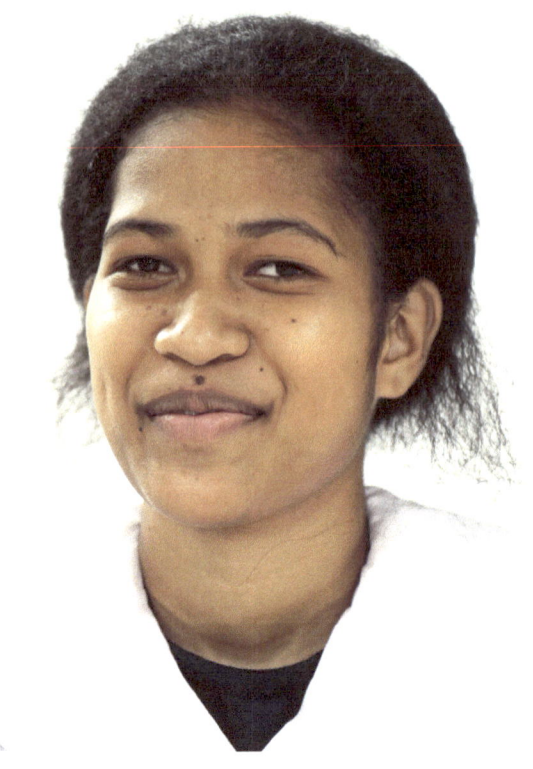

Caroline Tinan (Yap)

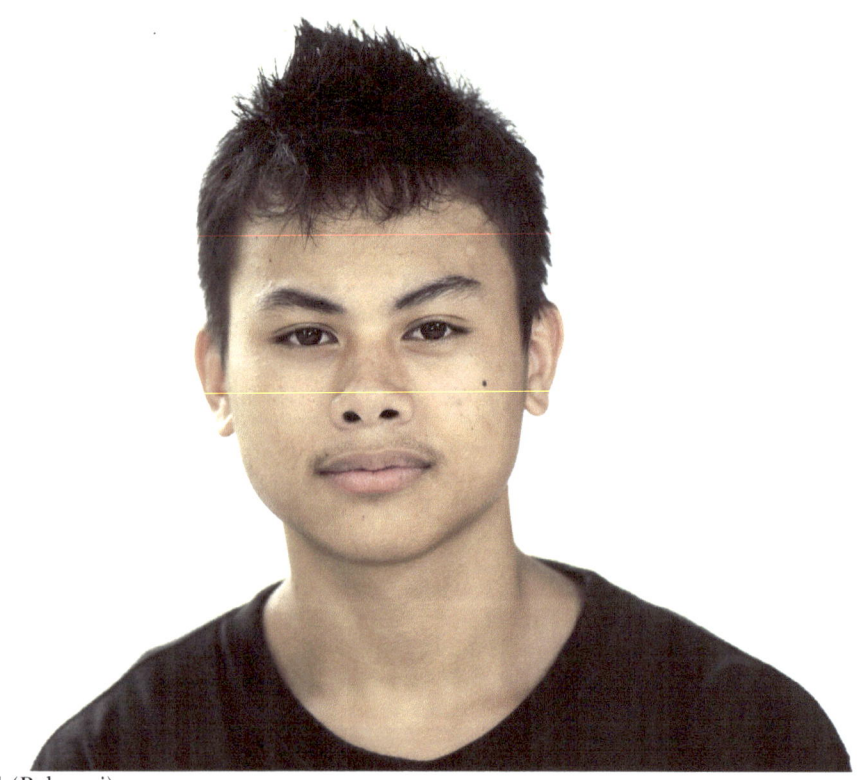

Kenneth Edmund (Pohnpei)

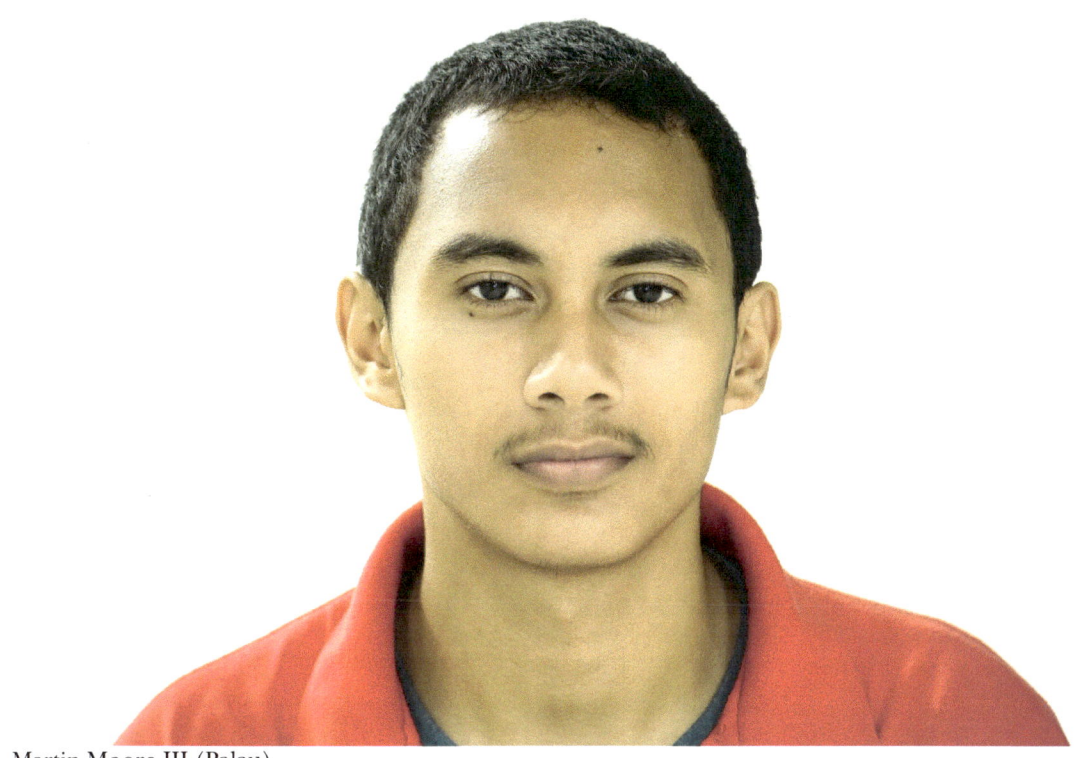

Martin Moore III (Palau)

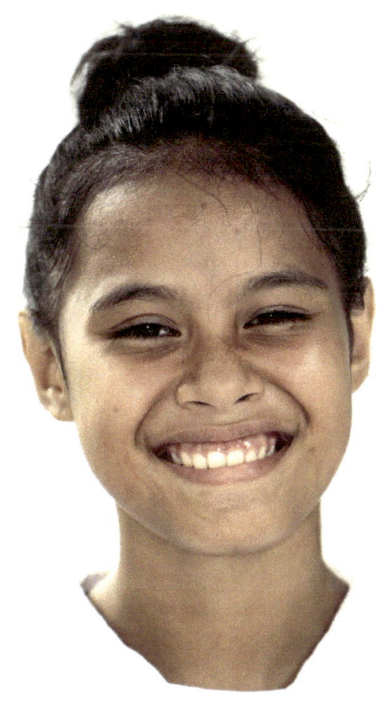

Ferleen Mallarme (Pohnpei)

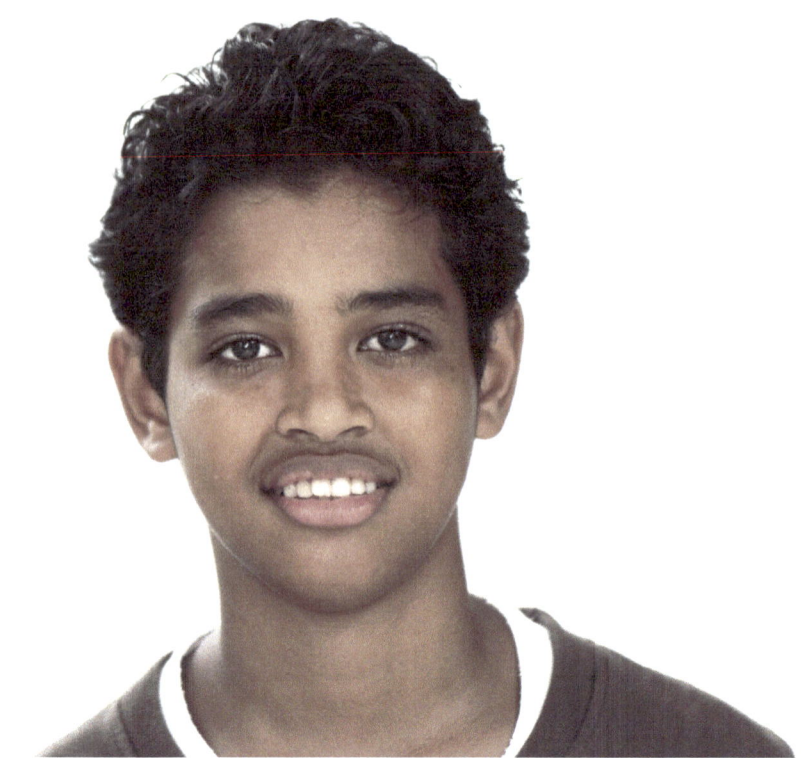

Sato Foruw (Yap)

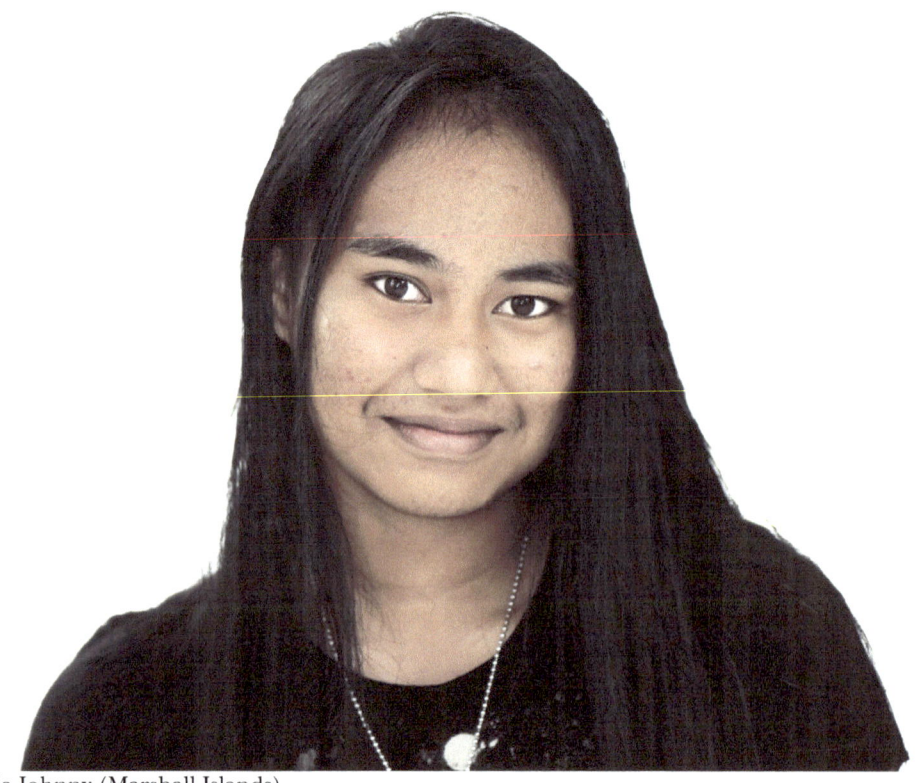

Alexandria Johnny (Marshall Islands)

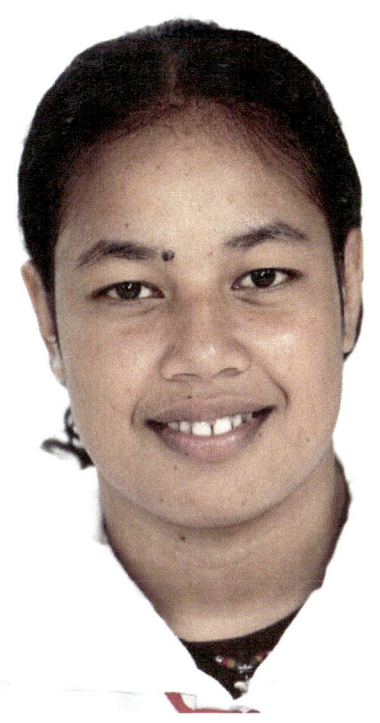

June Joy Lemaisei Laibeyal (Yap)

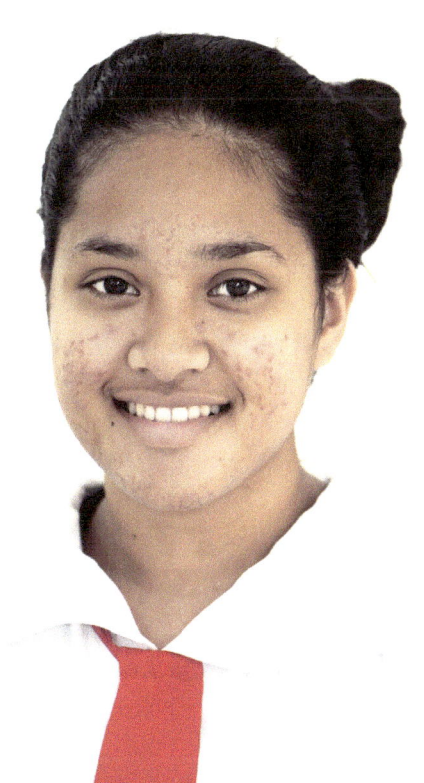

Jeanelle Omisaol Adelbai (Palau)

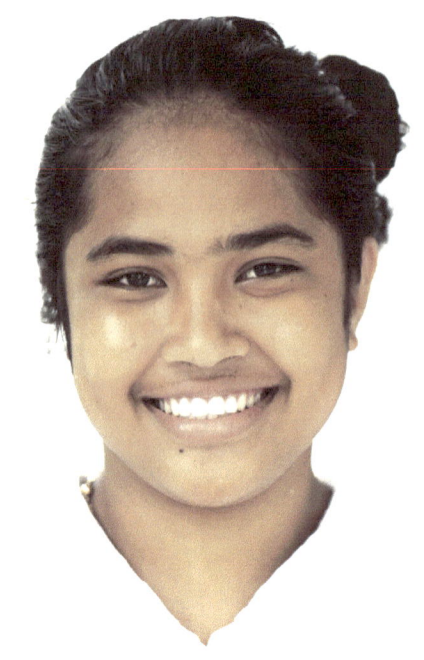

Luan Gilmete (Pohnpei)

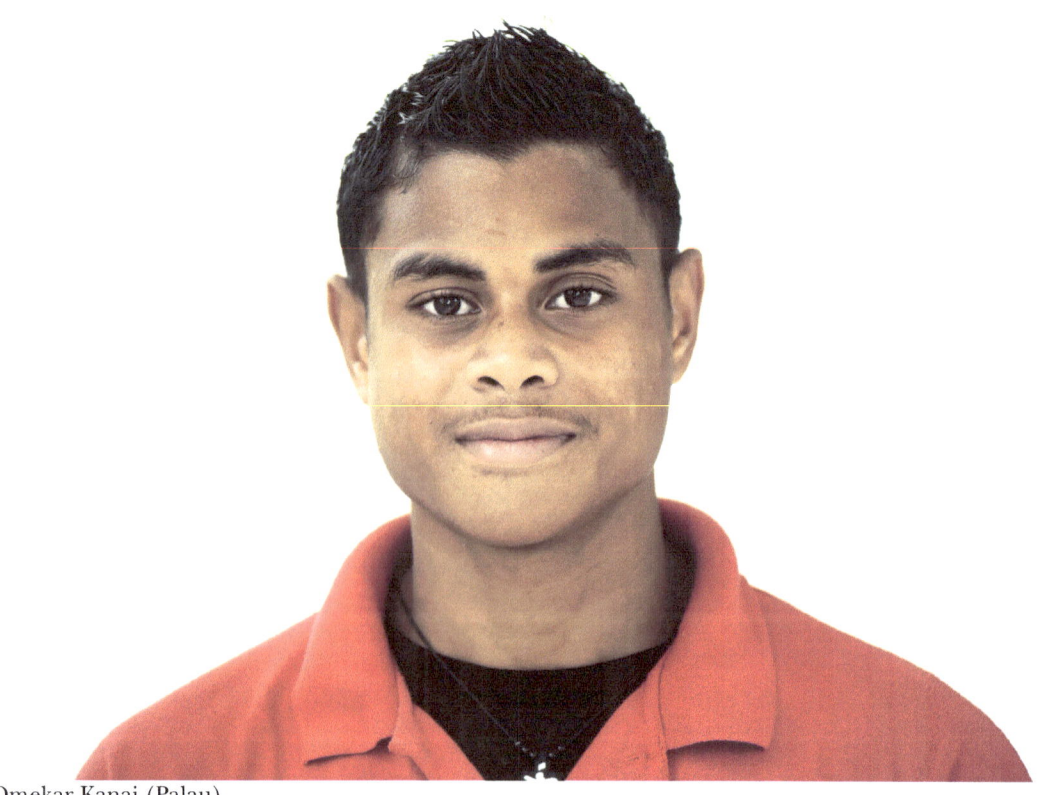

Omekar Kanai (Palau)

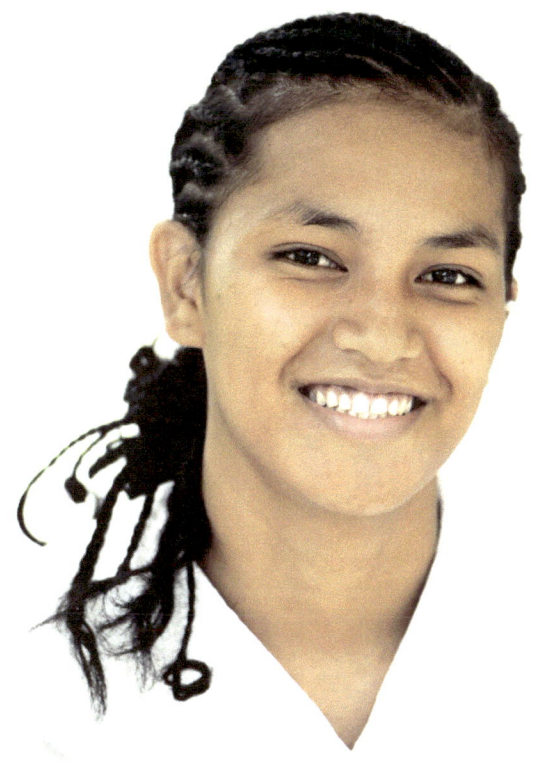

Roxie Moya (Pohnpei)

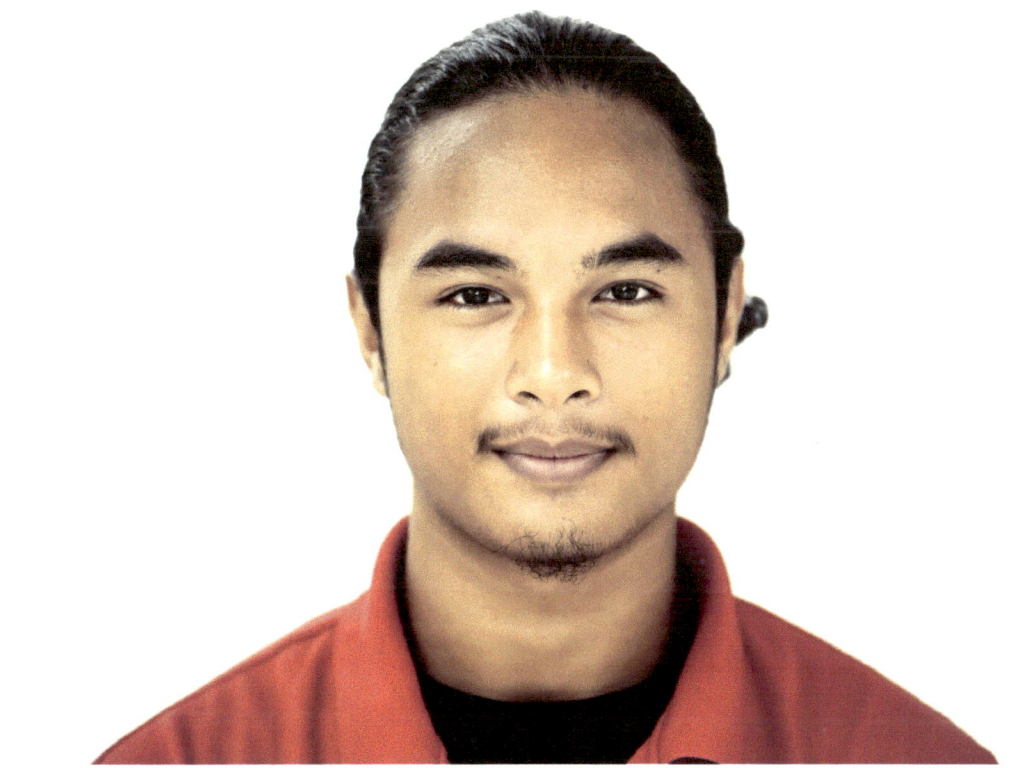

Benigno Sablan (Palau)

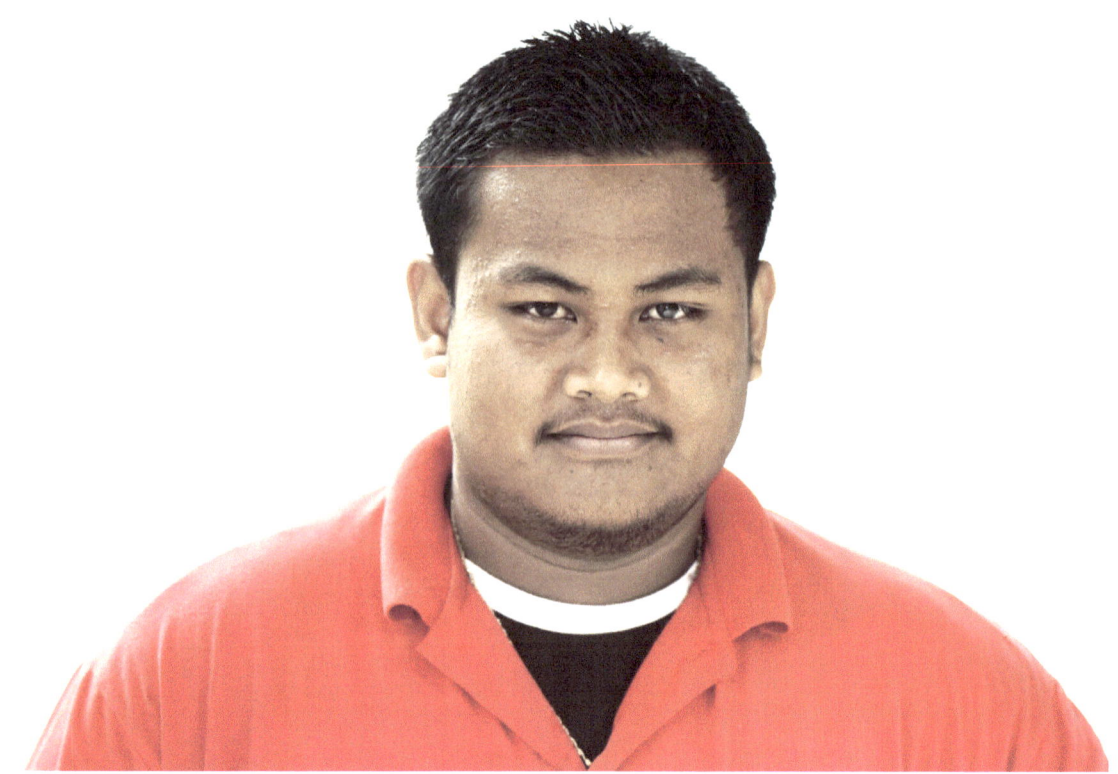

Tommy Abraham (Pohnpei)

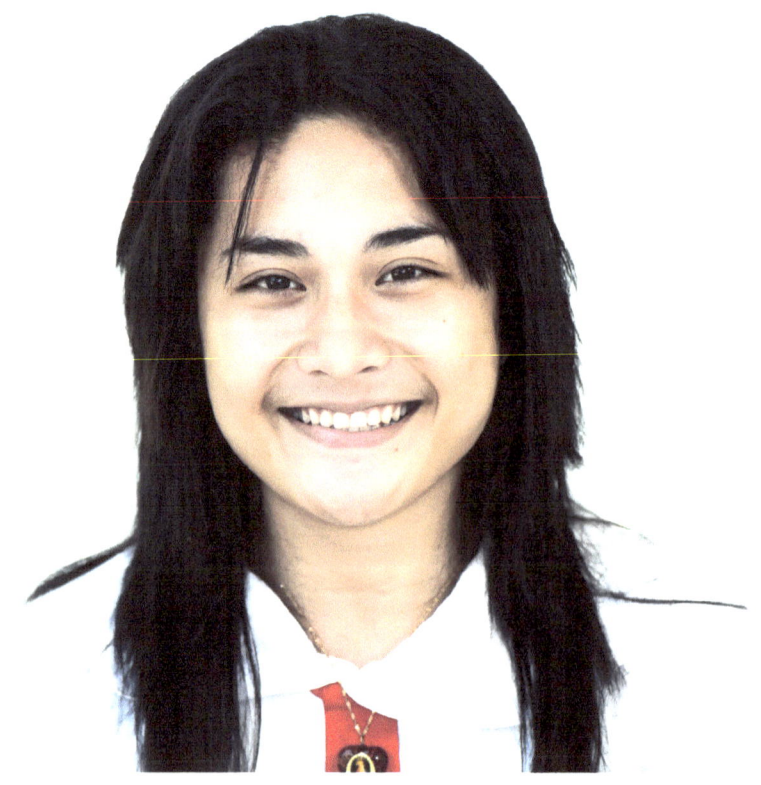

Shanna Paul (Chuuk)

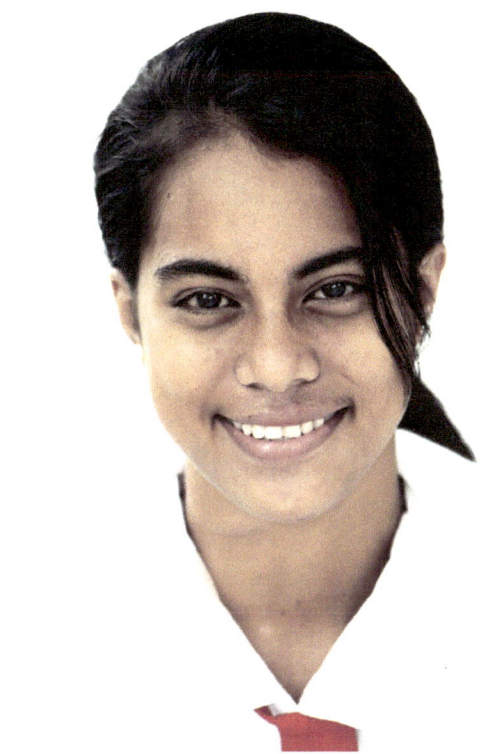

Leola Susaia Primo (Pohnpei)

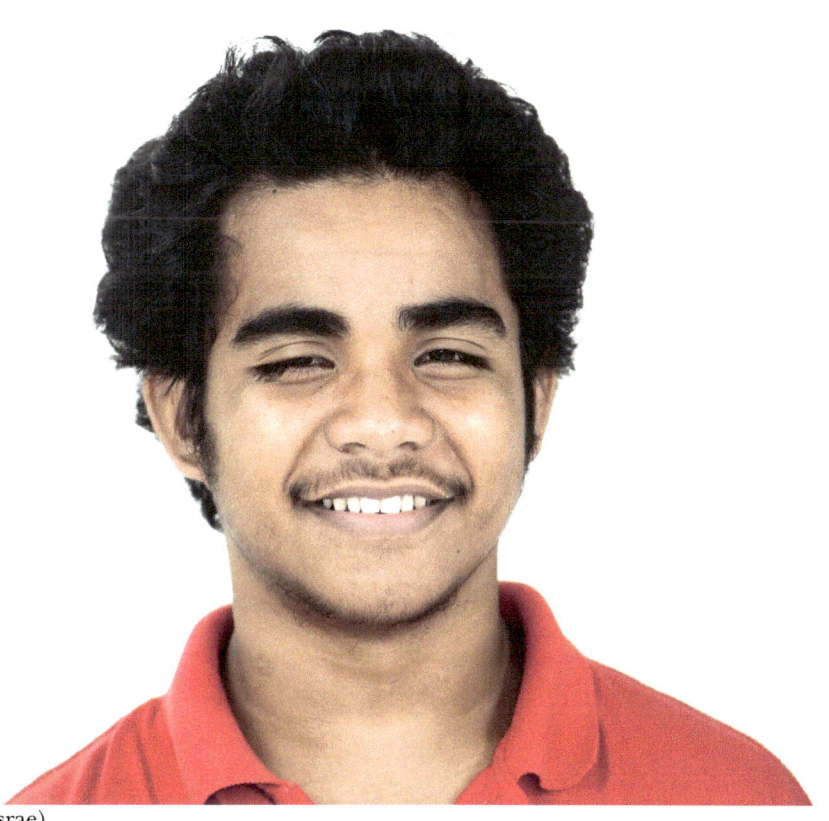

Marson Elley (Kosrae)

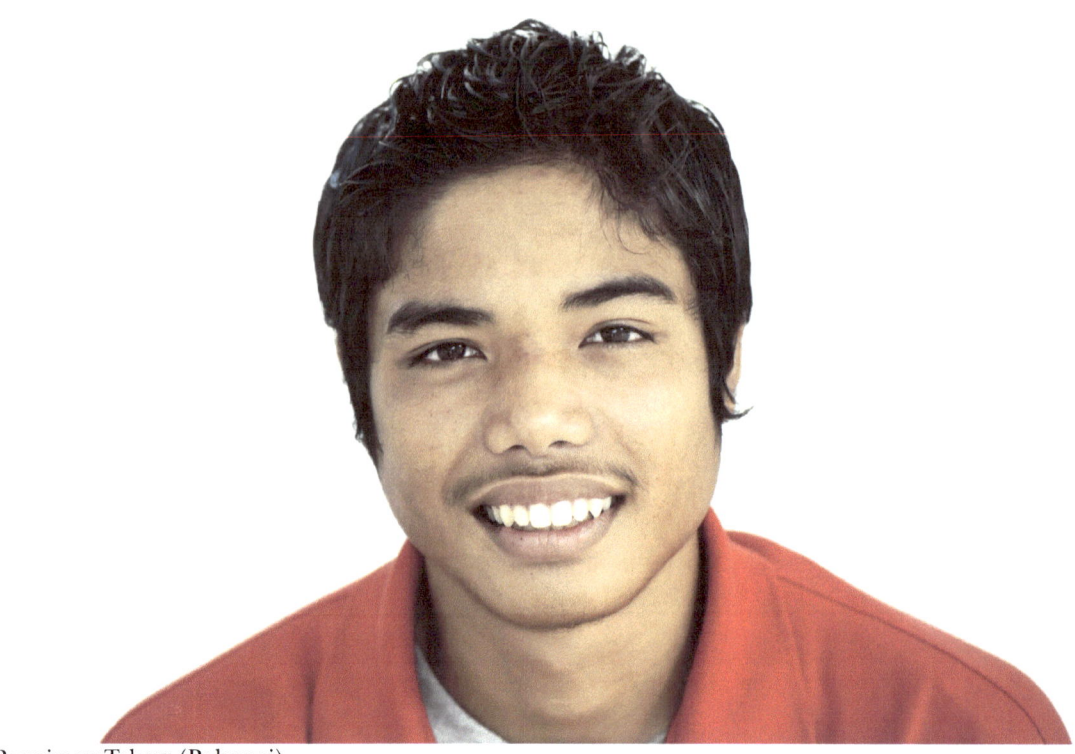

Repeimau Takesy (Pohnpei)

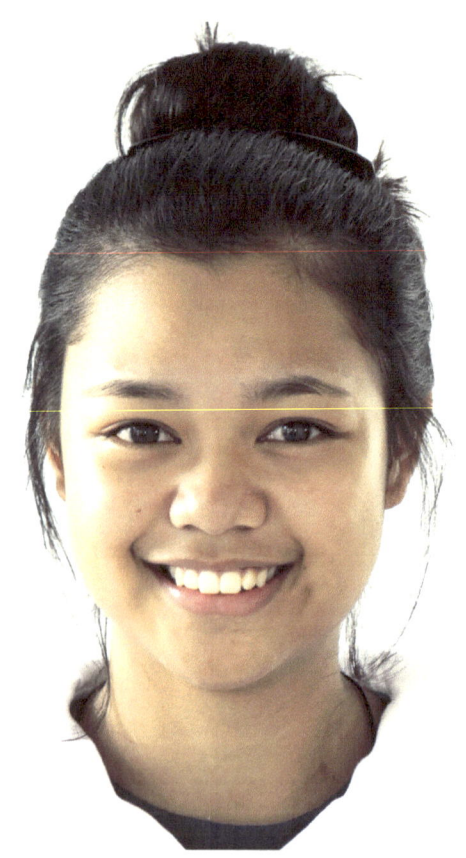

Lisette Yamase (Pohnpei)

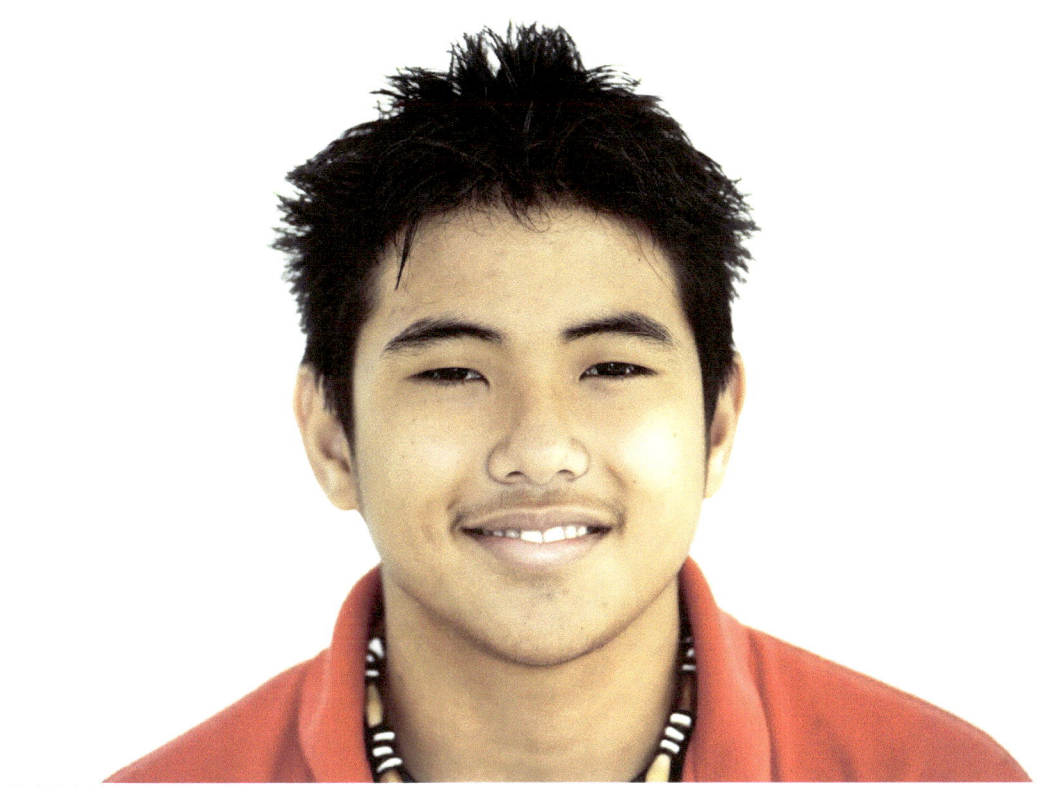

Hideichi Mori (Chuuk)

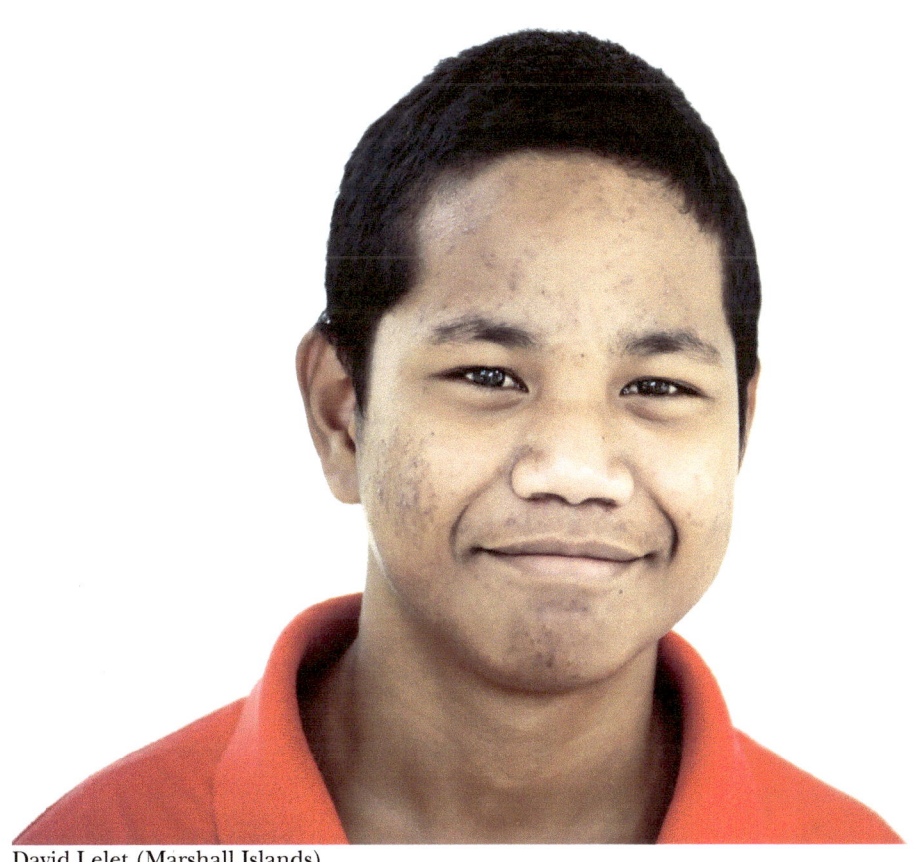

David Lelet (Marshall Islands)

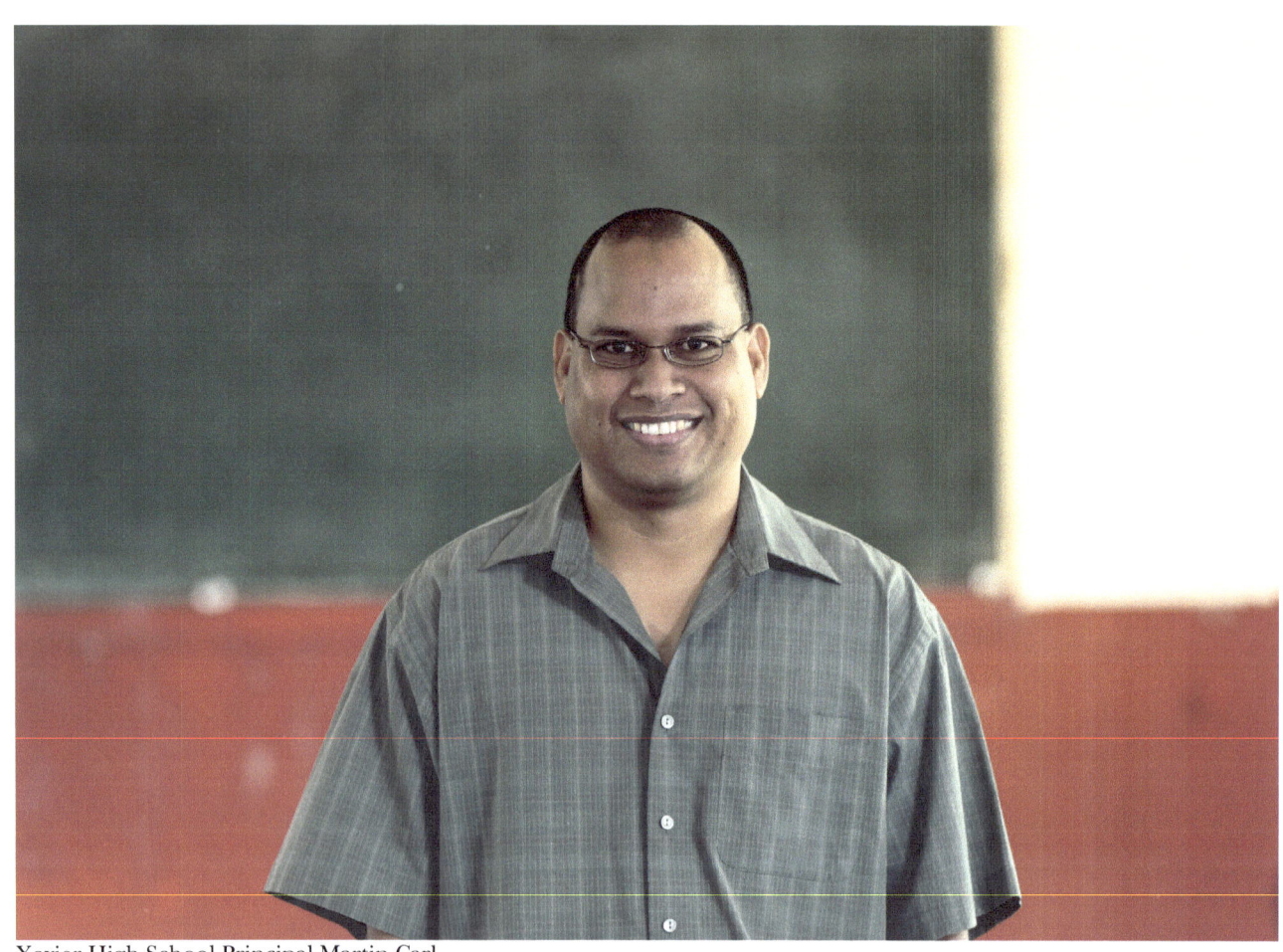
Xavier High School Principal Martin Carl.

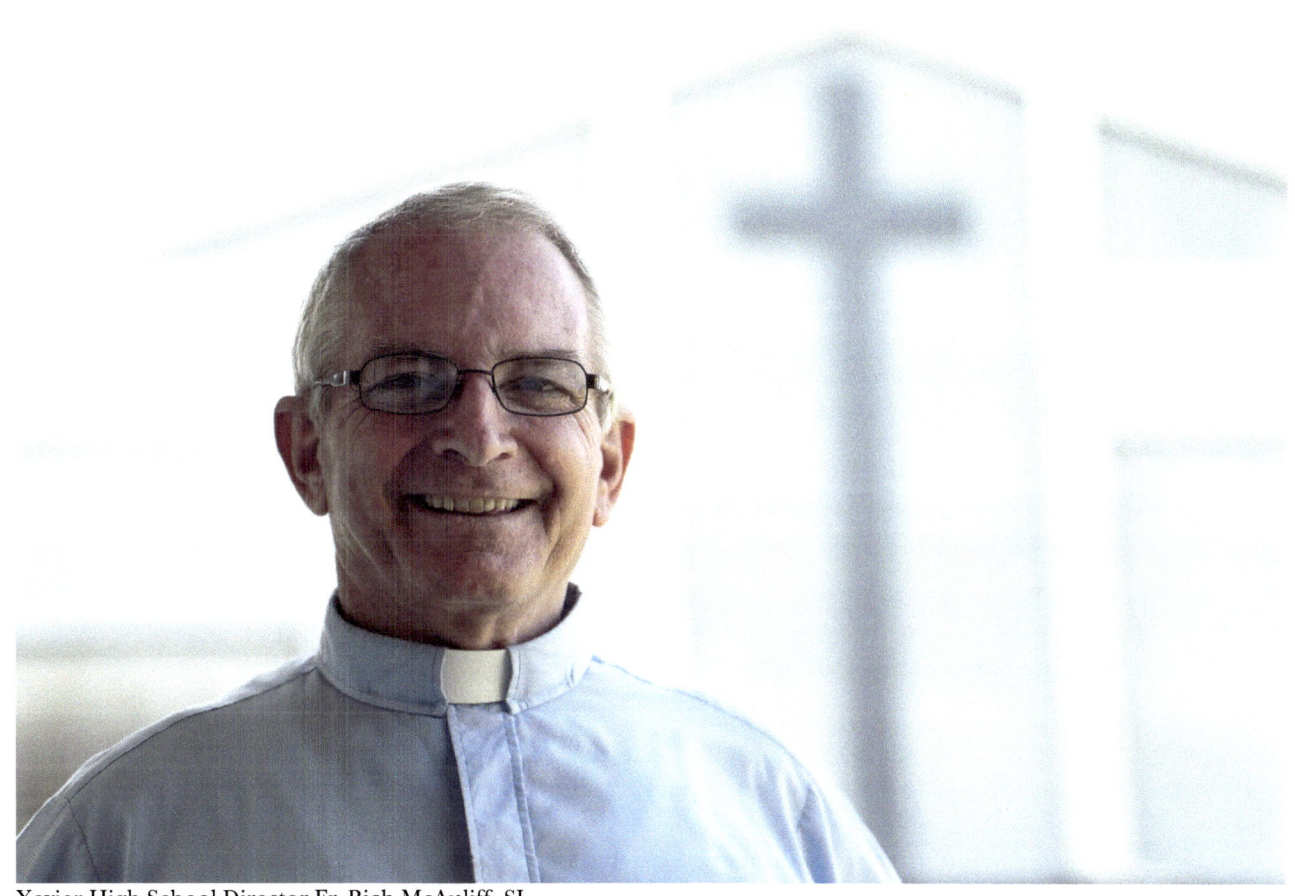

Xavier High School Director Fr. Rich McAuliff, SJ.

Retreat

Each year, the junior and senior classes at Xavier High School go on retreats. These are held off campus on islands that are scattered across Chuuk Lagoon. The students might approach the outings as picnics, but it soon becomes clear that there is serious business to discuss at retreats. For their final retreat, seniors traveled by boat to Pisar Island, a leisurely two-hour trip across the lagoon.

For the members of the Class of 2010, the retreat was also the last time that they would gather as a group before graduation. And for students who spent four intense years with their classmates, and had seen nearly half of their class leave for various reasons, there was intensity to the retreat knowing that Xavier would soon be a memory.

The senior retreat has a spiritual focus. Students are asked, over two and a half days, to look deep into their hearts to understand their spiritual journey at Xavier. They were also asked to meet, one-on-one, with the priest who led the retreat, former Director Fr. Jim Croghan, SJ, or any of the teachers who also attended the program. Those sessions were part discussion, part confessional.

The class also divided into groups, and was asked to meet in groups to discuss individual journeys. I attached myself to one group, as I was by now an expected diversion with my camera. But as the students talked about their spiritual journeys, I put down my camera and listened. I won't reveal his name, but one student's story particularly moved me. He said if it wasn't for the strength of his faith, and the support of his classmates, he was sure he would have been kicked out for academic reasons. His faith, he said with quiet certainty, gave him the courage to try harder in class.

I'm not sure what moved me the most – the strength of his faith, the courage he showed in discussing his fears and faith with others, or the unqualified trust he placed in all of us to treat his story with respect? I know that at his age, I had nowhere near his self-awareness or strength and conviction of values.

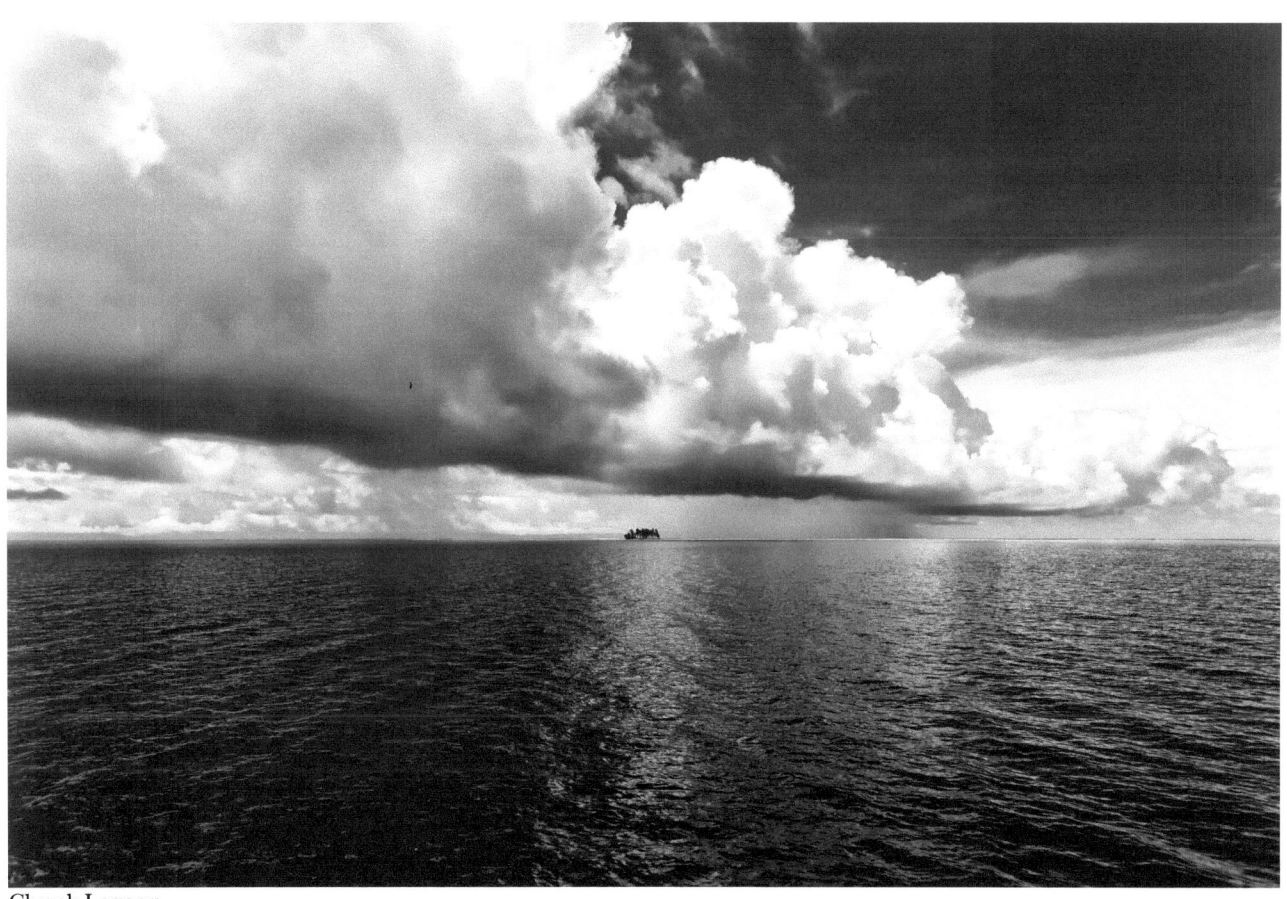

Chuuk Lagoon.

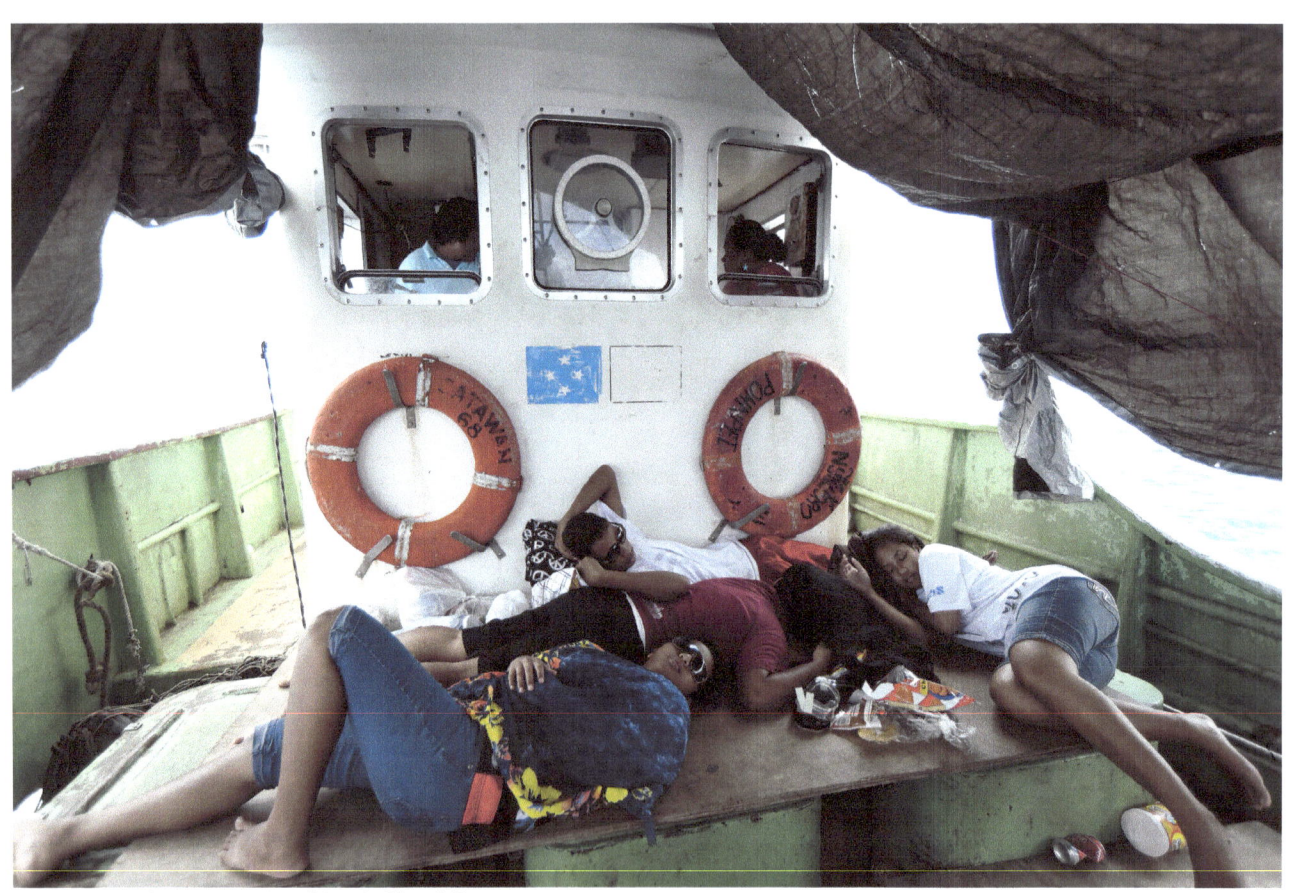

Sleeping on the way to Pisar Island, Chuuk Lagoon.

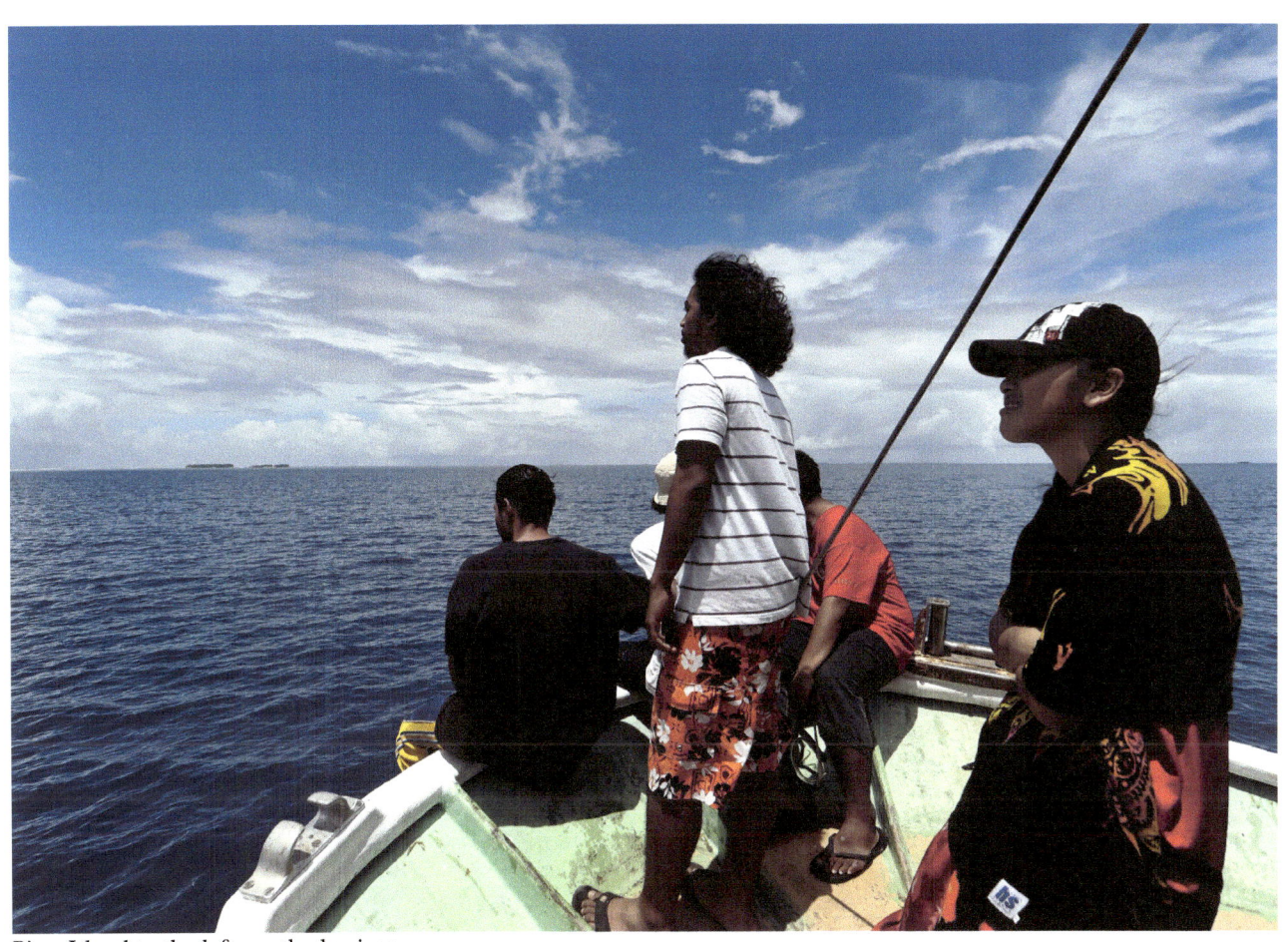

Pisar Island to the left, on the horizon.

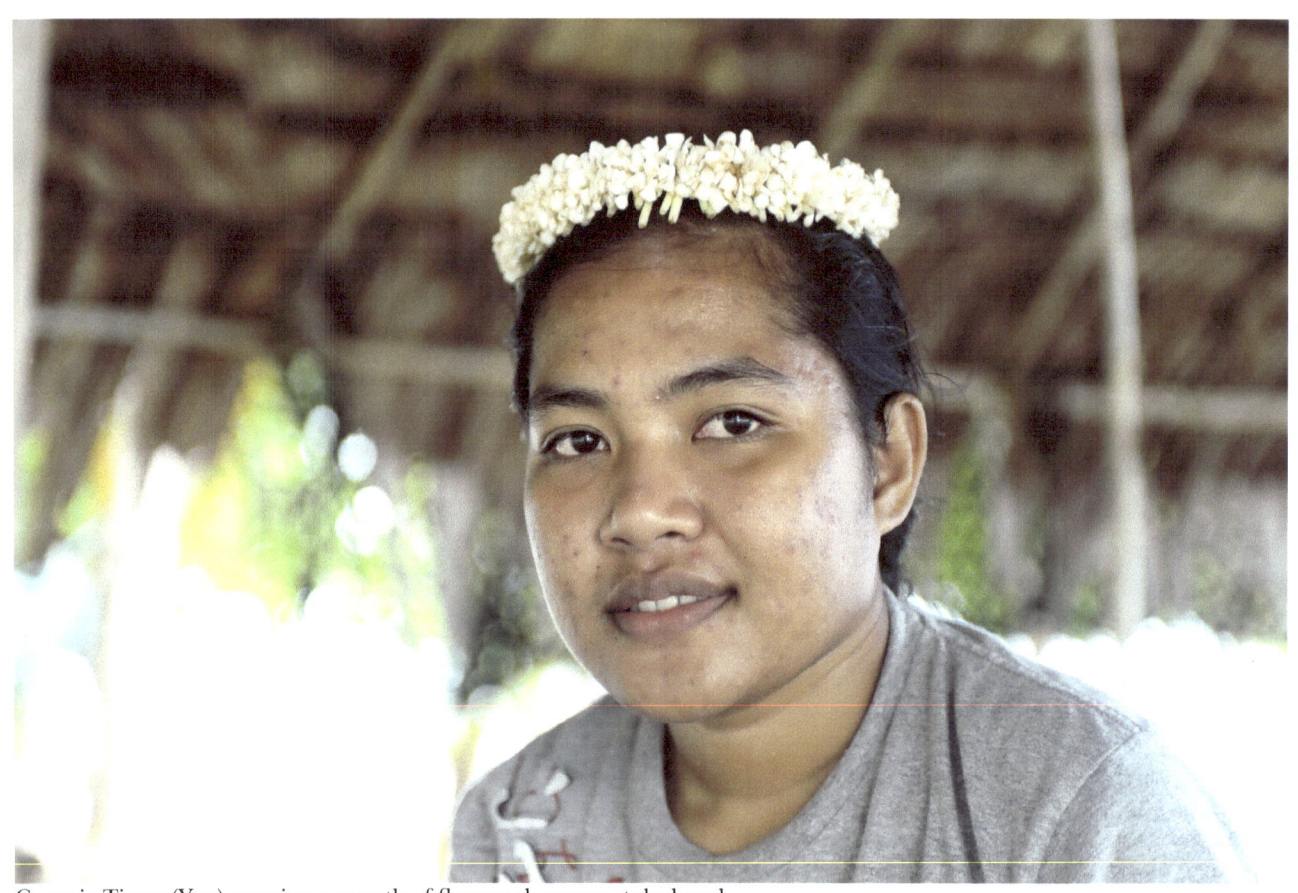

Georgia Tinag (Yap) wearing a wreath of flowers she wove at daybreak.

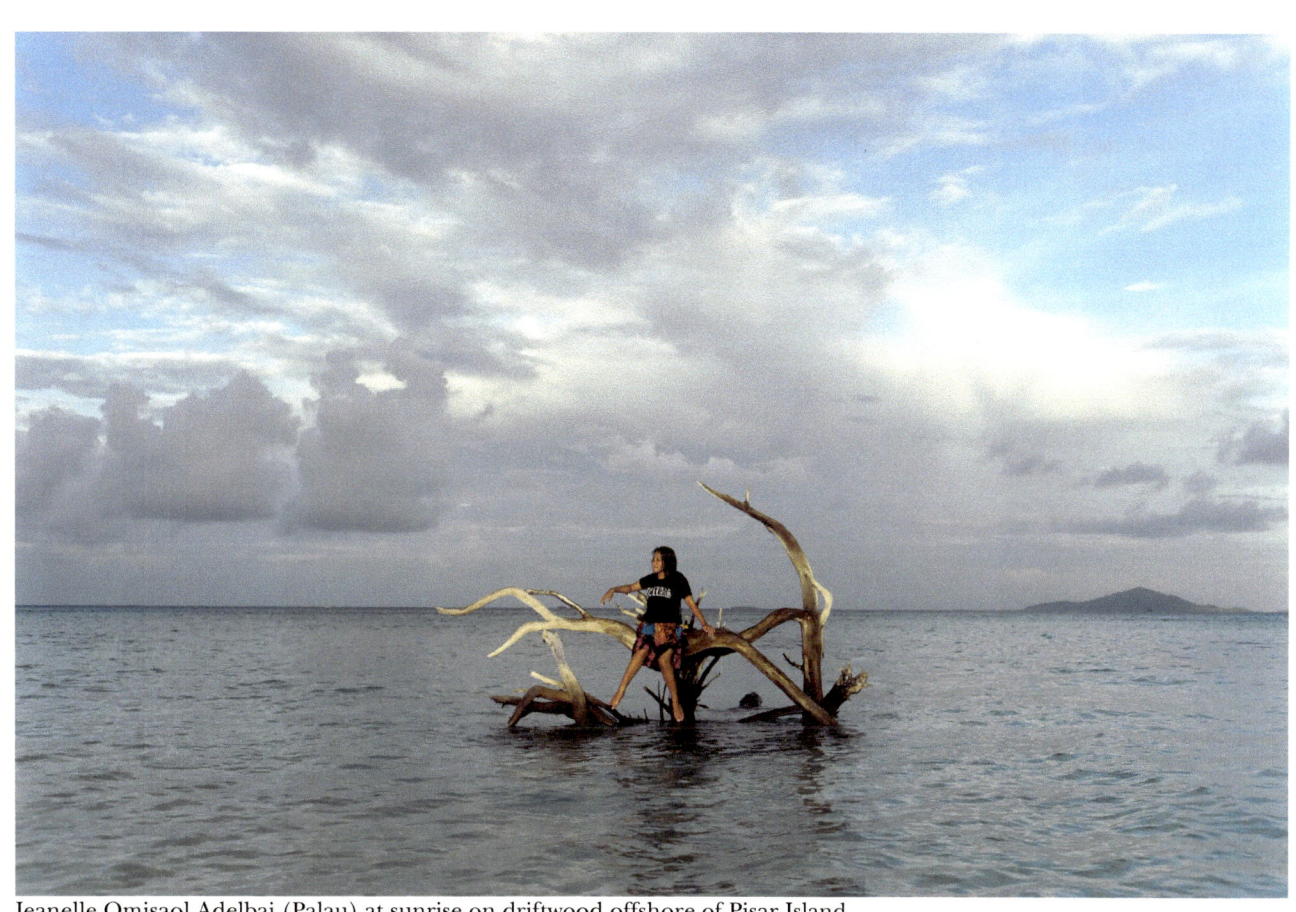

Jeanelle Omisaol Adelbai (Palau) at sunrise on driftwood offshore of Pisar Island.

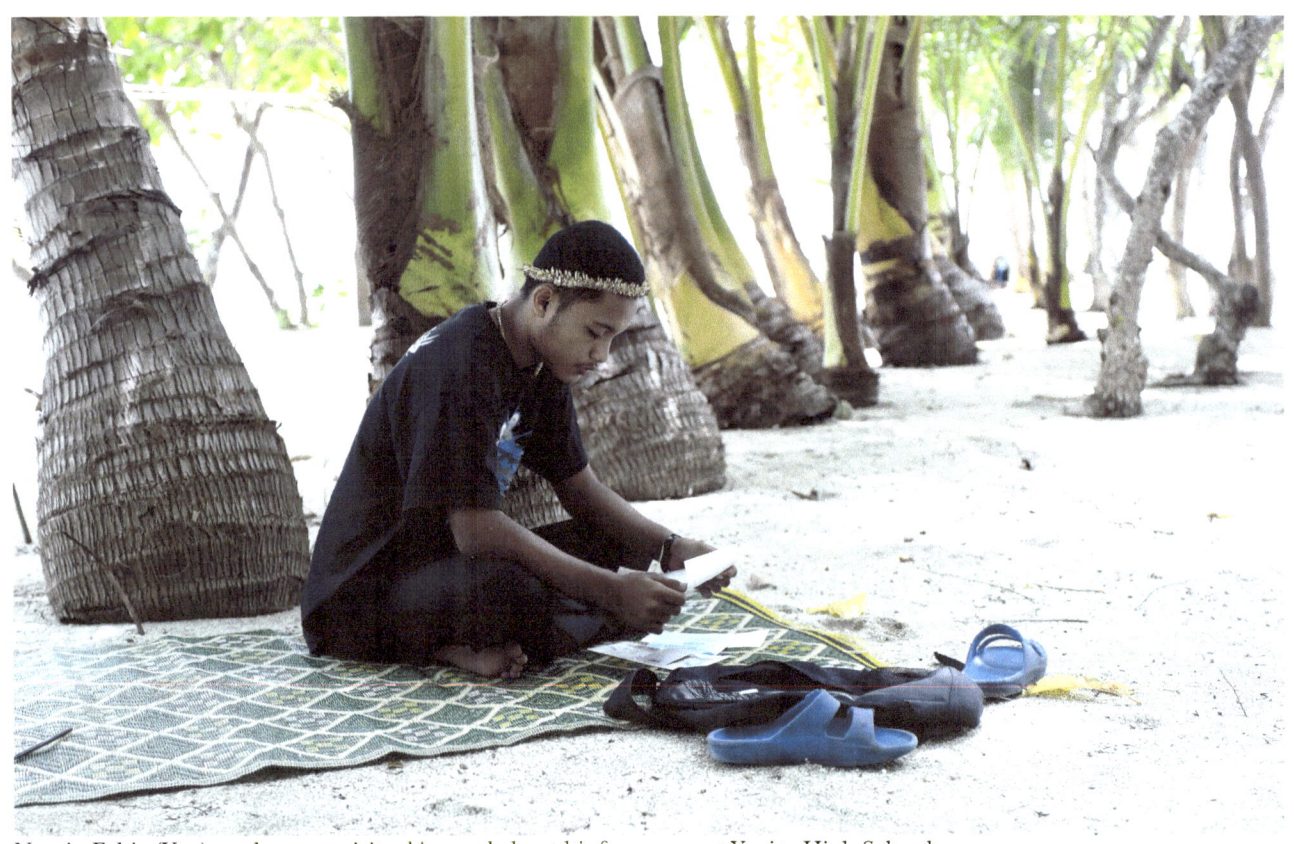

Norvin Faltir (Yap) works on a spiritual journal about his four years at Xavier High School.

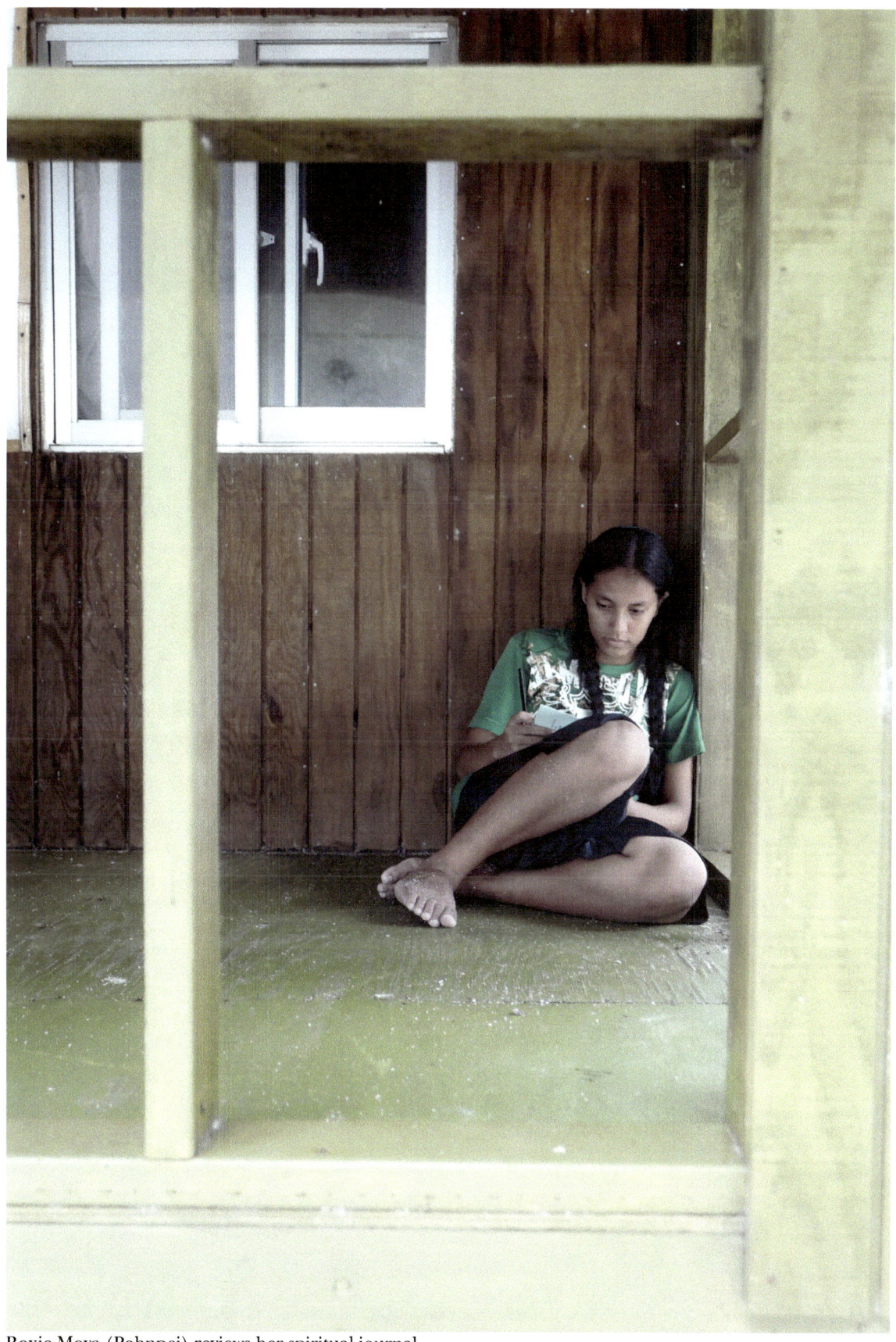

Roxie Moya (Pohnpei) reviews her spiritual journal.

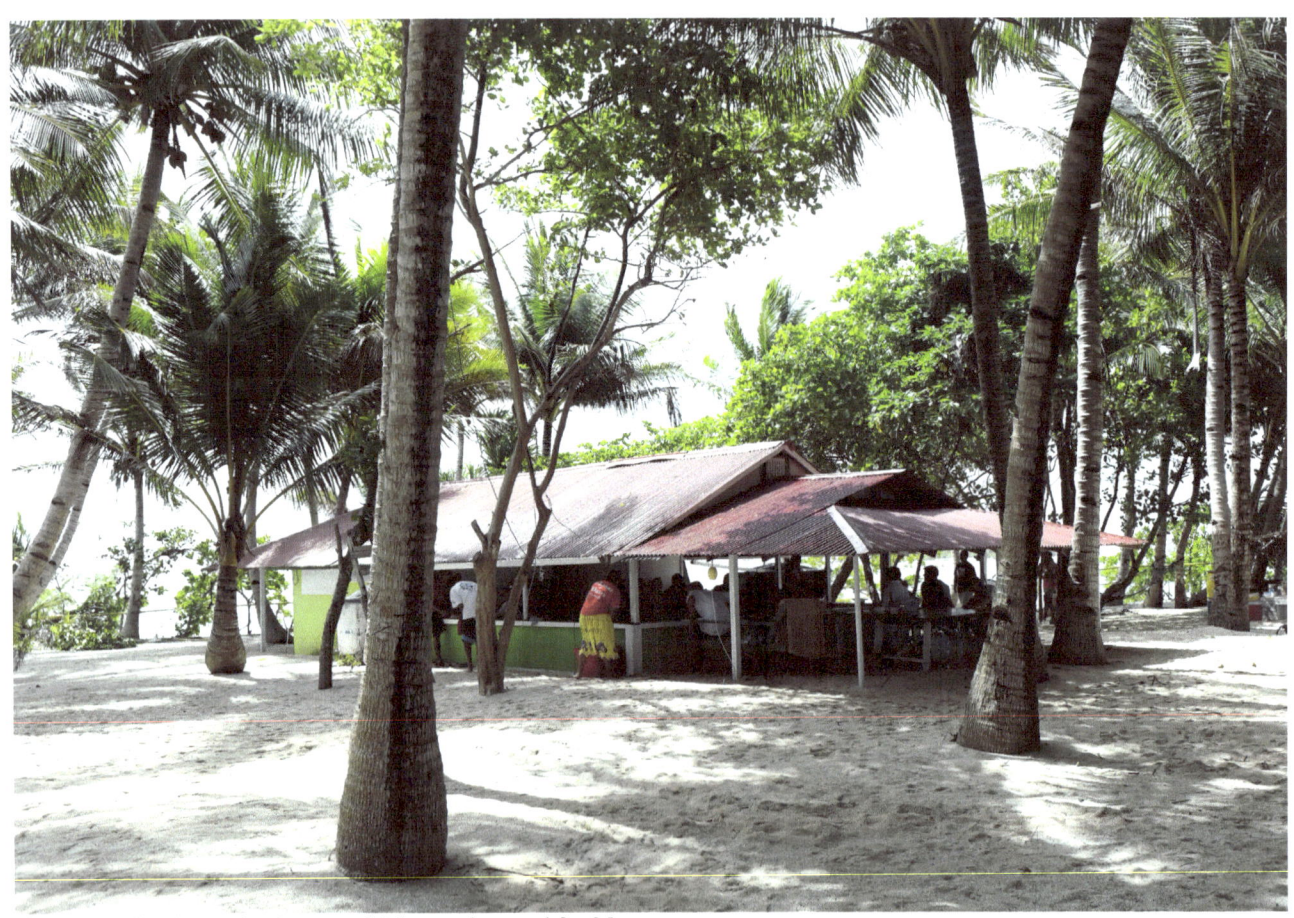

The Pisar Island meeting house, which was also used for Mass.

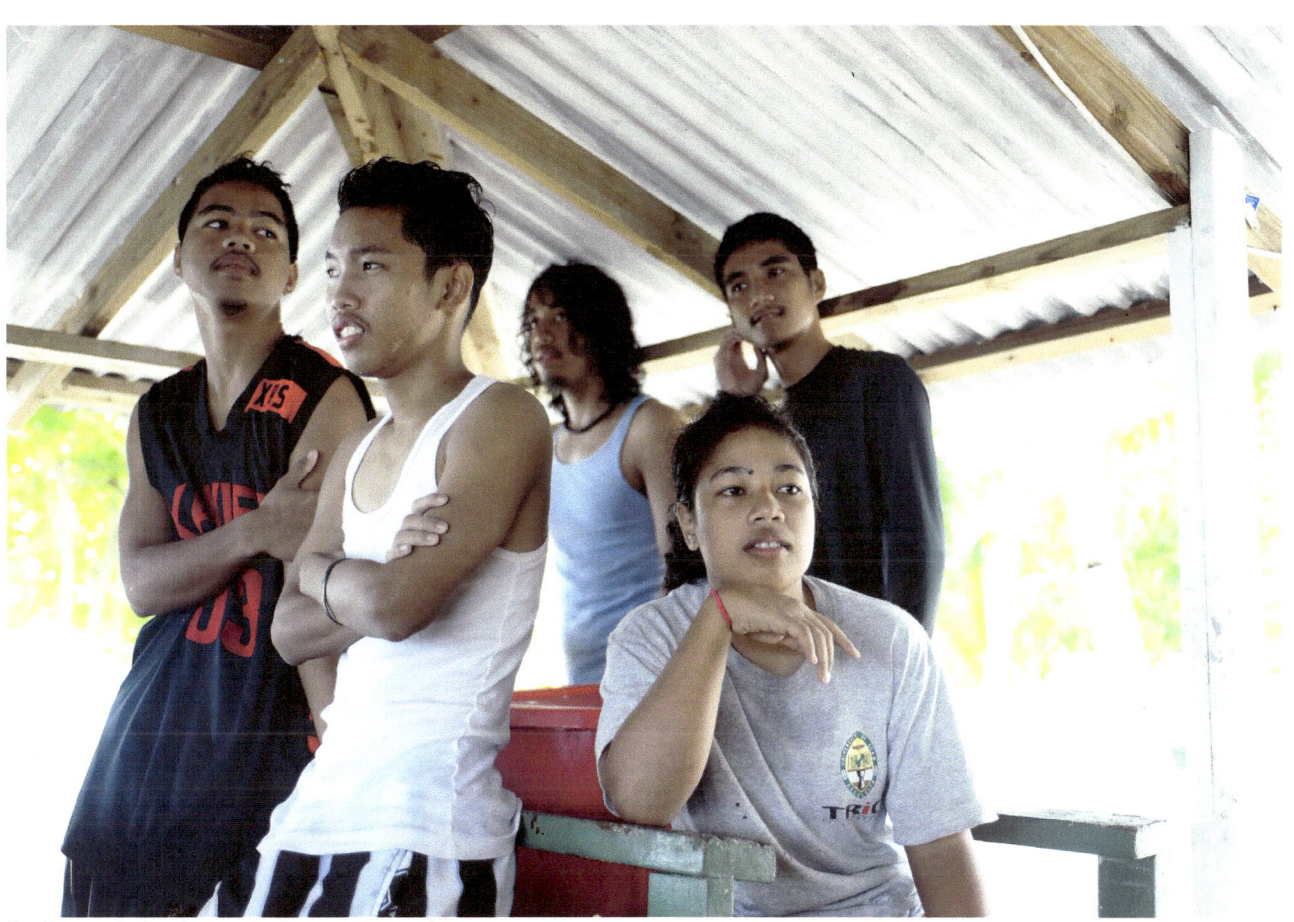

Seniors wait for the start of a group meeting.

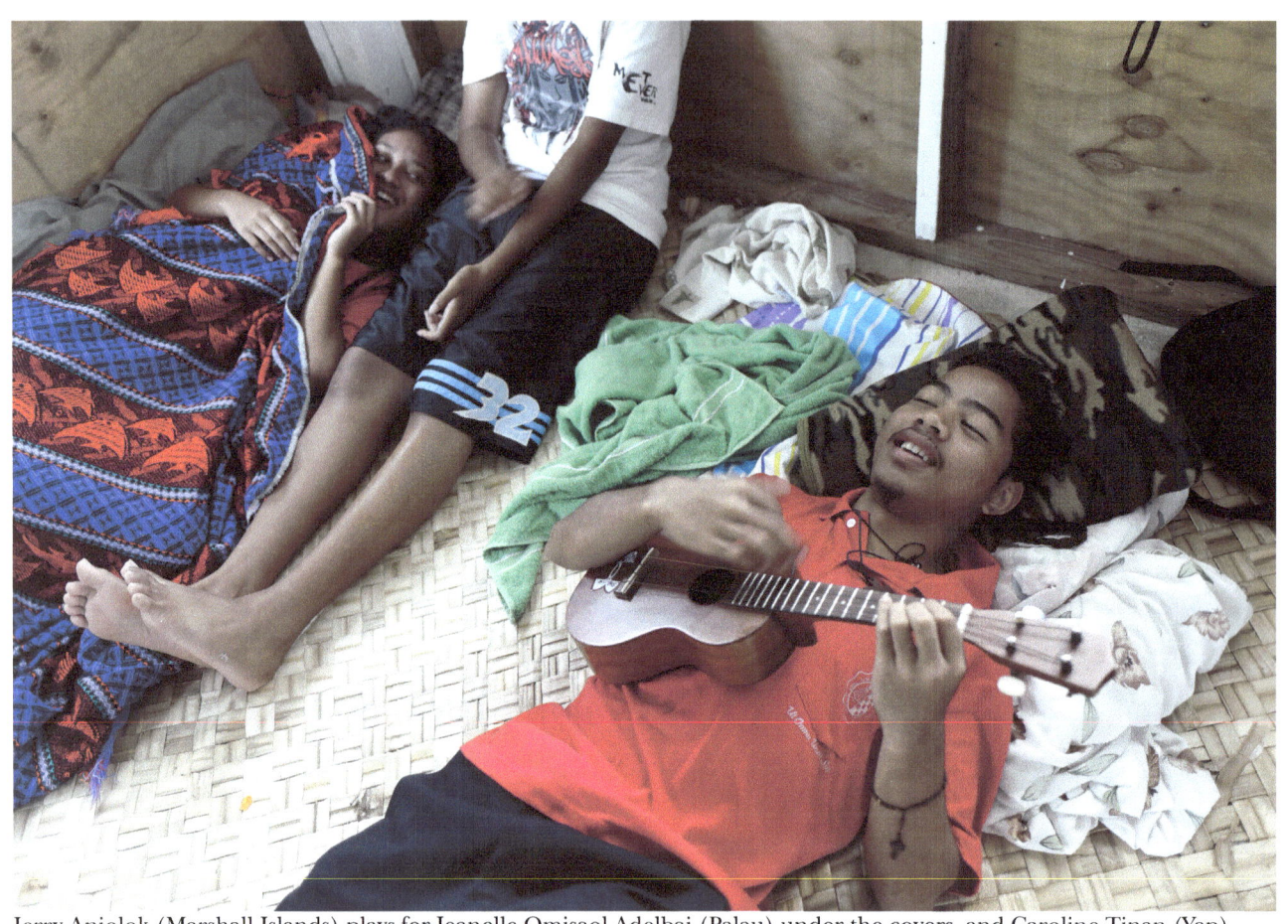

Jerry Anjolok (Marshall Islands) plays for Jeanelle Omisaol Adelbai (Palau) under the covers, and Caroline Tinan (Yap).

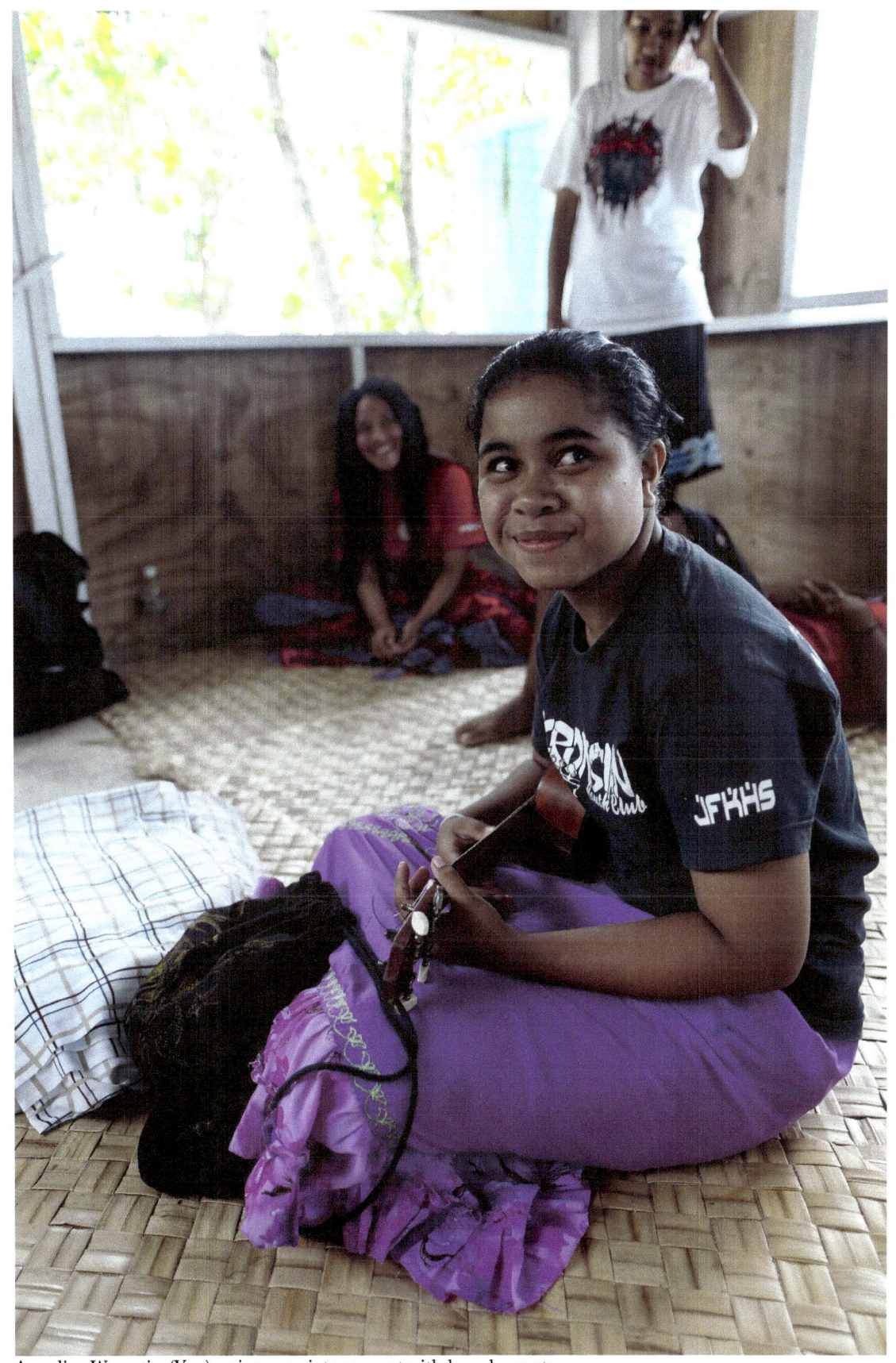

Angelica Waamtin (Yap) enjoys a quiet moment with her classmates.

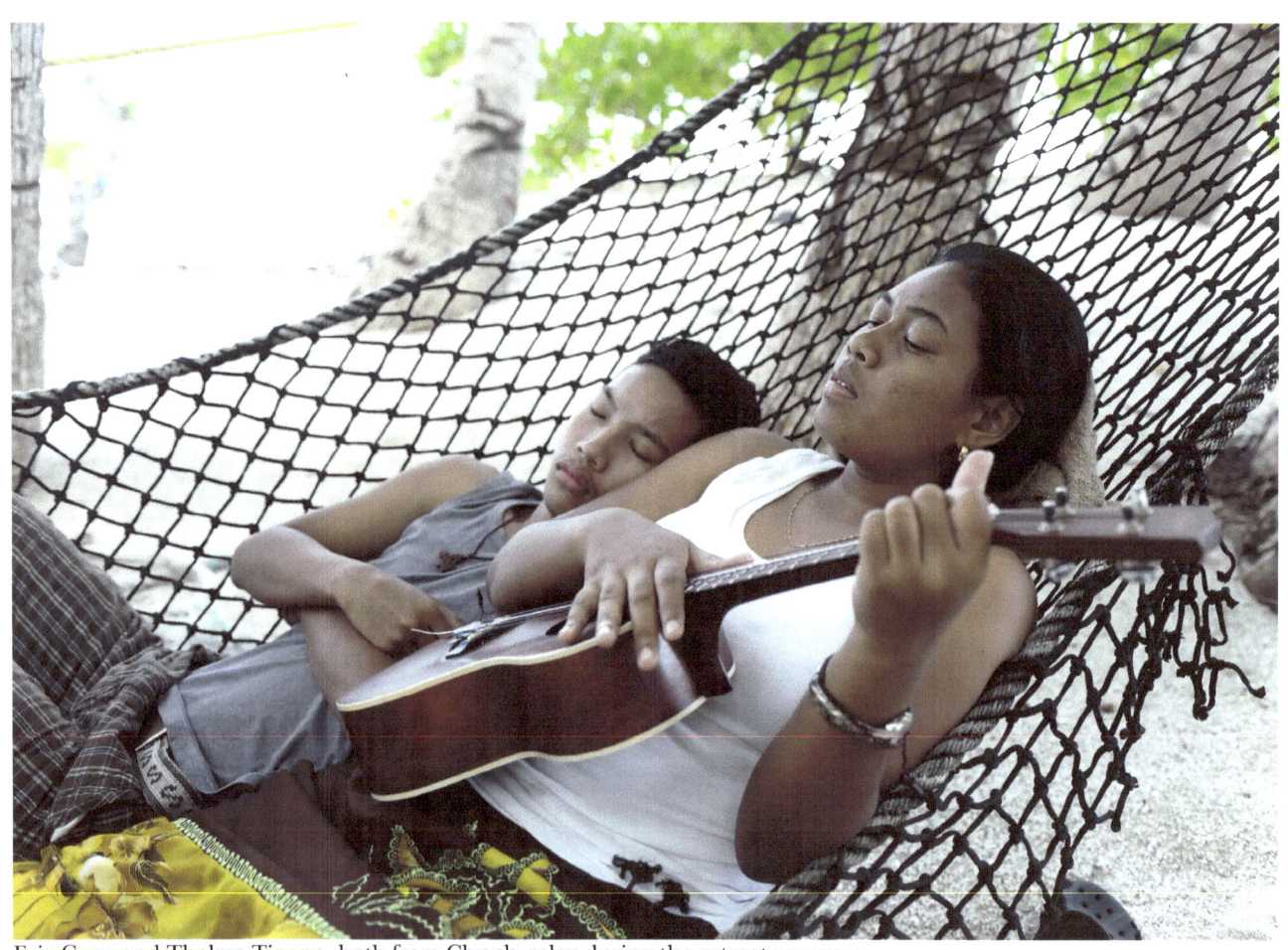

Eric Cano and Thelma Tipeno, both from Chuuk, relax during the retreat program.

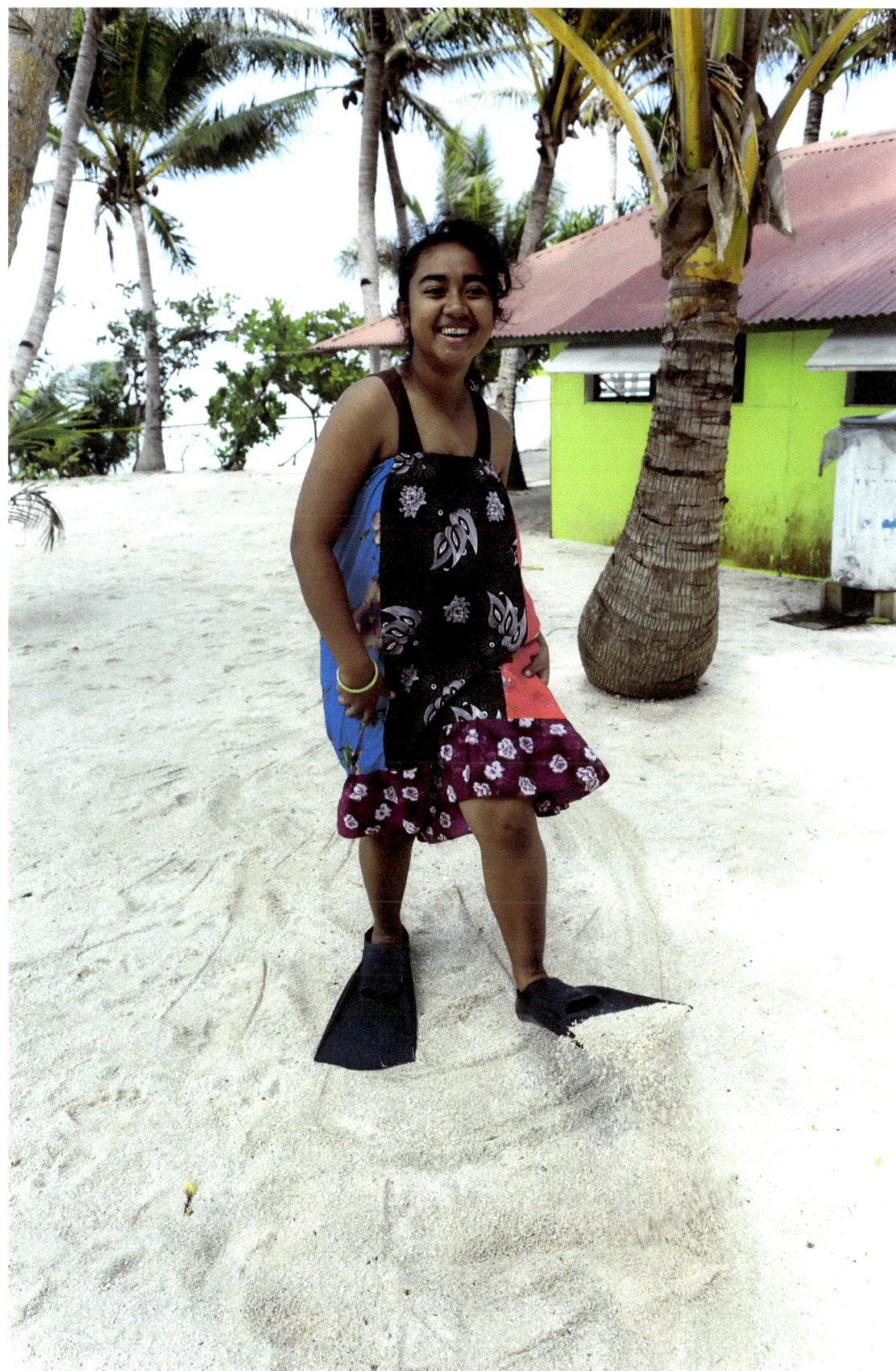

Stephanie Ham (Chuuk), who cannot swim, prepares to enter the ocean.

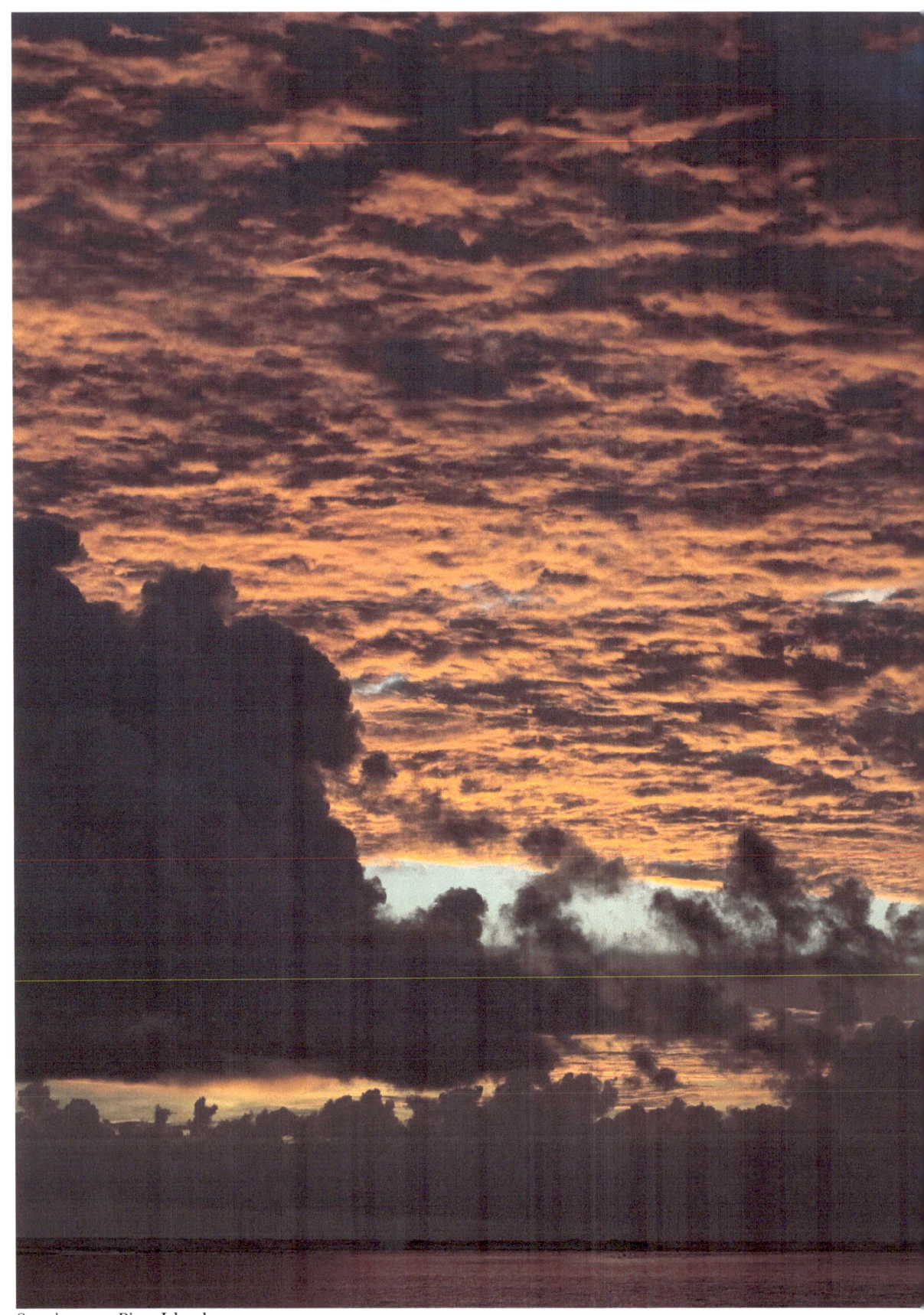

154 Sunrise over Pisar Island.

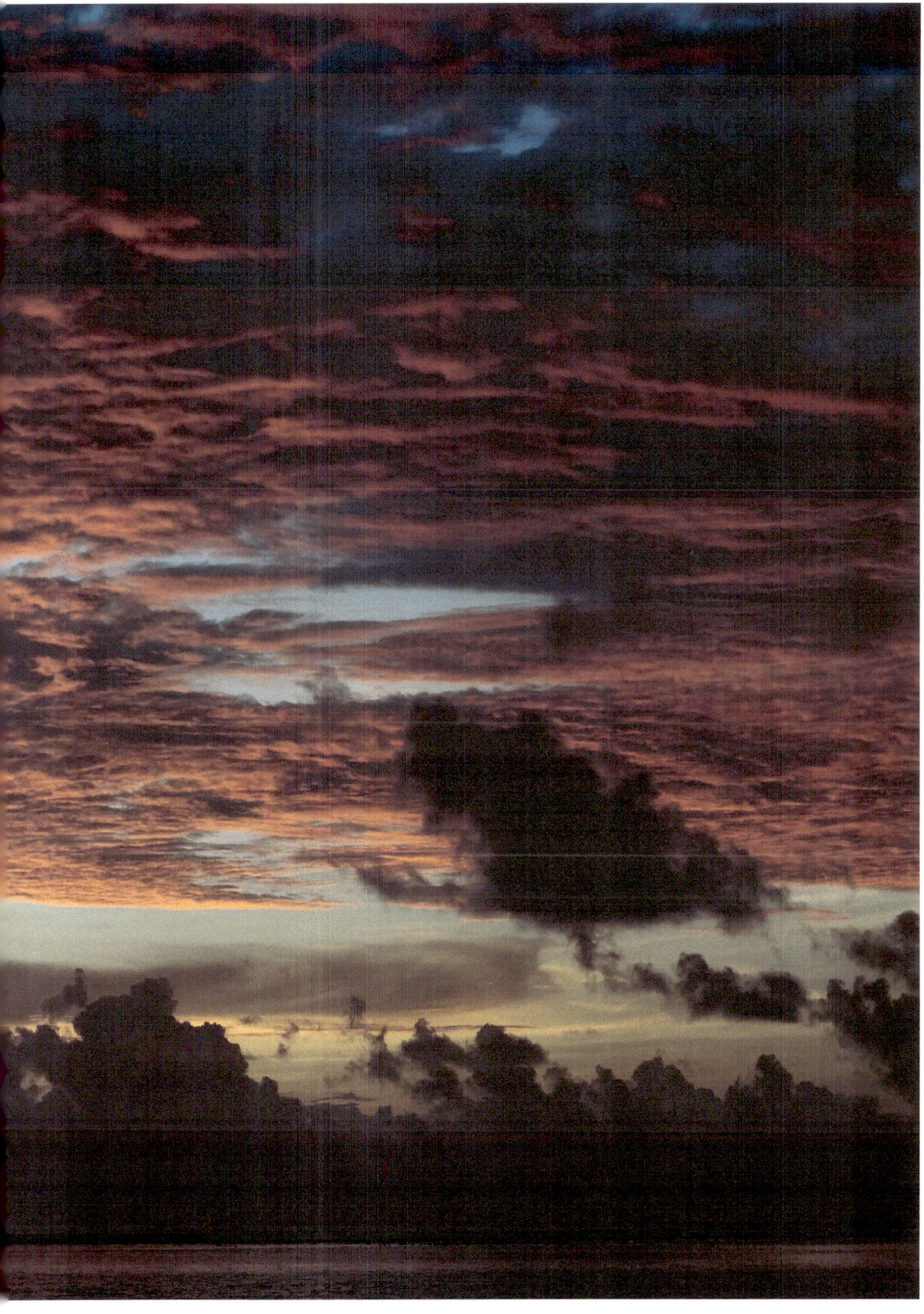

Commencement

Commencement marks the act of beginning, an appropriate way to describe the journey that seniors start on the day they graduate from Xavier High School.

The formal journey to commencement begins the day before at the Baccalaureate Mass, which is held at Chuuk's Roman Catholic Cathedral. The all-school Mass, which includes parents and relatives of graduating seniors, is a uniquely island mix of pomp and circumstance, Catholic spirituality and local color.

The color begins on campus, when girls in the lower classes don their Sunday best. (The seniors wore white and black.) The congregation was a sea of bright muumuus, as bright as the red paper bunting that students hung on the entrance to the Cathedral. The Baccalaureate Mass blessed those who were about to graduate, and reminded them of God's love and constant presence in their lives.

The next day's graduation ceremony seemed to me to be almost an anti-climax. Was it my imagination, or did I see in the faces of some seniors' bewilderment and fear of the unknown, of leaving best friends? It was as if the seniors' parents, siblings, relatives and friends who made the tortuous drive up to Mabuchi and Xavier, had intruded on a special and private place.

But, of course, the end did come. Diplomas were conferred. Graduates lined up and were greeted by family and friends. And a last party and dance was held on campus to mark the conclusion of one journey, and the commencement of another one.

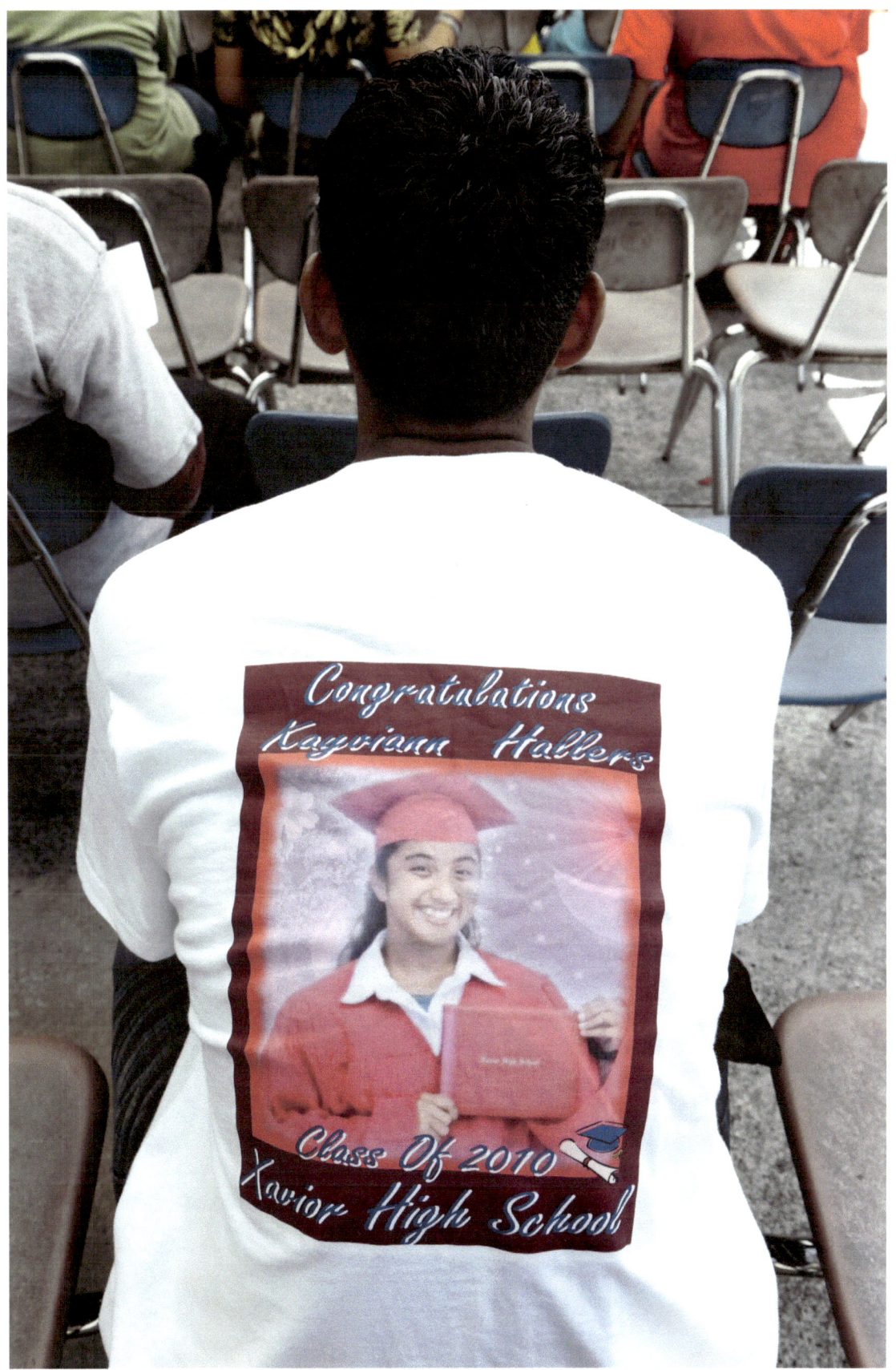

Celebrating the graduation of Kayviann Hallers (Chuuk), valedictorian of the Class of 2010.

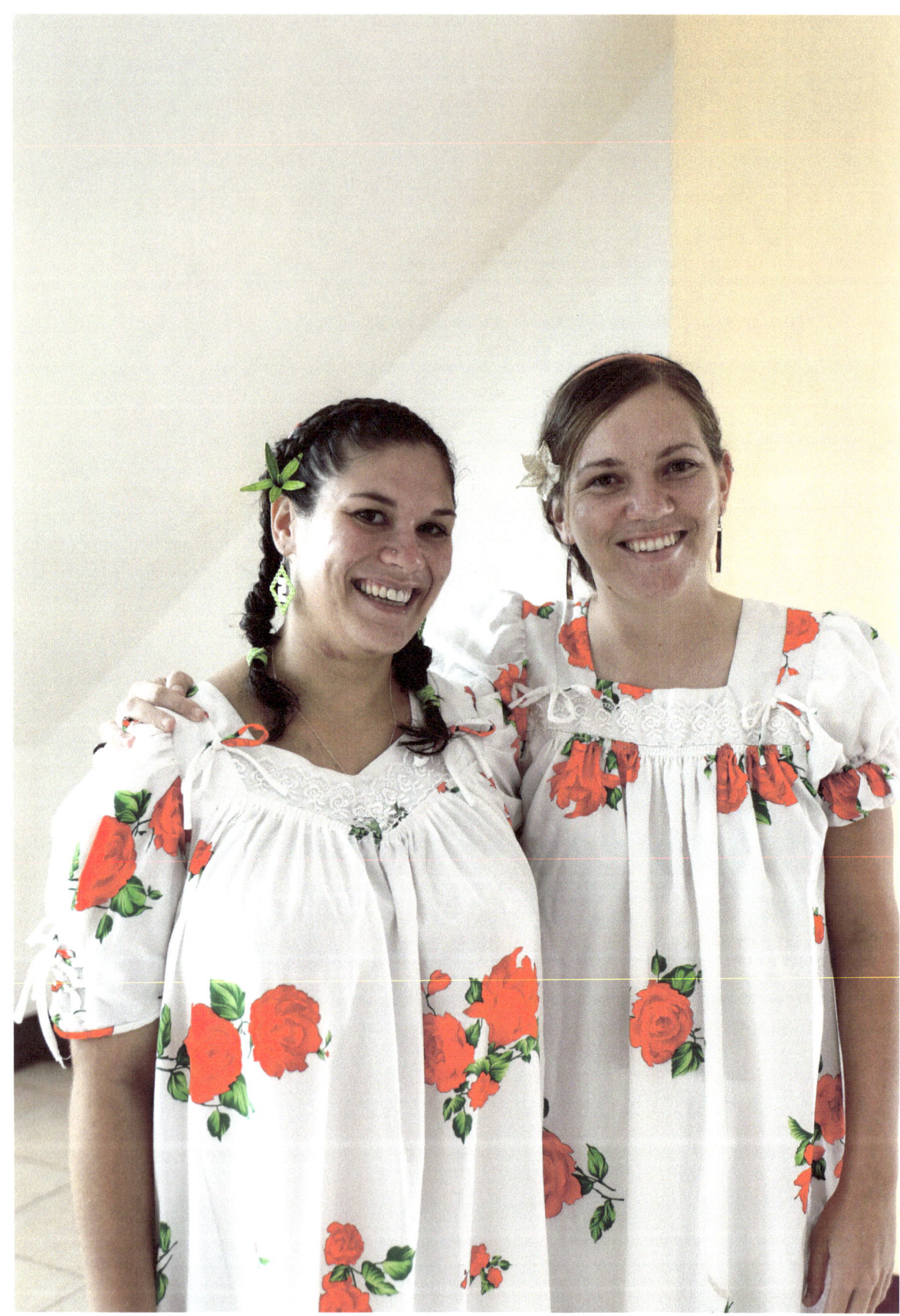

Teachers Stephanie Osborne and Megan Bell at the Baccalaureate Mass.

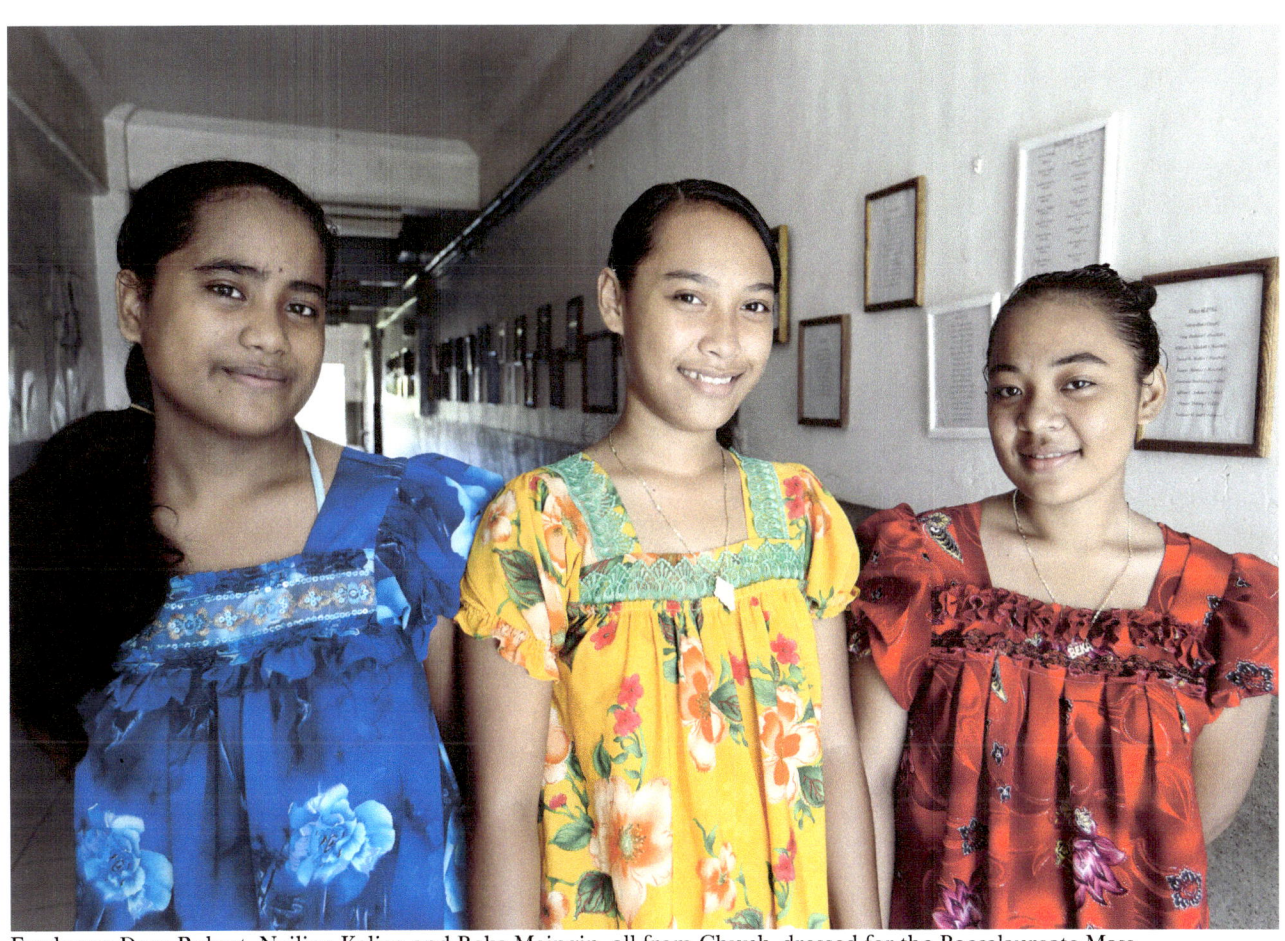

Freshmen Dece Robert, Neilien Kaliga and Beka Meingin, all from Chuuk, dressed for the Baccalaureate Mass.

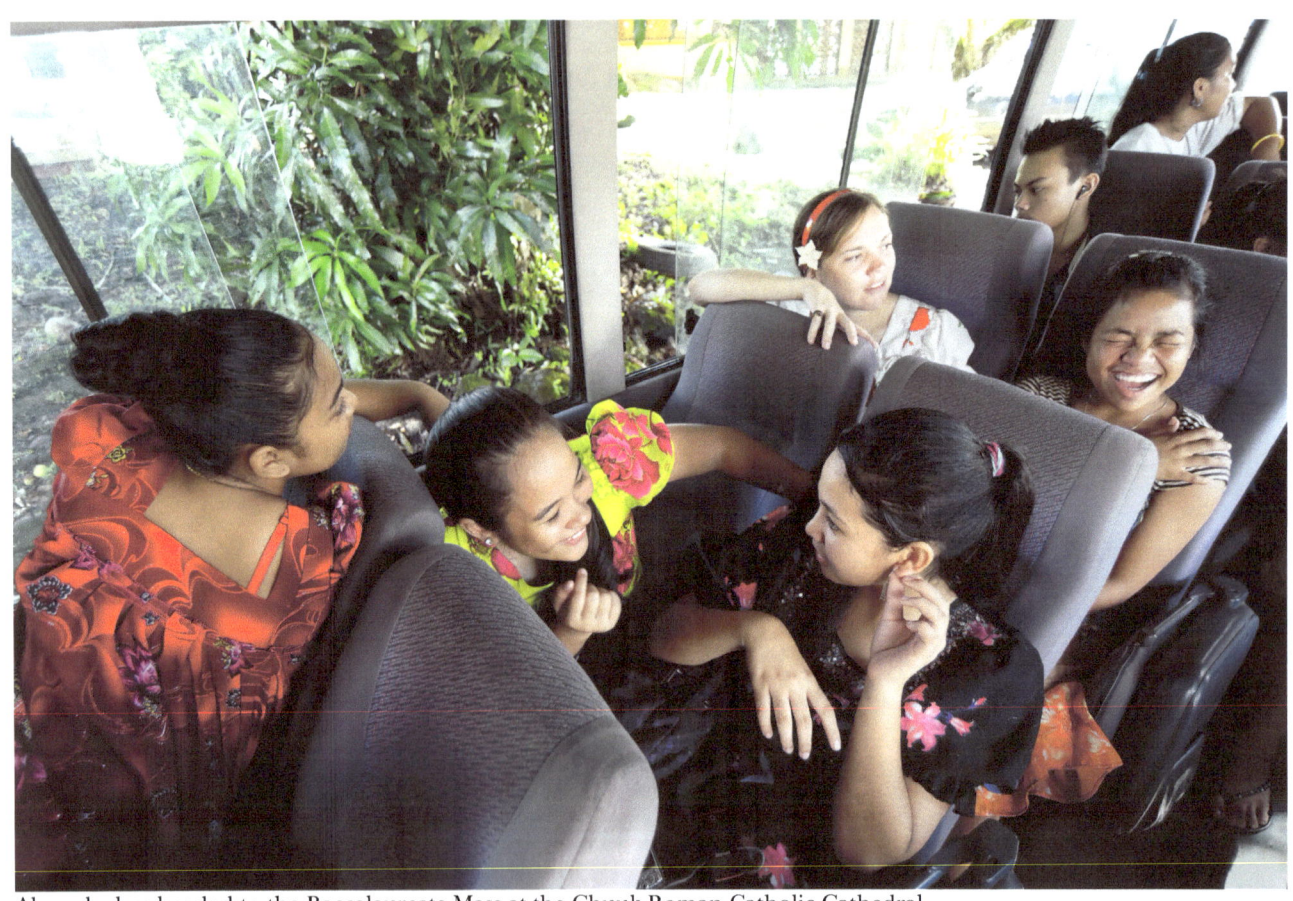

Aboard a bus headed to the Baccalaureate Mass at the Chuuk Roman Catholic Cathedral.

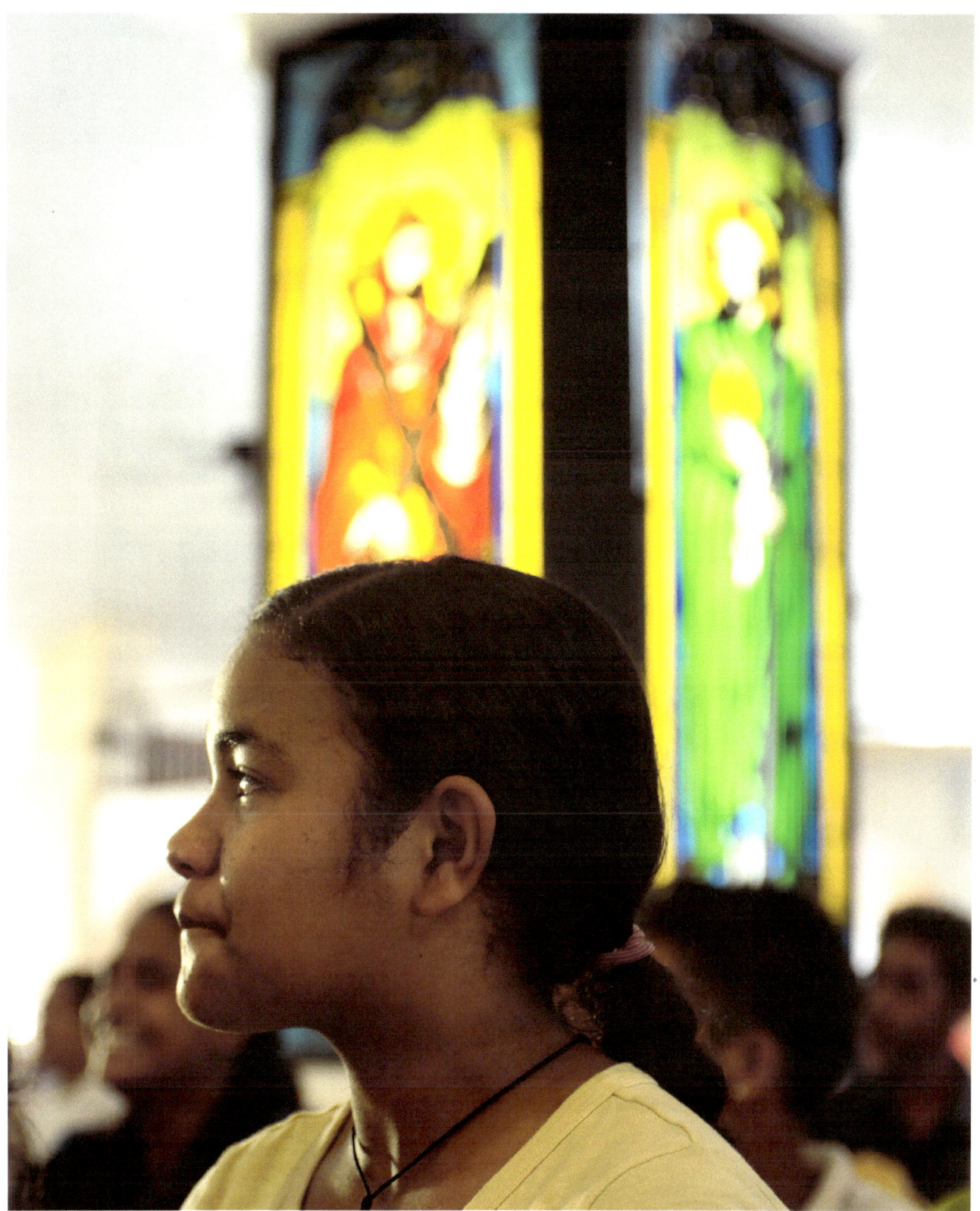

Freshman Zoe Kintaro Rechelulk (Palau) at the Baccalaureate Mass.

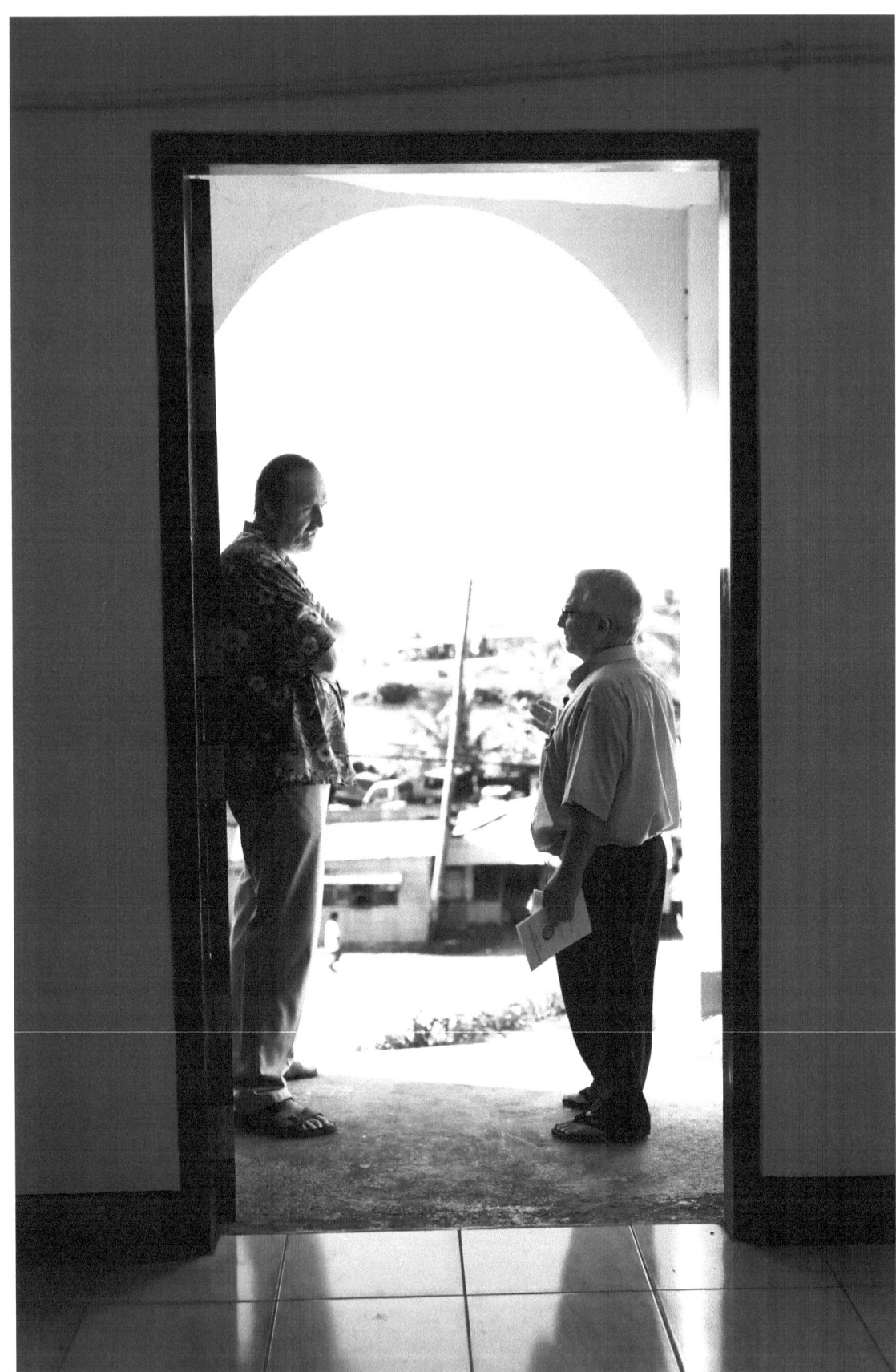

Fr. Jim Croghan, SJ, and Fr. Rich McAuliff, SJ, confer at the Baccalaureate Mass.

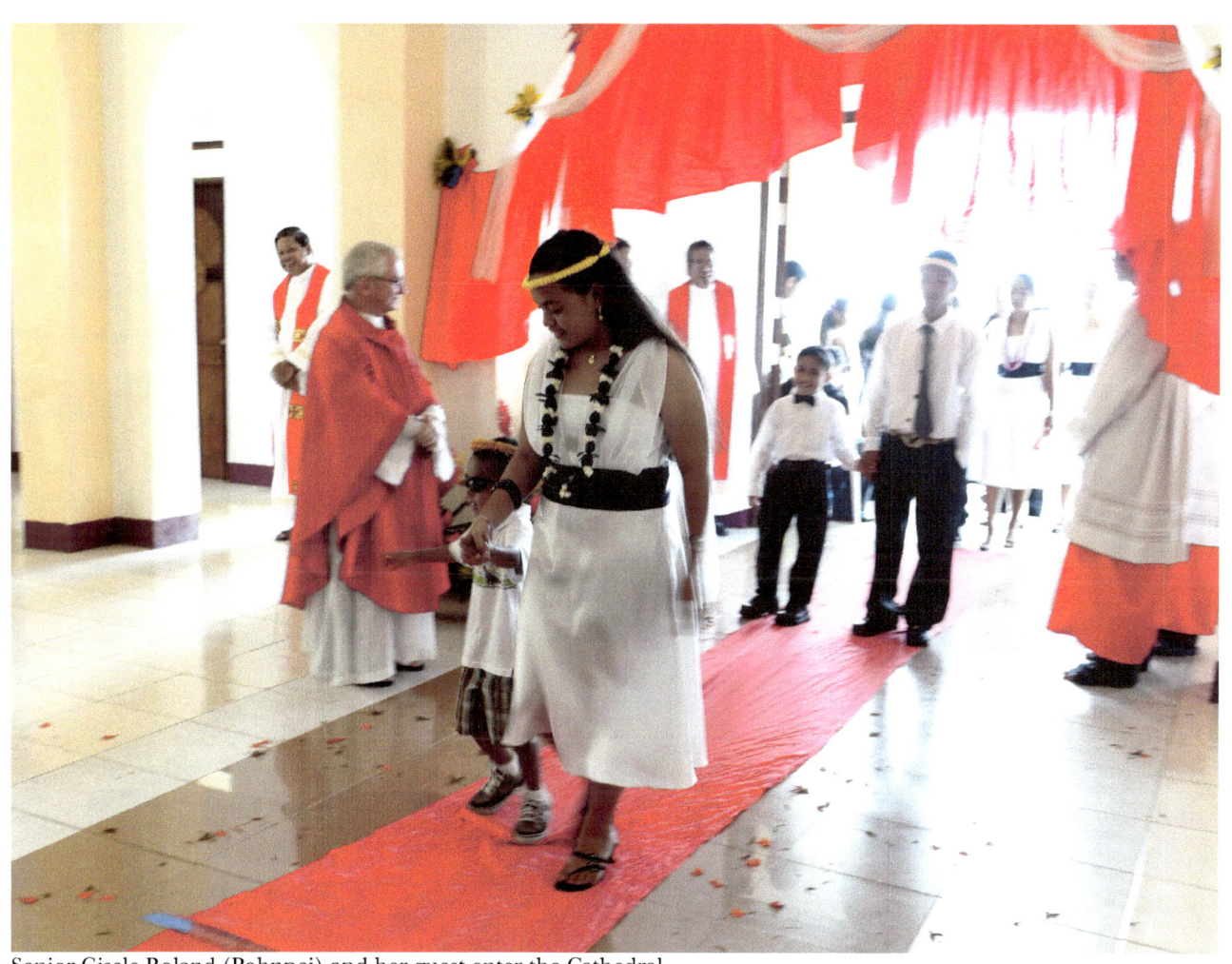

Senior Gisele Roland (Pohnpei) and her guest enter the Cathedral.

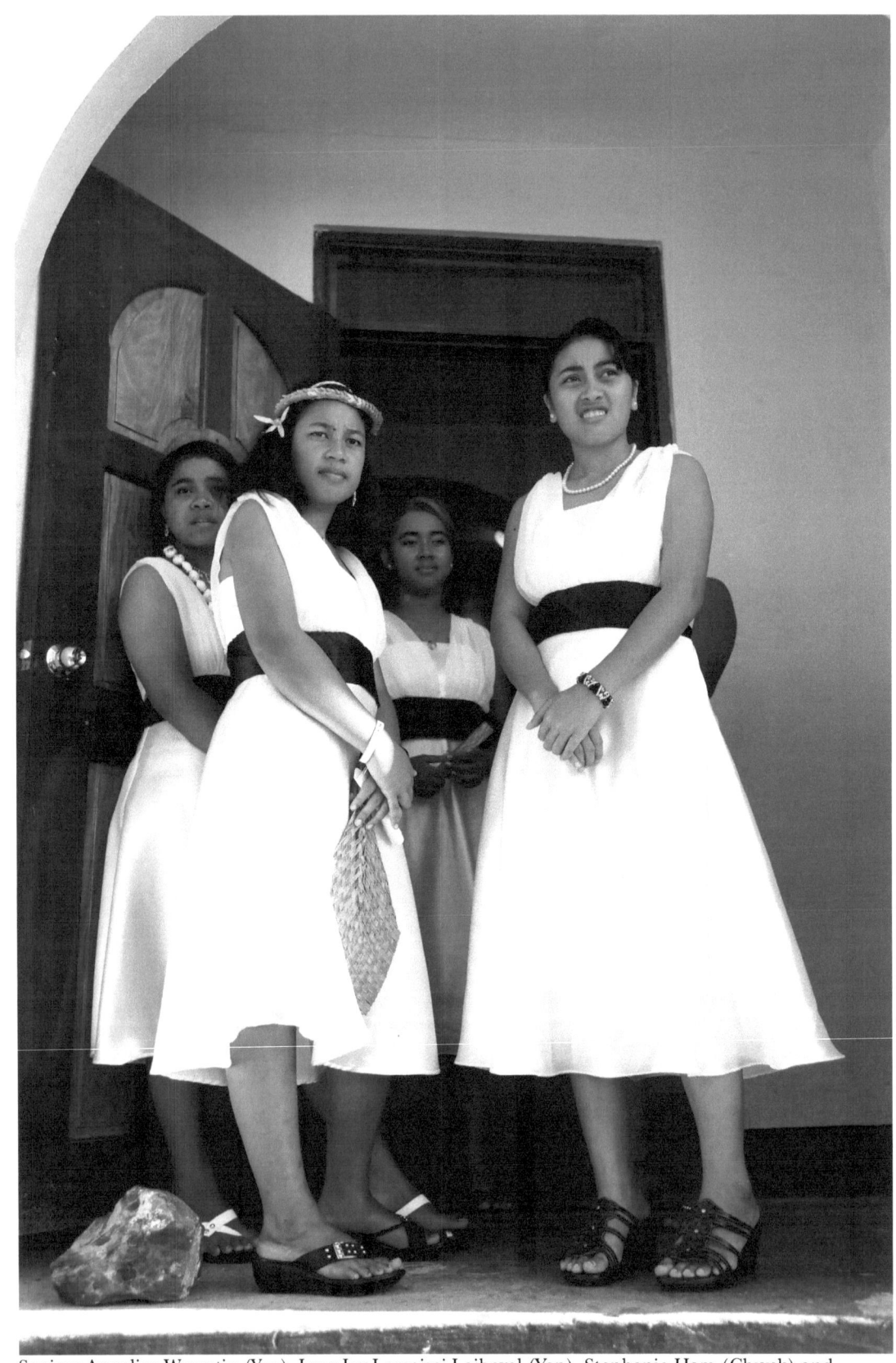

Seniors Angelica Waamtin (Yap), June Joy Lemaisei Laibeyal (Yap), Stephanie Ham (Chuuk) and Lucy Irons (Chuuk).

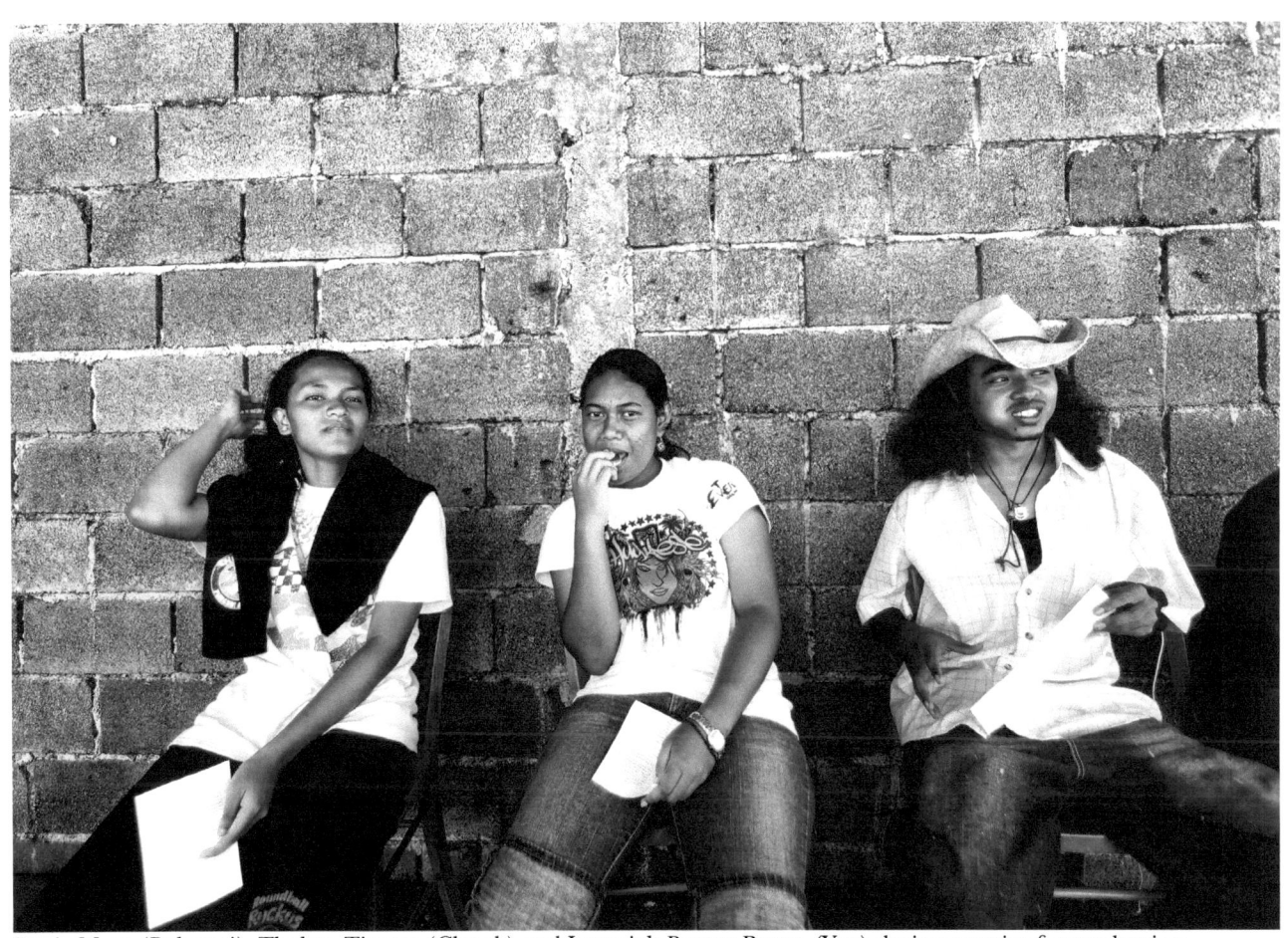

Roxie Moya (Pohnpei), Thelma Tipeno (Chuuk) and Jeremiah Bugun Rutun (Yap) during practice for graduation.

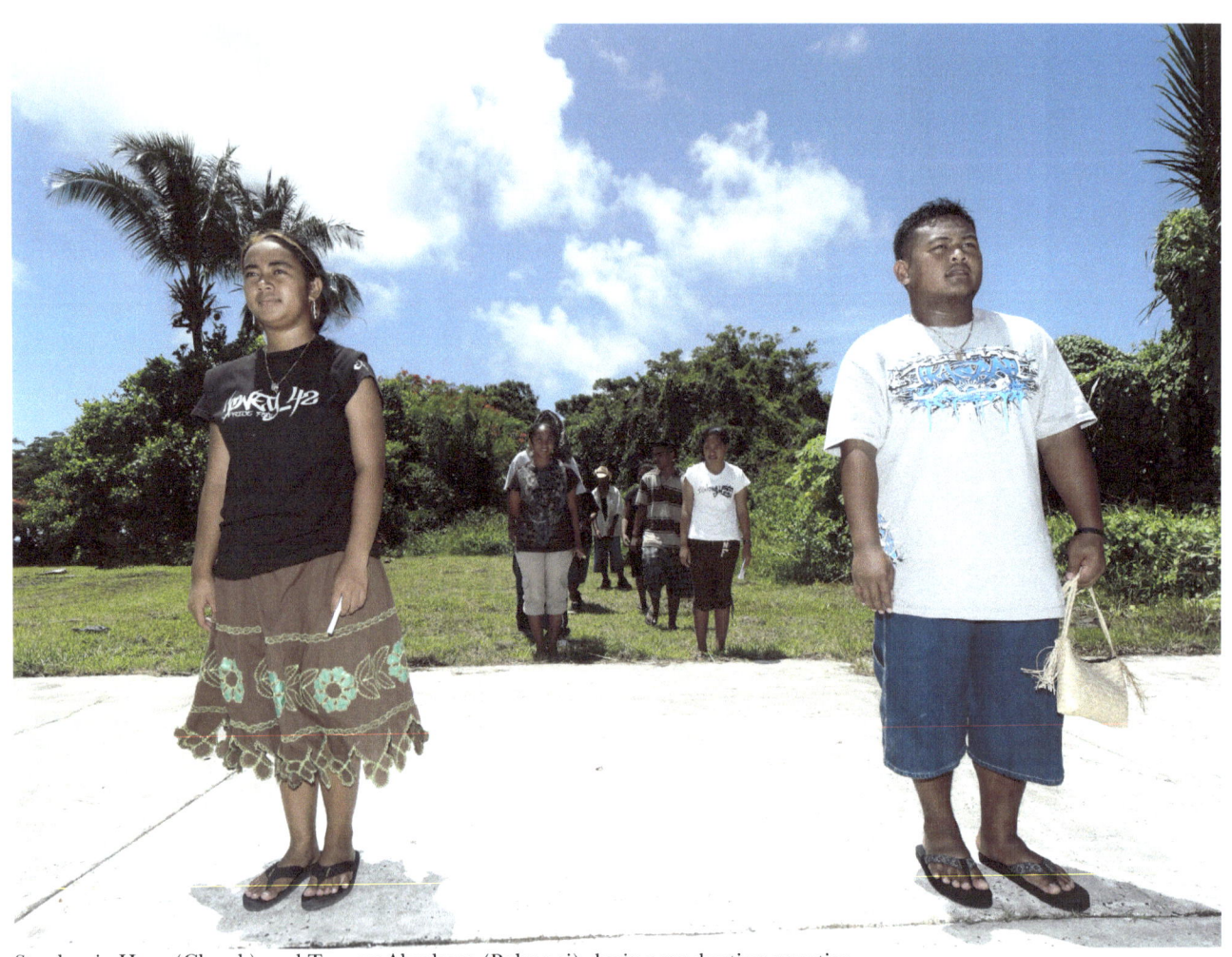

Stephanie Ham (Chuuk) and Tommy Abraham (Pohnpei) during graduation practice.

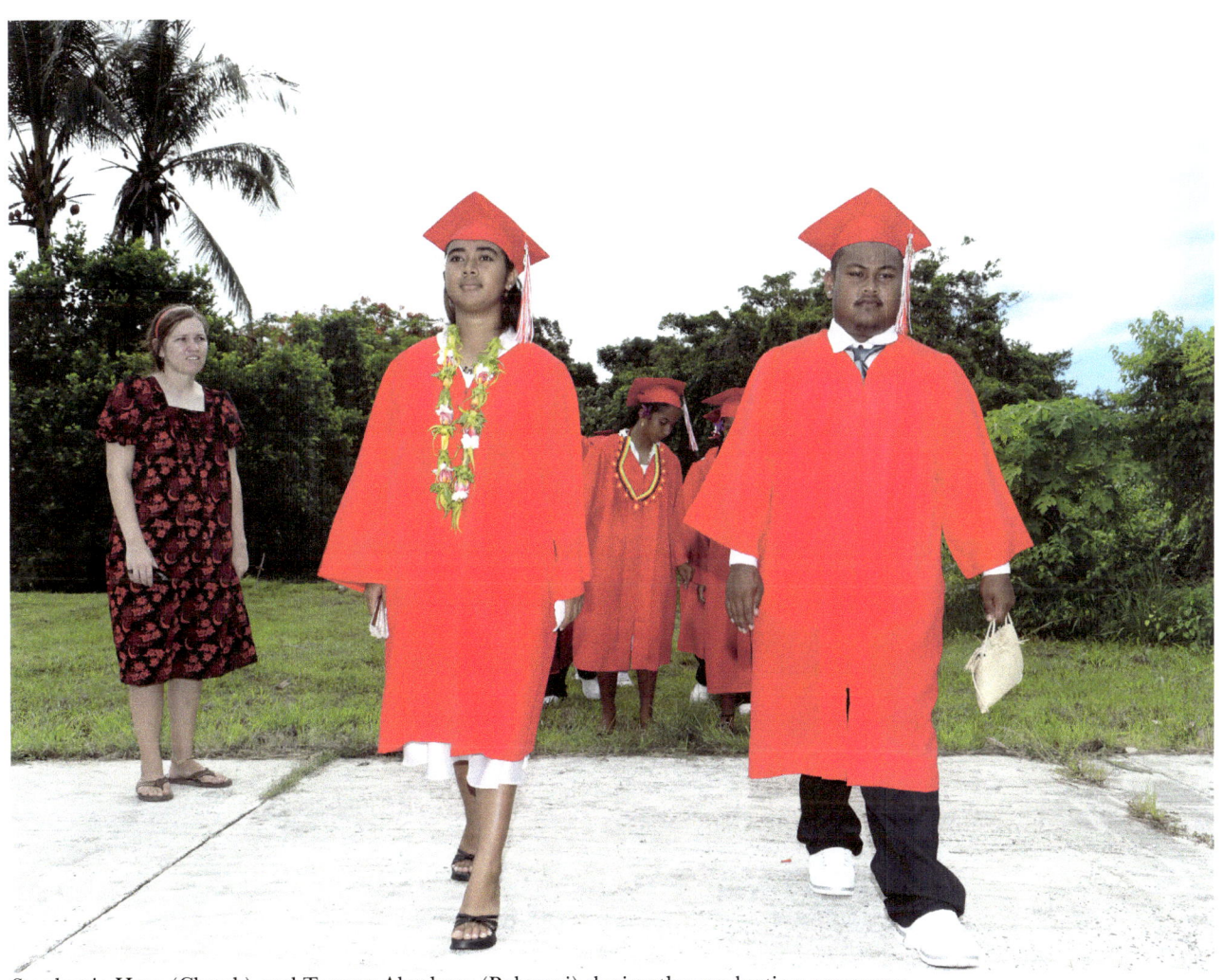

Stephanie Ham (Chuuk) and Tommy Abraham (Pohnpei) during the graduation ceremony.

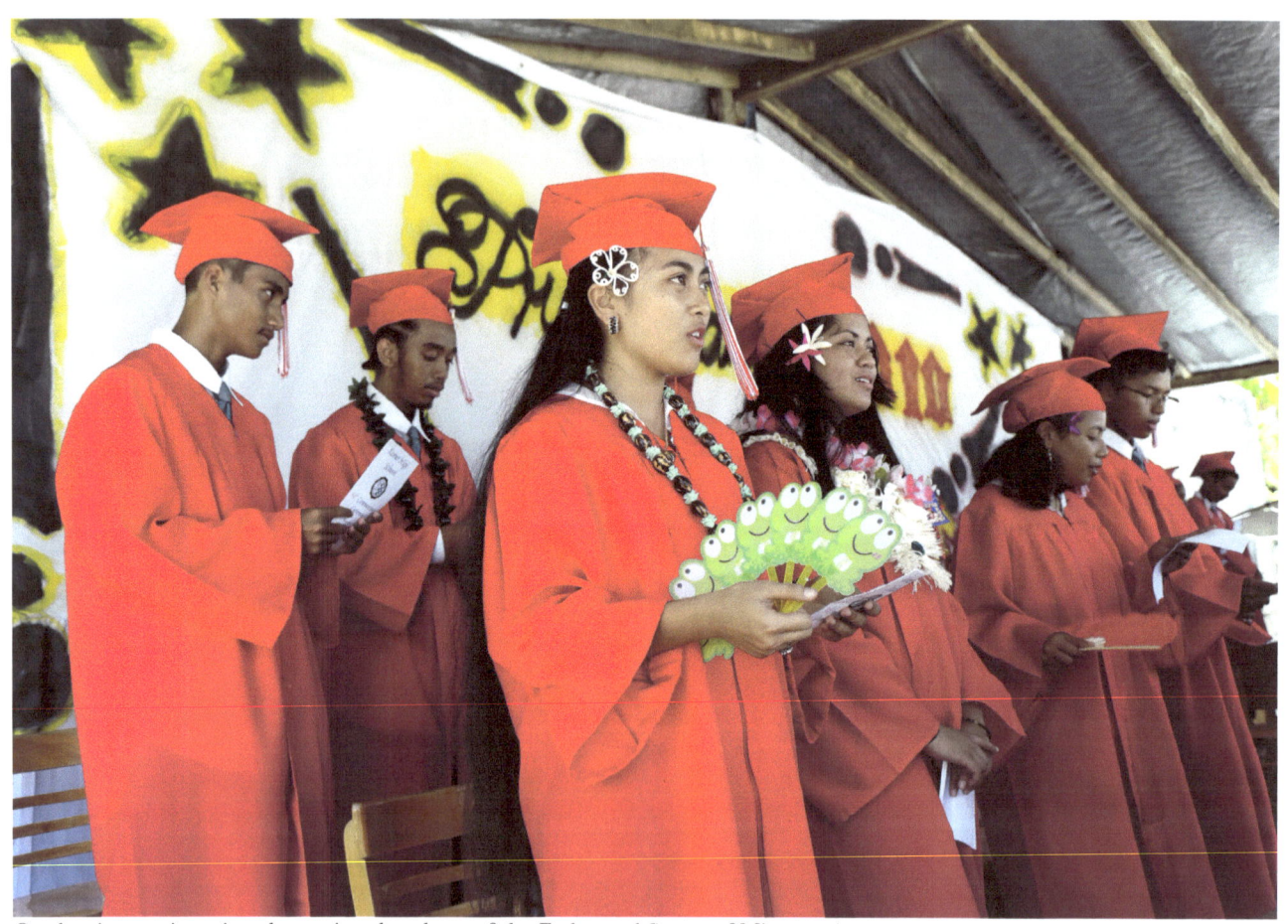

Graduating seniors sing the national anthem of the Federated States of Micronesia.

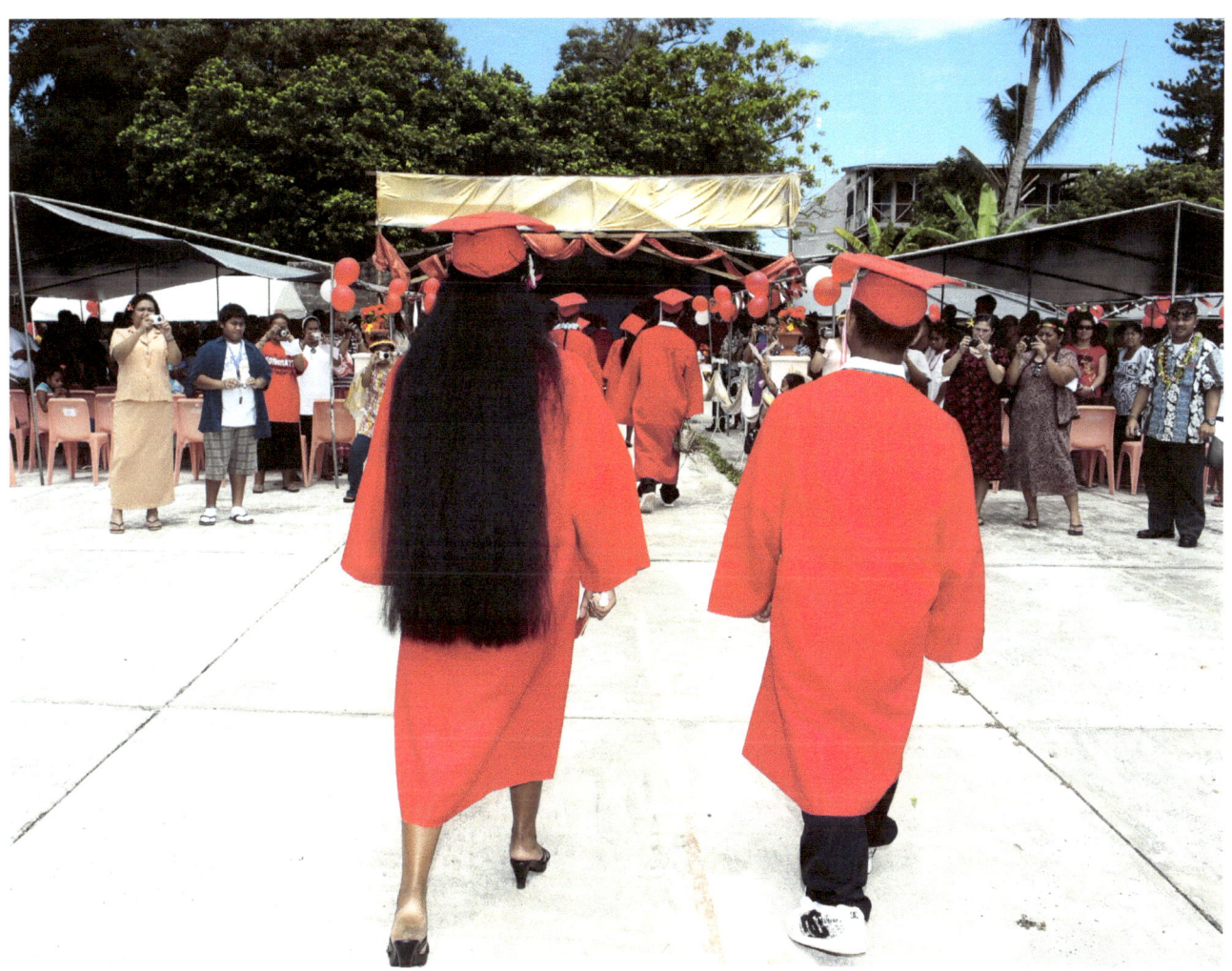

Polita Dil'Ungil Asanuma (Palau) and Marson Elley (Kosrae) are the last two seniors to march onto the graduation stage.

Senior Tommy Abraham (Pohnpei) and sophpmore Naiomy Lohn (Pohnpei) at the graduation party.

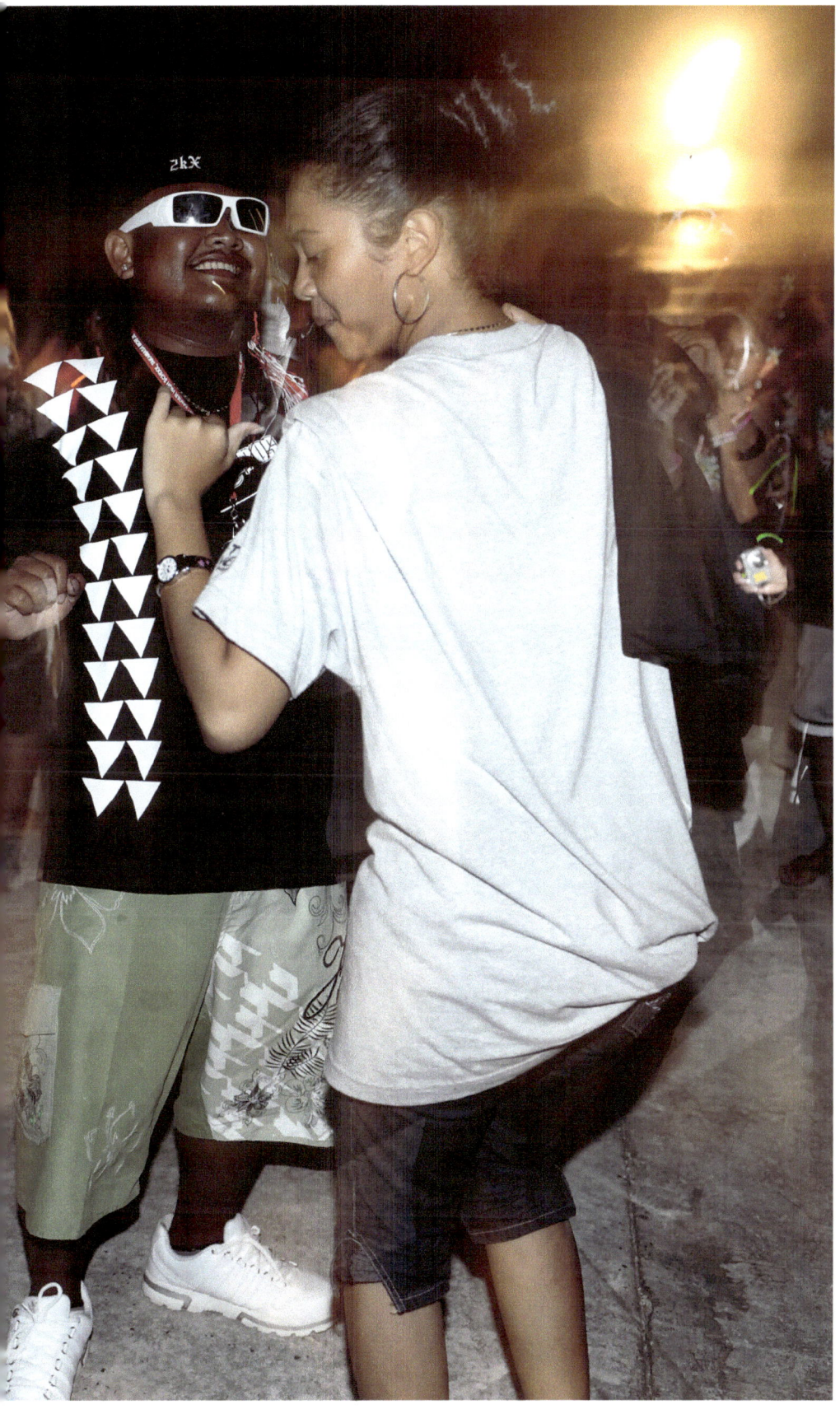

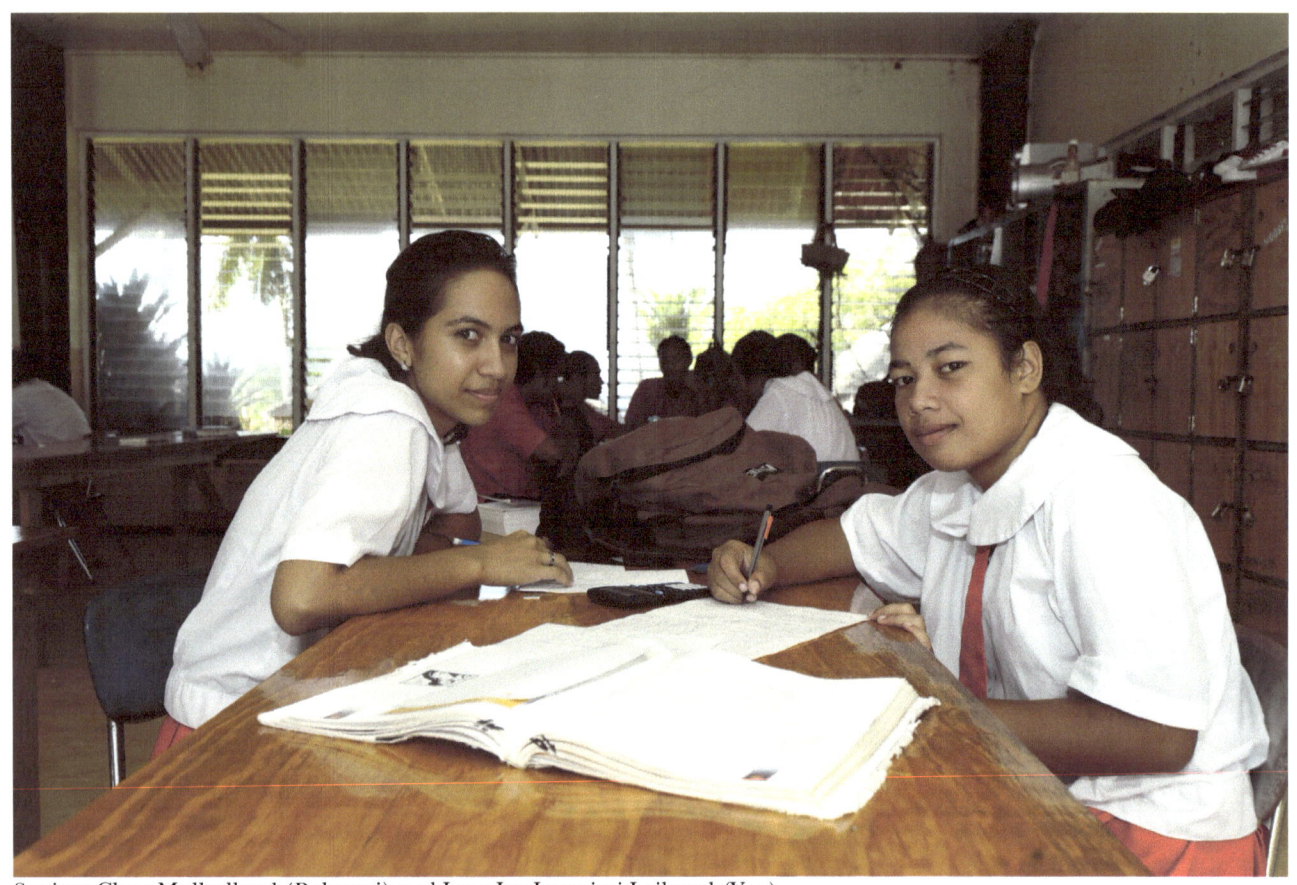

Seniors Clare Mulholland (Pohnpei) and June Joy Lemaisei Laibeyal (Yap).

Acknowledgements

This book would not been possible without the support and friendship of the Rev. R. Richard McAuliff, SJ. Father Rich – as he is known by friends, students and parishioners – is the Director of Xavier High School. He responded with his usual enthusiasm when I sent him an email expressing my interest in doing an extended photographic essay on Xavier. Father Rich's response? How soon could I get to Chuuk!

When I did arrive, Fr. Rich arranged a formal welcome at the airport, put me up with him at Jesuit House on the campus, allowed me to share meals with the faculty and staff, and gave me unrestricted access to every aspect of Xavier life. I spent more than a month at Mabuchi, as the hill where Xavier sits is known, divided between two trips. I was there for so long that some Chuukese Catholics took to greeting me as "Father," a great honor, but somewhat embarrassing for a married Episcopalian.

I must also thank the faculty, staff and, most importantly, the students at Xavier High School. They were remarkably patient with me as I intruded into their daily lives with my camera.

Two colleagues played key roles in helping me produce this book. Neil Sananikone, a digital imaging guru who owns Kaimuki Camera in Honolulu, helped me manage post-production imaging with a number of challenging photos. Malcolm Mekaru, who is also a photographer as well as a computer whiz, translated my layout ideas into the book you hold in your hands.

Finally, this project could not have been undertaken without the support of Kris Tanahara, my wife and biggest fan. I would not be able to traipse around the Pacific with my camera bag without her love and enthusiastic support. I remain surprised and grateful that the locks haven't been changed every time I return from another long trip.

Floyd K. Takeuchi
Honolulu, Hawaii

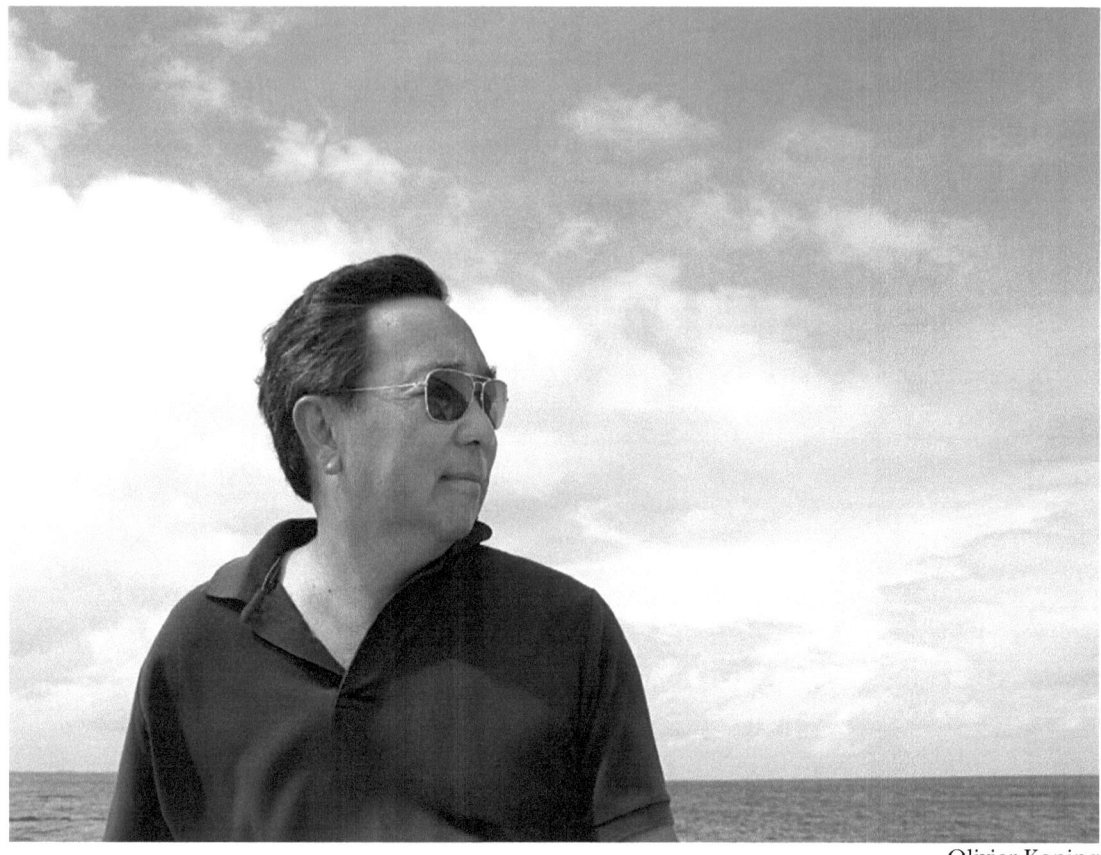

Olivier Koning

The Author

Floyd K. Takeuchi is a writer-photographer who specializes in the Pacific Islands. He has traveled to nearly every corner of Oceania, and worked as a journalist in many of the islands. His experience includes serving as a reporter at the *Pacific Daily News* on Guam, and managing editor of *The Daily Post* in Fiji. He has also been a reporter, editor, radio and television anchor and publisher in Hawaii and Japan. He also worked in Washington, D.C. as a senior staffer for a Member of the U.S. House of Representatives. He is the co-author of *Majuro – Essays from an Atoll*, which is sold exclusively at Amazon.com. Floyd was born and raised in the Marshall Islands. For more, see www.floydtakeuchi.com.

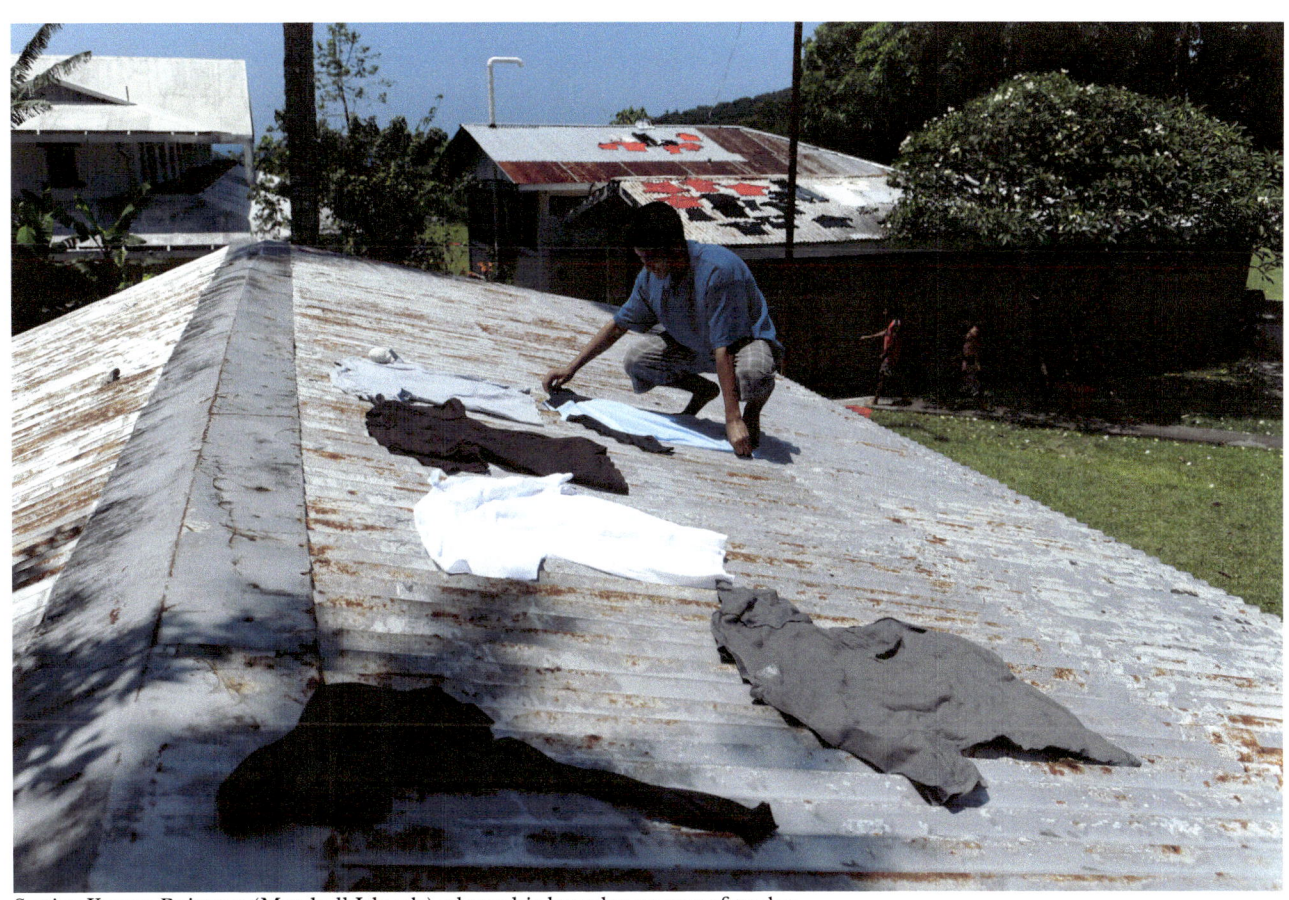

Senior Keanu Reimers (Marshall Islands) places his laundry on a roof to dry.

www.ingramcontent.com/pod-product-compliance
Lightning Source LLC
Chambersburg PA
CBHW051017180526

45172CB00002B/380